Why England Sleeps

WHY ENGLAND SLEEPS

JOHN COCKCROFT

London ∽ Arlington Books

WHY ENGLAND SLEEPS
First Published 1971 by
Arlington Books (Publishers) Ltd
15 Duke Street St James's
London SW1.

Made and printed in England by
The Garden City Press Ltd
London and Letchworth

© John Cockcroft 1971

ISBN 0 85140 142 2

TO MARK

in the hope that by the time he is grown up the
Britain which this book looks for has come to pass

'I would now emphasize . . . the excessive "overseas" orientation among the upper reaches of British policymakers, which gave priority to the maintenance of a world role the country could no longer carry. Although parts of the Treasury shared too much of this orientation for too long the, basic weaknesses of policy reflected deep-seated attitudes among a much wider circle. Here, in my view, is to be found the common factor behind our failure to join the European movement when we could have got in on our own terms, the crippling of the economy in the Korean armament drive, the failure to fund the sterling balances after the war, the disdain for fiscal export aids while other countries still had theirs, the neglect of "fall-back" means of protecting the balance of payments, the long delay in rethinking both the international role of sterling and its exchange parity, the investment of large resources in a series of military and aerospace projects, many of which had to be cancelled before completion, and the growth of overseas defence commitments, which has only recently been checked . . . The thinking concerned was so intimately connected with the idea of a special relationship with the United States that this gives one pause before advocating too warmly any North Atlantic Free Trade Area, irrespective of the narrower economic arguments.

While British leaders rushed from capital to capital on self-appointed international peacemaking missions, the rest of the world was more conscious of the rustle of their begging bowl, their utter dependence on the USA, and their inability to impose their will on the breakaway Rhodesian regime, still less affect the course of events in the Middle or Far East. The climax came in November 1967, with Devaluation: followed by the second French veto on the Common Market application—this time on the plausible pretext of Britain's economic unreadiness.

The best that Governments can hope to do to help people recover a healthy patriotism and sense of national pride is to concentrate on the welfare of the inhabitants of these isles. Britain will eventually find a new and worthy role among the nations, but the sooner the present preoccupation with the subject ceases, the sooner this role will be found.'

From *Steering the Economy*, Samuel Brittan

CONTENTS

PREFACE

Mr Cockcroft's book traces the mistakes and successes of the last quarter of a century and contrasts Britain in 1971 to what she was in 1945. He makes full allowance for the revolution from 1951 to 1955, the freeing of markets and the opening up of the economy.

In particular the author is critical of the lost opportunities to enter the Common Market. He criticises our not taking part in the Messina negotiations to which, ultimately, we were not invited. There is no doubt that the major offices of state, namely the Foreign Office and Treasury, were not advising their ministers at that date to make any further move towards European entry. This leads the author to be somewhat critical of the civil service and to regret the lack of attempt which our major civil servants have in keeping pace with outdoor events. He considers that the Fulton Report should give an opportunity for a review and revision of the civil service. The latest structure, with an independent head of the civil service and with the reorganisation of government in Whitehall, all coincide with the author's recommendations. He is particularly keen on entry into Europe and puts this policy in contrast to an excessive overseas orientation of Britain's position. To emphasise this he puts as a Frontispiece Samuel Brittan's comments in "Steering the Economy". The book stresses in detail some of the changes in policy necessary to make a success of our entry into Europe.

In discussing industrial relations and their reform the book is very much *à propos*. Its publication will coincide with the drive being made by the new Conservative Government to legislate on industrial relations. The book also coincides with the desire of the new government to reorganise the tax structure. It will be interesting to see whether the author's proposals in this field coincide with those of the new Chancellor. It does not appear that either this book or the new government have yet found a solution of how to dispose of nearly £600 million of revenue by abolishing SET, and what is to be put in its place. The main tenor of the book is in tune with Conservative philosophy in wanting to introduce more competition and to reduce the influence of the State.

Perhaps the book is best summed up in the words on the last pages:

"It cannot possibly be predicted in advance with any certainty that the British people would respond to the challenge of going into Europe. If they did not do so their country could conceivably become even more of a backwater than it will be if present trends continued, and if Britain remained relatively isolated outside the Common Market on the periphery of the Eurasian land mass. By the same token, none can be certain that they would react favourably to any of the other radical changes suggested in this book—such as more competition, more flexible exchange rates, more incentives through lower taxation, much greater selectivity in the social services, a drastic reduction in the power and influence of the State, a streamlined machinery of government, and a legal framework for industrial relations."

These are indeed the objectives of the present government so one may conclude by wishing well to both this book and to the government.

Butler

INTRODUCTION

The concept of this book was conceived over two years ago, with the idea of attempting to show why it was that Britain should make radical new departures if she were ever again to be a credible power n the world, and if she were to become a more satisfactory place in which to live. The book's sins of omission and commission are entirely my own, its merits if any conceived in long walks on the Yorkshire moors near my birthplace and parents' home, and in the fields around a village not a thousand miles from Cambridge; and in verbal debate at Peterborough Court, Fleet Street.

I hope that *Why England Sleeps*—with apologies to the memory of John Kennedy for adapting so topical a title—will at least stir controversy, and that it will stimulate its readers to think afresh from first principles what British politics should be about in the 1970's. Those who are inclined to dub this book as "absurdly right-wing" in its economic, if not in many of its views on social issues and world affairs, might pause to reflect that most o the things which it advocates are but the small coin of life, almost universally accepted, in comparable civilised countries.

JOHN COCKCROFT

The Cottages
Crowtree Street,
Great Gransden,
2 February 1971

ACKNOWLEDGEMENTS

My heartfelt thanks are due to Maurice Green of the Daily Telegraph *for allowing me the time at short notice to write this book; to Lord Butler for writing so graciously of a book which in places sharply criticises the Governments in which he served; to Ian and Helga Raitt and Tessa Shepley for their invaluable help in "processing" this book; to Mrs King-Harman for the use of her "one-off" typewriter; to Pamela Creasey for so expeditiously and efficiently typing an often raw text; to Douglas Houghton who, although of a different political persuasion, has for so long kindly borne with youthful enthusiasm and pointed out the practical limits on political action; to those who have read and kindly commented on the synopsis of this book or the proofs; and to my family and friends who have listened patiently, if at times contentiously, for a decade and more to a thesis on which, over dinner, some wine has fallen.*

CHAPTER ONE

1945 and 1971—Triumph and Decline

Nations rise and fall but seldom has any fallen so far so quickly as Britain. Only a quarter of a century ago she ruled the largest empire the world had ever seen; her writ still ran from Rangoon to Georgetown. The British Empire and Commonwealth had emerged from six years of war victorious and the old adage that Britain lost every battle except the last (which she assuredly won) seemed to have been triumphantly vindicated. There seemed nothing that the British peoples, in alliance with the Great Republic beyond the water, might not achieve together.

There were even hopes that the distant, forbidding, brooding Russian peoples, partners in the war-time Grand Alliance, would look on benignly at such a prospect—might even play a part themselves in the joint construction of a better world. Britain's greatest war leader since Chatham, abruptly voted into opposition at the moment of victory, it is true, had deep forebodings about the intentions of Communist Russia. But he had not in 1945 despaired that all might yet be well; and on every possible occasion he spoke of how much Britain and America might together achieve in the world—and, later, of the need for the historic enemies of a thousand years to unite in building a new Europe.

There were indeed reasons for believing that Britain had some further service to render mankind. In 1945 it was not yet apparent that the ill wind of war had in an economic sense blown more strongly on the victors than on the vanquished. Within a decade Germany and Japan were to rise phoenix-like from the rubble of the Ruhr and Nagasaki to such effect that men spoke of their "economic miracles". But all this lay in the future. For some time after the 1939–45 war, Britain appeared to have benefited greatly from the devastation of her chief competitors. Most of Europe was shivering, hungry, dislocated, close to despair until America in "the most unsordid act in history", offered Marshall Aid in 1948 to rebuild her shattered economies.

In contrast, twenty miles across the Channel Britain seemed a country much to be envied. Despite the punishment certain of her cities, such as London, Coventry and Plymouth, had taken from German bombing, she was relatively intact after the holocaust. Her standard of living was still the fourth highest in the world. Her navy, despite the U-Boat losses, with America still dominated and controlled the world's sea routes. Her vast Empire and Commonwealth was apparently intact while the German and Italian attempts at colonialism lay in ruins; the French domains had been bitterly divided between the de Gaulle and Vichy Governments and the running sore of Indo-China already showed signs of bleeding France white; the Portuguese were still—grimly—in Africa; but the Spanish had long ago been thrown out of Latin America; and the Dutch were trying desperately, and as it transpired, unsuccessfully, to re-establish themselves in Indonesia.

Yet the British were not content with their comparative good fortune. They rapidly beat their swords into plough shares and switched their war industries back to producing consumer goods for the home market and to exporting. There were enormous opportunities for filching the export business which her competitors had enjoyed before the war—and her Commonwealth trade preferences in markets comprising nearly a quarter of the human race remained intact.

At the same time the ambitious, pioneering proposals of the war-time Beveridge Report for social welfare were implemented. By greater State spending and more sophisticated "Keynesian" monetary and fiscal techniques it was hoped that the pre-war spectre of mass unemployment (so demoralising, so wasteful of men and machines) would be banished for ever. And lo, the long-predicted slump did indeed fail to materialise, largely owing to the success of the Americans in keeping their giant economy moving steadily forward, with nothing worse than minor setbacks in expansion.

Moreover, there were no obviously immediately unfavourable results of Britain trying to do so much in such a short time (ambitious nationalisation measures were superimposed on the rapid expansion of social welfare). Indeed, the crutches of

American Lend Lease, the American-Canadian Loans and even Marshall Aid, were dispensed with by the end of the 1940's. Britain used her hard-won war-time expertise to good effect and, with America, pioneered the peaceful use of atomic energy for producing power. New "growth point" industries were set up and once-depressed towns, such as Burnley in the old Lancashire textile belt, were born again under new management.

On a wider world scene, not surprisingly, the shattered countries of the Continent looked to victorious Britain as a model of social success, economic progress, and as the natural leader of a uniting Europe. When Churchill returned to power in 1951, although he disappointed these European hopes, his Chancellor "set the people free" and for a time the economy appeared to respond impressively to the belated abolition of war-time controls.

What then went wrong? Could there be a greater contrast between Britain in 1945 and 1971? Much of what has happened in the intervening quarter century was of course inevitable—notably the withdrawal of imperial power, and the relative attrition of Britain's economic and political might as other nations "caught up". Even the over-slow adjustment of her leaders to her changed position in the world was no doubt in part unavoidable. The inevitability of much (but not all) Britain's relative decline is discussed in Chapter Two. It is also true that most British people are much more prosperous in material terms than they were a quarter of a century ago, and that in a sense Britain has recovered remarkably well from the scars left by the 1939–45 war.

Yet no one can really be happy with things as they are. That this is so is indicated eloquently by the high emigration figures. Young and not-so-young people have "voted with their feet" by leaving Britain and there is no sign of this changing: on the contrary. Such disturbing trends have a volition of their own. If enough people think that a nation is in decline, and that their own prospects if they stay there are unduly depressing, then the thought is in a sense father to the fact. In the longer run it cannot be good for Britain that she is losing so many highly skilled, expensively-educated people and has been receiving in return immigrants of much lower average quality—whatever her undoubted moral obligations to do so, whatever the debt London Transport and British hospitals owe to Jamaicans, and whatever the undoubted and considerable merits of East African Asians as skilled craftsmen and entrepreneurs.

Nations do decline, but not only in the sense of the imperial withdrawal discussed in this and the next chapter. They also can decline "psychologically"—although not inevitably so—in the sense that a sequence of events, maybe some of those nations' own making and maybe some not, reduce their morale so much that there is no place for that morale to go but down farther, as it were. It is unwise to be categorical about the experience of other countries, but it could certainly be argued that, for instance, Spain's long relative decline, both culturally and materially, into an isolated backwater on the edge of Europe since her heyday of colonisation, mass conversion of Latin America to Roman Catholicism, and gold riches, was in part a psychological phenomenon. The reasons for her economic decline were complex and will always be debated. But as that decline gathered momentum the Spanish people somehow seemed to lose the wish to be a significant power or influence in the world. Although now a holiday paradise on account of its sun, beaches, cheap food, wine and ancient ruins, Spain has not, to say the least, in living memory been in the van of economic, political or democratic progress. And the same is true of Portugal, a more often quoted example of backwater-manship—although she was never as great as Spain and so the subsequent fall seems less dramatic.

Britain is, as the British and a growing number of foreigners agree, a most delightful place in which to live, for those with enough money. For those who live on the bread-line, such as certain pensioners, for the third of the population which does not even have access to a bath and inside toilet, for the masses of the great, sprawling, ugly, industrial revolution cities of the Midlands and North, it is not a good place to live in in material terms and never has been. That, in short, is why Britain needs economic growth. Those who argue otherwise tend to be relatively well off already and to have little conception of how many of their countrymen live: "I'm all right, Jack." It is after all an ever-growing bore to have the roads cluttered up with more and more of "these people's" cars; to be embarrassed by hordes of uncouth Britishers on the beaches of the Mediterranean; to find domestic help increasingly difficult to get and expensive to retain. Things were not always ordered thus.

The next step in the argument that growth is unimportant is to say that even if Britain does decline relatively in material terms into a backwater, the country will continue to be as it is now for the better-off minority, a pleasant place in which to live. But why should this necessarily be so? After all nothing stands still for ever. The relative decline of Britain and people's increasing awareness of this trend could set off in its train all sorts of undesirable consequences. A society which was becoming relatively—or even absolutely—poorer might, for instance, become a more violent society as everyone sought to grab for himself a larger slice of that famous but by now shrinking national cake. The big increase in strikes, largely unofficial, after the pay freeze, and in particular after the Labour Government's climb-down on its proposed trade union legislation in 1969 was a timely reminder of how unpleasant, and in economic terms self-defeating, such a grab-for-all could be.

There would be, too, all the side-effects of a poor but "quaint" country making the most of its remaining assets (tourism? the monarchy? Dingley Dell? see Chapter Sixteen). Britain is already poor by Continental European standards, although this is not yet generally recognised here. If she were to become a second Portugal, catering for wealthy Texans by providing cheap services—domestic help, tours round the Tower of London, chauffering Rolls-Royces, re-learning the dialects of the countryside—surely the class-conscious British would be the first to object to their new-found servile status.

Yet in a metaphorical and not *necessarily* too literal sense, that is precisely the prospect. In economics, as in life, it is a good rule to assume that a trend will continue until it is seen to do otherwise. It is not necessary to know much about compound interest to see where present trends are leading Britain. An economic growth rate of only 2 to 3 per cent, with a tendency of late to fall towards the former figure, compares with twice that rate or more for most of Britain's main competitors, for most nations at a comparable stage of development. And Japan, with a growth rate at least four times that of Britain, will be far more powerful within a decade, barring the totally unforeseen.

In popular British folk-myth, despite the evidence that this country is now fourteenth in the international league table of living standards, other countries are merely "catching up". There is, indeed a sophisticated but admittedly rarer version of this argument which asks who won the war (a quarter of a century ago)? Germany and Japan have apparently been rebuilding their shattered economies, with American aid, for most of the last twenty-six years, and may indeed still be doing so for all that is known about them here. But, marvellously, the argument can be inverted. Sweden and America, two of the richest countries in terms of income per head in the world, whose industries were unscathed by the 1939–45 war, are apparently so much better off than Britain precisely because they were neutral for part or all of the war. So according to these flexible arguments-for-all-seasons Britain was virtually the only country which actually suffered in economic terms from the war!

These points are emphasised (at the risk of this book being labelled by the reader who gets no further than the first chapter another boring, depressing, introspective "condition of England" analysis, even though it is optimistic about Britain's longer-term future) for good reason. For the contrasts between a triumphant Britain in 1945 and 1971; and between Britain as she is now and as she *could* have been in 1971, are too striking to be ignored. And, although almost everyone in Britain is ostensibly tired of morbid introspection and "knocking Britain" there is no doubt that there is still a lot of misapprehension about just how much ground this country has lost relative to its main competitors in recent years; and by the same token about the degree of change, some of it unpleasant in the short-term for a lot of people, which is now necessary if recent trends are to be reversed—as they certainly can be over a period.

One must ask again, and try to answer in this book: why is it that in a generation the British have sunk from Gibbon's "happiest state of man" to their present unhappy state? Notwithstanding the late 1969–70 improvement in the balance of payments (which may prove to have been only too transient, as other "turning points" have in the past), how is it that Britain in such a short time has come to be regarded as a by-word for economic inefficiency? Why has the "English sickness" passed into the language as a synonym for continuous, almost unrelieved, economic failure, whether rightly or wrongly?

Almost everywhere the traveller goes he hears the same stories. They may, but they should not, lose their force by repetition. Tales of British exporters not using the languages of the countries to which they are exporting, not answering letters, providing poor or no servicing, packaging badly or inappropriately for the market concerned, and not doing their market research. Why, for instance, is there *still* no British car suitable for East African, and indeed most "under-developed" countries—which does not at once fall apart on dirt tracks? Why, for that matter, has not British Leyland got an all-night car service station in Nairobi (Volkswagen has)? Why has no small British car (except sports cars in relatively small numbers) ever swept the American market as Volkswagen did in the 1950's and Japanese Hondas are doing now?

It is embarrassing when abroad, however much the traveller may patriotically take issue, to hear a constant denigration of Britain's economic performance; this country was after all, and in some products still is, the home of quality products and good workmanship. There is little awareness in, for instance, America that Britain's balance of payments improved out of all recognition in the years 1969 and 1970. This turn-round may prove to be short-lived, it may have been bought at fearful cost. But at least it happened. At least Britain is no longer in that respect "the sick man of Europe" in need of the crutches of repeated foreign aid injections to survive. People abroad should know about the improvement: if they do not, British public relations and salesmanship are at fault.

It will be argued—it is often argued—that much of the gloom about the so-called English Sickness is over-done, not least among the British themselves. That is partially, but only partially, true. But to the extent that it is true, that foreigners have an unjustifiably gloomy view of Britain's past economic performance and future prospects, it is not their fault but that of the British. How can anyone without a particular interest in Britain, living in another country, be expected to spend more than a minute or two of the day at the most thinking about her fortunes? Hence it is up to British salesmen travelling abroad, British Government export services, and British journalists, to point out more effectively the considerable achievements of this country since the 1939–45 war. It is after all poor salesmanship in the widest sense which has contributed to Britain's bad economic reputation.

Yet it is not only poor salesmanship which has done that. The argument that "every country has its problems" and, by implication "ours happen to be economic" and, sometimes, "even *they* are much exaggerated" is only valid on the first score. It is not necessary to know much about America, the richest country in the world, to realise that she has major problems, such as race, and dissent, and violence, which dwarf anything yet seen in Britain or indeed anywhere in Europe. It is even true that every country also has its economic problems—such as Belgium's poor (by Common Market standards) economic growth rate, the relative backwardness of much of French industry, Germany's high-cost, remarkably inefficient farmers, the difficulty even America is having in reconciling reasonable price stability with a satisfactory rate of economic growth and so on. But Britain's problems happen to be more economic than most countries': for decades she has needed intermittent foreign financial support, she has one of the lowest growth rates known to modern man, and net emigration has increased alarmingly.

That is the answer to those who say that Britain's economic difficulties are no worse than anyone else's. The subjective impressions of the way too many British firms do business abroad, already mentioned, can at a pinch be discounted. So, too, can impressions of British inefficiency at home be brushed aside—such as the unbelievable London telephone service; Heathrow baggage handling procedure; the legion of business people who say they will ring back and never do so; the collapse of public services at the first arrival of more than one half-inch of snow; the stolid refusal to explain to the inconvenienced public what is happening or, more usually, not happening on such occasions; the sheer idleness or forced inactivity of so many junior office staff; the number of businessmen who never take their staff into their confidence, and the many who take days off for frivolous reasons. All these examples, and many more, can individually be discounted. All or most of them happen elsewhere, too. But their total result, the fact that Britain gets relatively poorer year by year, certainly cannot be so discounted.

Hence it is important and urgent to consider the various aspects of this problem and to suggest possible solutions.

CHAPTER TWO

A Process of Adjustment

There have undoubtedly been extenuating circumstances (see Chapter Three) for Britain's relatively poor economic performance in the last quarter century. And it is indeed depressing for the worst aspects of that performance to be constantly reiterated. It could even become counter-productive if the effect of too much brooding on Britain's ills, real and imagined, was to discourage further effort and initiative. This is unlikely. Every thinking person knows that there are enormous reserves of talent and ability waiting to be liberated in Britain, given the right conditions. And meanwhile it is still in many ways one of the most civilised societies in which to live that the world has ever known: witness the rapid increase in tourism to Britain and the large number of foreigners who have chosen to make their homes here.

A gloomy view of Britain's long-term future can really only be sustained on the view that national characteristics change over a period—or that her relative decline has reached the point of no return. It could be argued that, even if the right conditions, notably a more competitive environment, were created for the British to prosper in, they are now so sunk in relative economic failure and psychological depression that they would not react in the prescribed, text-book, manner. An analogy might be the behaviour of the Irish after British Governments had removed most of the economic constraints, notably the absurd system of land tenure which had caused so much misery in Ireland in the nineteenth century. The Irish economy remained a by-word for backwardness, however, for decades, indeed until the late 1950's, before it took off into a more than respectable growth rate. But Ireland's economic problems have probably had more to do with such constraints as the dominance of the Catholic Church and its attitude to birth control, the high average age at which the Irish marry, her lack of raw materials, and her dependence on the British market for her agricultural exports.

The British have after all already had an economic hey-day. A hundred years ago this country was ahead of any other in overall economic performance. The looms of Lancashire, the screw machines of Smethwick, the nut and bolt manufacturers of the Black Country, the coal mines of South Wales and the steel works of Lincolnshire poured out their products on a scale never seen before. It is true that even in 1870 Germany and America in particular were already eroding Britain's head start in the industrial revolution. It is true, too, that the economic dynamism which the British evinced a hundred years ago reflected in part the natural, comparative advantage they enjoyed in, for instance, Lancashire's damp climate which was ideal for cotton, and the reserves here of raw materials such as coal and iron ore.

Yet it also reflected the dynamism, the willingness to innovate and to take risks, of the British people themselves. The late eighteenth and nineteenth centuries saw an extraordinary flowering of inventive genius in this country. Every schoolboy knows about Hargreaves's spinning jenny, Kay of Bury and his flying shuttle, Arkwright's spinning frame, James Watt's steam engine and the agricultural improvements of Coke of Holkham, for instance.

Yet familiarity should not breed contempt for these long past achievements of the British. They are relevant to the present, and more important, the future of this country. For fortunately there is every indication that this inventive streak is still strong in the British. A country which can produce the hovercraft and the Concorde, has pioneered nuclear physics, can stretch end-to-end more Nobel prize winners in relation to its size than almost any other country—this nation should not lack a bright future. If our economic performance is poor now compared with most of our competitors then this is surely of our own making and therefore rectifiable. Even the fact that so many young and not-so-young British scientists, engineers, doctors, dentists, architects, business school graduates and other professional people are leaving this country to find what are usually first-rate jobs in the countries of their adoption, although a sad commentary on the present economic state of Britain, must also, paradoxically, be taken as a hopeful sign for the longer-term future. If more of them could be persuaded to stay in this country how much brighter might not her economic future be?

Even so it really is necessary to look again at Britain's more recent past before deciding what needs to be done to put things right in the future. The economic successes have been so relatively few, and the failures so many and so obvious and in some ways so repetitively similar, that although history may not repeat itself exactly, the lessons of the 1940's, 1950's and 1960's do have some bearing on the shape for Britain of the 1970's and 1980's.

If in some ways they have been locust-eaten years for Britain since 1945, there is, of course, no one reason for it. And it can be persuasively argued that the British have made the adjustment from being the mightiest imperial power the world has ever known to a medium-power-status (still near the top of the second eleven division, but certainly not playing in the first) with remarkable aplomb. The voluntary withdrawal from India in 1947 was, of course, the classic example of this massive adjustment to a reduced role in the world. British people not yet middle-aged remember as children maps showing a large part of the world still painted red. And nearly a quarter of the human race in 1945 still paid homage to the King-Emperor. Large numbers of the British middle and professional classes served him in faraway places from Lusaka to Rawalpindi, from Simla to Kingston. Administrators, lawyers, soil erosion experts, engineers, scientists—many were cut off in the prime of their careers by a withdrawal of the Raj which often came much sooner and more abruptly than there seemed to be any reason to expect in, say, 1945 when the victorious Empire stood bloodied but unbowed.

Many of these "colonial types" and particularly the older ones, have found it virtually impossible to get comparable jobs in Britain, or anywhere else for that matter. Where does one find in Europe or North America an assignment comparable to administering—sitting under a mango tree, dispensing white man's justice, the critics used to say—for instance a large tract of Nigeria, perhaps with one European assistant? However well the job was done (and it usually was) even the most benign and well-disposed potential employer here at home would find it difficult to offer anything even remotely comparable. So many former District Officers have, sadly but inevitably, ended up running chicken farms or public houses or golf clubs, activities far below their abilities and training.

There have, of course, been other massive imperial withdrawals; and other nations have been cut down to size by the long march of history, by the force of changed circumstances. But such adjustments to reduced circumstances have seldom been on such a scale, nor so rapid. The decline of Spanish influence in Latin America, for instance, was a long drawn-out affair, and it was well over a millenium from Gibbon's Antonine Age of Rome to the fall of Constantinople. Yet within a generation Britain has withdrawn from all her vast empire except for a few unviable fortresses and tiny dependencies.

The change has been completed without a complete collapse of morale, or serious break-down of the social fabric, as happened in France, for instance, between the world wars, in the aftermath of the blood-letting she suffered on the Somme and at ("ils ne passeront pas") Verdun. Crime has increased in Britain since 1945, but so it has in most countries. Many of the middle and professional classes remember with nostalgia those golden summers of the 1930's when there were few cars on the roads (except one's own), servants were still cheap, £2,000 a year still went a long way for a family of four, and "who's for tennis?" was still heard on select vicarage lawns and at weekend country house parties—and indeed all over the vast imperial fief, from Nairobi to Rangoon.

They naturally regret the passing of all (or most of) this, but they have not become Fascist. Indeed many of them have accepted the social changes of their lifetime with remarkable equanimity: that one's son should do science rather than history or the classics; that public-school-induced "leadership qualities" have no longer such great importance; that in the future whether Britain sinks or swims will depend largely on the quality and competitiveness of her advanced technology; that she may soon have to link hands with her enemy of two world wars across the Rhine; that for the first time ever the great majority of the population can enjoy, because they can afford, many of the good things of life. To that extent, and to the extent that people are no longer persecuted for what they do in private and young people have opportunities (to exploit or to squander) which their parents barely dreamt of, Britain is a more civilised and more worthwhile society for the majority than it has ever been before. Roy Jenkins's speech of 19 July 1969 on "the civilised society" is well worth re-reading in this context.

Yet that society has retained its homogeneity. Enoch Powell

sees the Tiber foaming red at some unspecified point in the future, and in particular in his own Black Country. But the fact remains that now, whatever the precise projections of the buoyant immigrant birth rates, little more than 2 per cent (a tiny proportion by, for instance, American standards) of the British population is not indigenous in its origins, concentrated though this percentage is in certain places. And a high proportion of that 2 per cent is treated with a decency and equality which would be impossible in many parts of the world.

The social aspect of Britain's readjustment since 1945, the symbolic passing of P. G. Wodehouse's Lord Emsworth and his Empress, has been emphasised in order that the mistakes of British economic policy since then may be seen in their right perspective. Serious mistakes there have indeed been, which the first part of this book is largely about. But they could have been worse. And they had much to do with the difficulty that those who ran Britain's affairs—usually, as is normal here, relatively elderly men—had in adjusting sufficiently rapidly to her changing position in the world. Not surprisingly, but disconcertingly.

Many of those lessons have now been well learnt—as evidenced by, for instance, the enthusiasm and persistence with which the Foreign Office has rightly but belatedly, and at times unskilfully, sought entry to Europe. And it could be argued that to the extent that they have been so learnt, the past has little bearing on the present or the future. Yet that is surely not so. For the process of re-adjustment of people's attitudes to Britain's relatively reduced role in the world is still not yet complete, as this book hopes to show. This is, for instance, still a relatively xenophobic country. It is still true, as it was in 1962 when Dean Acheson said it (to the accompaniment of absurd protests in Britain from the Prime Minister downwards), that Britain has lost an empire and not yet found a role. And there is also the fact that a persistent streak of the British character, an unwillingness to look too far ahead and to acknowledge soon enough hard and unpleasant facts—which was so apparent in the Nazi-dominated 1930's and which has contributed to some of the mistakes of economic policy since 1945—still exists today and must be guarded against in future policy-making.

CHAPTER THREE

Twilight of the Raj: Aid and Defence

Are there, were there, special reasons for such a relatively poor performance by Britain? It could be after all that those reasons had little to do with the British, who put on a remarkable economic spurt after the 1939–45 war. Despite or because of export drives ("export or die" was a well-used post-war slogan), the proportion of imports covered by exports rose to a much higher proportion than ever before. This was essential, of course, to compensate for Britain's substantial sales of foreign investment during the war. And the unexpectedly sustained boom in world trade, in stark contrast to pre-war experience, was a great help. Nevertheless, it happened, and it was a considerable achievement.

So, too, was the rate of economic growth achieved. Minimal unemployment and a much fuller utilisation of resources, coupled with a more sophisticated use of monetary and fiscal policy than before the 1939–45 war, were the main reasons for this more rapid creation of real resources. Britain's post-war growth rate of about 3 per cent a year (falling to 2.2 per cent in 1964–69) is good by historical standards, not even excluding the Victorian hey-day of 1850–70. And the growth of productivity seems to have made, in this country as elsewhere, a sustained, and it is to be hoped permanent, breakthrough to a higher plane.

Yet there is no escaping the fact that over a quarter of a century Britain's economic performance—however it is measured: whether in terms of relative economic growth, share of world trade, level of capital investment, or improvement in living standards—has been unusually poor. Over this long period hopes of an improvement in this record have been almost consistently shattered. And, as time has passed, it has become progressively more difficult for the British to persuade themselves that others are merely catching up with the head-start they enjoyed in 1945. There was, moreover, the growing realisation that some of the apparently easy successes of the immediate post-war years were based on ephemeral, and as it turned out, transient factors.

In 1945 the Ruhr had been reduced to rubble and Germany, Britain's natural competitor in Europe since the end of her long Victorian economic hegemony, had perforce to spend several years putting her house in order. Not before the early 1950's could she begin to become a significant factor again in international trade. And Japan, which had made remarkable strides in exporting cheap consumer goods before 1939, was similarly (though less) disabled. Moreover, the whole pre-war pattern of trade was distorted by the notorious "dollar shortage" and the lack of convertibility between currencies. And Britain still had significant tariff preferences in most Commonwealth countries. Her departure from India, it is true, hastened, but far from destroyed, her traditional trading links.

All these factors helped to prolong the illusion of Britain's economic Indian summer. So soon after a war in which she had, almost single-handed for a while, helped to save mankind, it was difficult indeed to foresee that she would soon become a second rank power with perennial economic difficulties. Up until the time of the Suez mis-adventure in 1956 it was possible to believe that such setbacks as the 1949 convertibility crisis and subsequent devaluation, the constant need for foreign economic support such as Lend Lease, the 1946 American loan, Marshall Aid, the intense inflationary pressures created by the post-Korean re-armament programme, and the retention of rationing and economic controls long after most other countries had abandoned them, were all in their different ways flashes-in-the-pan, "one-off" crises or misadventures inevitable in Britain's return to "business as usual". But after Suez it was no longer possible for even the most diehard Tory back-woodsman to believe that Britain was still a super-power which could go it alone.

Yet the argument can, in part at least, be inverted. Have there not been particular factors which most of the last quarter century made it difficult, if not impossible, for Britain to perform even averagely well economically? Perhaps her very success in the more distant past made it inevitable that she should appear to lag as the Victorian golden age became a distant memory?

Certainly the imperial legacy, which in its time had provided such useful assistance in war, and raw materials and captive markets in peace time, in a sense went sour on Britain after 1945. The cost of administering India, by far Britain's most important imperial possession, for instance, had been a charge on the Indian taxpayer and on the Indian balance of payments and not on the British taxpayer. And such major British industries as Lancashire cotton had vast, albeit poor, tailor-made markets for their goods. After the British withdrawal the full cost of maintaining a defence posture (for instance the great sprawling, expensive base at Singapore), fell on the British taxpayer and on the British balance of payments. Moreover, imperial interests like Aden and the Suez canal zone, and even the Arabian sheikdoms before they struck oil, had been regarded basically as staging-posts to sustain the long supply routes to India. When she left India the question was asked what precisely was Britain's *raison d'être* in a changed world?

Closely linked with this theme of imperial withdrawal, which by the beginning of the 1960's had left Britain bereft of most of her former enormous colonial empire (still ostensibly intact in 1945), were the controversial sterling balances. Latterly much was made, not without reason, of how they represented a millstone round Britain's neck, a major constraint on economic growth, a cause of balance of payments instability, a curse of which no man could see the end. And the cost of servicing them grew a lot as interest rates increased substantially over the years since 1945. Moreover, there was understandably a good deal of resentment in Britain, unspoken and at times spoken, that they were largely debts incurred by Britain towards her former colonies for defending them in the 1939–45 war. It was even suggested that they should be "forgotten" in a general moratorium on 1939–45 war debts. Certainly their very existence, at least until the 1969 "Basle dollar guarantee" by the richer countries of the world against a further devaluation of sterling, made the task of negotiating Britain's entry into Europe that much more complex. The problems they raised were a favourite horror story of Gaullist mythology.

Yet the existence of the sterling area and of the sterling balances in London since the 1939–45 war was in other ways a source of strength to Britain—and particularly so in the earlier post-war years. The balances were largely invested in British Government securities and thereby substantially helped the Government broker in his job of selling gilt-edged stocks and maintaining an orderly market. In fact, the balances themselves represented a tailor-made market for those stocks. The overseas sterling area countries were remarkably loyal, even unto the end in the shape of the 1967 forced sterling devaluation, in maintaining their bank accounts in London and not switching their resources elsewhere as they could have done, individually if not collectively, over a period. After the 1967 devaluation, which represented a default by Britain on her obligations to these countries, not surprisingly they became nervous and started to diversify their assets away from London. Hence the need for the Basle guarantee.

More important though than the stability of the London gilt-edged market was the assistance the overseas sterling area countries gave to Britain's balance of payments, in good times and in bad, in her many post-war crises. It so happened that the sterling area countries (roughly the Commonwealth, minus Canada but plus certain other countries, such as South Africa, Burma, Israel, and Eire) were by and large producers of raw materials and food. Traditionally these were traded for manufactured goods from Britain. And it is a fact of international economic life that just as all farmers are never happy with the weather at the same time all sterling area countries are not prospering equally well. So when primary producers were thriving and depositing their hard-earned, scarce foreign currencies in London, Britain benefited indirectly. And those overseas sterling area countries similarly benefited when the economic pendulum swung the other way, and Britain's relatively sophisticated manufactured exports sold well overseas and the proceeds were credited to the collective account of the sterling area.

Yet there can be no doubt that, for the reasons already mentioned, the sterling area in the 1960's became progressively more of a "con" and less of a "pro" in Britain's balance sheet. There were also to be weighed in the balance the imponderables, such as the extent to which the existence of the sterling area persuaded Britain to make investments, and to incur defence expenditure at least in part to protect them, which she would have otherwise avoided. Certainly much money was invested on the basis of strictly non-commercial criteria. There are certain major British companies, for instance, which rue the day they ever invested in India. They tend to claim, in mitigation of past errors, that although they cannot afford to invest there, they equally could not afford not to have at least a foot-hold in such a vast potential market. No doubt they will be proved right in the *very* long run. No doubt the great potential of India, like the famous economic possibilities of Brazil, will one day make her an economic giant. Meanwhile, however, many foreign investors are on a tread-mill (as they are in many so-called under-developed countries in that they have to run faster merely to stay in the same place). Under the pressure of successive development plans they must, to retain the good will of the host Governments, keep investing heavily in their local subsidiary. Yet restrictions on remitting profits often make it virtually impossible legally to get much money out of the country concerned in order to remunerate existing investments. Retained profits, it is true, increase the value of the investment. But what use is that if in a socialist or semi-socialist economy there is only one potential unenthusiastic, ungenerous buyer—the "host" Government?

Much of the money invested in the Commonwealth by Britain might well have been more profitably employed either at home or in the dynamic markets of Europe and North America. There are big British investments in North America, much greater than many people in Britain realise, but clearly they could have been even larger by now. And for a long time after the 1939–45 war Europe was relatively neglected by British industry (with some notable and honourable exceptions such as ICI's vast chemical complex at Rotterdam).

Perhaps more important, however, is the question, to which we shall never know the exact answer, how much more might Britain have prospered since 1945 if some of the money invested by business abroad, and in particular spent overseas by the Government on "prestigious" defence projects, had been spent at home on building up and renewing the infrastructure of a modern industrial nation? More motorways, more deep-water ports, more automated machinery, a sustained higher level of investment generally, might by now have made a considerable cumulative difference to Britain's economic growth rate and hence to her standard of living. Moreover, Britain's notoriously low level of productive investment over a long period no doubt has a number of causes—not least the reluctance of many British businessmen to invest in new machinery when the old equipment is still working, however inefficiently. But the out-pouring of money from this country over many years, which could have been profitably invested here, has contributed to the low investment rate.

That overseas investment has in a sense reaped a rich harvest, of course, has become apparent in the remarkable increase in Britain's overseas earnings in recent years. But the harvest had some of that money been invested at home, although equally invisible and more unquantifiable, might have been even greater.

What is certain is that much of the money spent abroad on Government account has been wasted. The sums cannot be quantified (no Government Department would have any interest in doing such sums even if they were possible). Just as the benefits of, for instance, the East of Suez posture, the imperial role without the Empire as it were, can never be accurately assessed. There have been notable (although in strictly commercial terms unprofitable) successes for Britain's policy of maintaining, relative to such competitors as Germany, a large overseas posture. She helped America to restore order in the Lebanon in 1958, for instance, she put down the East African mutinies in 1964, she defeated Indonesia's confrontation against Malaysia in 1967. And the benefits to the world of the latter achievement, using only some 10,000 men, are incalculable.

Nevertheless, it is clear in retrospect, if it was not at the time, that since the 1939–45 war Britain tried for too long to maintain the trappings of a great power without the economic basis with which to sustain it. The performance has resembled the "Skylon" at the 1951 South Bank Festival of Britain—an impressive, graceful, object suspended in mid-air with no visible means of support. Even after Suez the attempt was made (not without some success but at a high cost in the neglect of alternative investment opportunities) to go on appearing to be the super-power she no longer was.

Duncan Sandys' brainchild, the independent nuclear deterrent, largely duplicated the all-embracing American nuclear umbrella. It was difficult, at least until America started to show signs of wanting to withdraw from her post-1945 commitments, to see what this deterrent achieved except the appearance of great power status. Its real cost was undoubtedly high but immolated and submerged for all time deep in the Government's defence estimates. It is certain that this was, and is, a cost which Britain's NATO allies never asked her to undertake. Thus it prohibited her from doing desirable alternative things—such as honouring her obligation to maintain two full-strength divisions in Germany until the end of the century, being able to fly troops quickly to the trouble spots where they were needed, and being able to maintain a consistent defence policy which did not involve the constant need to cancel projects at short notice under dire economic pressure. No doubt there was a substantial technological "fall-out" from Britain's independent nuclear weapons armoury, but it was not sufficient to compensate for the high costs involved.

Linked to these facts of a Britain over-extended—the latter-day sterling area, the mis-direction of investment, the maintenance of world-wide, costly commitments, the expensive ostensibly independent nuclear deterrent—has been the financial burden of the actual process of imperial withdrawal. It was sometimes expensive for Britain to be in a country (for instance Cyprus during "the troubles"); it was also expensive for her to withdraw.

Thus throughout the post-1939–45 war period there was the incubus to Britain, albeit a morally desirable one, of aid and assistance to former colonial territories. These new nations were often, to say the least, unready and unprepared to assume independence without help. Apart from France, Britain had probably a greater moral obligation to assist more countries than any other major industrialised nation (if only because she had had more colonies). And in many cases, such as Kenya, she had not expected that she would have had to leave so precipitously. This meant that the "downside potential" for cutting aid, technical assistance, investment, and defence help was strictly limited. Indeed, aid at "x" millions over "y" years was often in effect written into Independence Day concordats.

These often ostensibly reciprocal agreements with newly

independent countries (Britain and Malaysia, for instance, promised to defend each other in the case of attack) "slotted into" the multilateral network of obligations around the world which Britain contracted in the post-war years. Membership of the United Nations, the North Atlantic Treaty Organisation, Western European Union, the South East Asia Treaty Organisation, and the Central Treaty Organisation was expensive for what was, it became increasingly apparent, only a medium-sized power.

The aid and defence burdens combined meant that Britain had to generate an overall surplus on her balance of payments of several hundred million pounds a year in order to break even. In many years Britain's "invisible" earnings did in fact bridge the gap. Had it not been for the heavy Government expenditure abroad already mentioned, which had risen to an average of over £450 million a year in 1964–69, the books would have been handsomely balanced every year.

Despite doubts about whether certain of the large sums Britain has invested abroad since 1945 might not have been more profitably invested nearer home, her foreign investments *in toto* have unquestionably proved a valuable nest-egg. There was an urgent need after the 1939–45 war to restore Britain's foreign "portfolio", that is share investments, which had been sold to pay for the war. British investment trusts, for instance, were forced to sell their American investments during the war, but have multiplied their subsequent post-war investments on Wall Street many times. This has been very much to the general good. Yet the Labour Government of 1964–70 forced them to surrender a quarter of the dollar premium on selling their American investments, and thereby much reduced the flexibility of their investment policy.

Britain has in fact been remarkably successful in buying other countries' inflation-proof assets with money which they have lent her on fixed-interest terms. In other words, she has borrowed good money and paid back bad : her investments have been redeemed in depreciated currencies. There is no moral issue involved except in so far as inflation itself is immoral. Britain has merely shown good business sense in the manner of an individual who borrows money from a company in order to buy shares in that company. His assets are real, increasing in monetary value with the fall in the value of money. His liability, on the other hand, is defined in cash, decreasing in real terms as inflation takes its toll.

Since 1945, by building up its portfolio investments, Britain has only sought to restore the status quo ante. For this country has never lived by trade alone and there have only been a handful of years, such as 1970, since 1800 when the visible trade balance, that is the gap between exports and imports, has shown a surplus. Moreover, Britain's highly successful trade in services, such as shipping, banking, insurance and broking, has seldom been enough in itself to bridge that deficit. It was remitted profits, in the shape of interests and dividends, from overseas investment which made the difference between national viability and eventual bankruptcy.

Indeed, the earnings from these investments have provided the most stable and the fastest-growing element in the British balance of payments. Although net new investment overseas was deliberately slowed down by Government restrictions, in the 1960's net interest, profits and dividends from existing overseas investments increased rapidly. Thus the present balance of payments situation is more favourable than it would otherwise have been, on account of past deficits which represented overseas investment rather than current spending. The Wilson Government apparently deliberately blurred this distinction in order to exaggerate the size of the balance of payments deficit inherited from the Conservatives in 1964. Thus only £393 million of the famous 1964 £800 million (since corrected to £747 million) deficit was accounted for by the current balance deficit.

Britain is still a substantial creditor nation. Indeed, despite the vast official borrowings since 1964, at the end of 1968 Britain's investments overseas exceeded other countries' investments here by about £2,000 million. And subsequent debt repayments have almost certainly improved the position further.

Nevertheless, the 1945–51 Labour Government incurred large overseas debts and the debts incurred by the Wilson Government still amounted to £3,255 million in March 1970, largely owing to the International Monetary Fund and central banks. Some of this money has since been repaid from Britain's balance of payments surplus and from "hot" money flowing in on account of her high interest rates. During the thirteen intervening Conservative years British net private overseas investment was over £1,300 million. The value of this investment has, of course, subsequently grown considerably.

The importance of overseas investment to Britain can be looked at in a different way. Thus the visible foreign trade of Japan, which (not without reason—see Chapter Fifteen) is often held up to the British as an example, is about 17 per cent of her gross national product, and her invisible trade about 5 per cent. Comparable figures for Germany are 30 per cent and 10 per cent. And for America 7 per cent and 4 per cent. The same figures for Britain are 28 per cent and 15 per cent.

The moral is clear. Both visible and invisible trade account for an exceptionally high proportion of Britain's national income—and the latter especially so. Might it not therefore be wise to put less emphasis on improving "visible" exports, and more on boosting invisible earnings from activities such as banking, insurance, broking and even further? A Government which read the economic entrails correctly might make a start by lifting the Selective Employment Tax, as the Conservatives are pledged to do, on such invaluable exporting industries. So-called invisible earnings, including notably the foreign earnings of the City of London, are after all now estimated at more than £600 million a year, and are probably still growing. Thus "invisibles" have a key contribution to make to the new Britain. The seed-corn of future prosperity, they must be encouraged in every way possible; for they are indeed something the British do well.

CHAPTER FOUR

A Persistent Lack of Foresight

The persistent lack of foresight in British economic policy-making in the last quarter century, mentioned in the last chapter, can be illustrated from a number of mistakes, and some near-disasters, over that relatively long period. No doubt there were special factors in each case. No doubt, as is often the case for both nations and individuals, the unexpected happened time and again and caught the policy-makers off-guard. The 1949 devaluation, for instance, is a relatively long time ago and especially so to young people. But the record of overall relative economic un-success is too depressing, and certain themes, such as the lack of foresight, too recurring for twenty-five years of British history to be written off, their lessons ignored, as but an evening gone.

The first post-war Labour Government was almost as racked by economic crises as its Labour successor. But perhaps with better reason. After all, despite the contrast in Chapter One between a Britain triumphant and ostensibly as great a world power as ever in 1945, the then Attlee Government had formidable economic problems to face. Which makes it all the more surprising in retrospect that it pushed ahead so rapidly with, and used so much parliamentary time (as again its Labour successor of 1964–70 did) for, expensive acts of economic policy. The nationalisation acts, for coal, gas, electricity and the railways, among others, and the legislation expanding the welfare state on the basis largely of the war-time Coalition Beveridge Report, were pushed through at high speed. No doubt Labour MPs regarded most of them as long-overdue. But they were expensive both of their time and of the taxpayers' money, when many other urgent problems pressed.

Moreover, it is at least possible that had the economy, and in particular Britain's external economic position, been handled with more skill, Labour would have had more time to push through its nationalisation and social legislation in a more carefully thought-out way. Many thoughtful Socialists regret the way in which the "Morrison formula" for nationalisation (in fact based largely on the earlier theories of Sidney and Beatrice Webb) of vast, monolithic State corporations with virtually no day-to-day accountability to Parliament, was foisted on them. It is certainly possible that had it run the economy more successfully the Attlee Government—albeit harassed as it was by the repercussions of the Korean War—might not have lost office in 1951. And so it would have been granted more time to make the changes on which it had set its collective heart.

That six-year Administration began, as it ended, in some economic gloom. In the shadow of a Europe devastated by war, with Britain's foreign investments depleted and her export trade largely disrupted, the Treasury's whiz-kid, Lord Keynes was despatched post-haste to America to negotiate a massive loan. The hope was that Britain's difficulties would prove temporary and the loan would provide sufficient time for her to convert her war industries back to exporting. The American and Canadian loans of £1,475 million were, however, by prevailing standards expensive: not even the great economist could persuade the Americans to accept the level of the British Government's opening bid. Indeed, the effort of the negotiations hurried him into his grave.

Had he lived he would doubtless have been distressed to see the loans exhausted within eighteen months. And, despite repayments of £469 million (deferments took place in 1956, and interest only was paid in 1957, 1964, 1965 and 1968), the loans outstanding, at £1,893 million in late 1970, were greater than they were when they were negotiated. (Although, of course, the remorseless march of inflation has made them worth less in real terms.) Since the loans were fixed in dollars, their value in sterling terms was substantially increased by the 1949 and 1967 devaluations. The loan ran out in a fraction of the time expected by the British authorities. Had not America's Marshall Aid, which was offered to the whole of devastated Europe, appeared in the nick of time there would indeed have been a débâcle.

Not that economic crisis was postponed for long. The many denials by Sir Stafford Cripps in 1948 that he would devalue the pound, although sometimes regarded retrospectively as inevitable in the difficult situation he found himself in, were not wholly deliberate dissembling. The Treasury and Bank of England appear to have been unconscionably slow in realising that the pre-war value of the pound could not be supported in Britain's changed post-war circumstances. So when the pound was devalued in 1949 under duress and in far from rational conditions (as in 1967), from 4.08 dollars to 2.80 dollars, there was an element of "over-kill" in the decision. In effect the foreign exchange crisis caused by Britain's short-lived attempt at convertibility for the over-valued pound, created something of a panic. It is clear now that a less drastic devaluation would have sufficed, at least for some time. Too great a devaluation unnecessarily moved the terms of trade, the ratio of the price of imports to the price of exports, against Britain. By unduly pushing up the price of imports, this large devaluation thus gave the prices-wages spiral an unnecessarily large twist. It also meant that for a given unit of imports, other things being equal, Britain had to find an unduly large unit of exports.

Morale was low after the 1949 devaluation débâcle. It had been low before it—and notably during the 1947 winter fuel crisis. Although no doubt in a sense an act of God, that severe shortage of coal over which Emanuel Shinwell presided as Minister of Fuel, was the first of many post-war winter crises in Britain: electric railway points freezing up, electricity cables collapsing, voltages reduced, a sprinkling of snow reducing traffic to a snail's pace and so on. These seem largely to have been unforeseen. A shivering Britain, superimposed on a still strictly rationed Britain, was a most depressing experience for a people who had a short time ago won a war through great sacrifice; they had naturally looked forward to happier times. There was, too, the Attlee Government's over-reaction to the Korean war—which admittedly was almost as unexpected in Washington as it was in London. Bevan turned out to be right, when he resigned from the Government with Wilson and Freeman (recently British Ambassador to Washington), in maintaining that a rearmament programme of £4,700 million over three years could not be sustained by an economy which was basically on a peace-time footing. The "war-monger" Churchill duly recognised this harsh fact when he returned to power in 1951 and scaled down the rearmament programme.

The economic sins of that Government, and of its Conservative successors under Eden, Macmillan and Home, were more those of omission than commission—apart from Suez. The implications of the slow economic growth rate which prevailed during 1951–64 are examined elsewhere in this book and even that growth compares favourably with Britain's experience since 1964. The Churchill Government with Butler as Chancellor was remarkably successful in dismantling the war-time and Labour paraphernalia of controls. But it sowed the seeds of mistakes in foreign and economic policy the results of which are with us to this day. In particular, Churchill's dream of becoming the great peace-maker, whom future generations would call blessed, achieved nothing in Moscow but it did divert attention from more concrete and more soluble problems nearer home. The memoirs of contemporary statesmen who served in that Churchill Government show clearly that the great man's obsession in his old age with "peace"—"the little children, what will they do if God wearies of mankind?" he asked in his last great peroration to the Commons—diverted his attention from his former European aspirations of Opposition days. "We must build a kind of United States of Europe" declined into *carte blanche* for his Foreign Secretary and Crown Prince, Sir Anthony Eden, to have a more or less free rein in foreign policy, with the exception of Summit meetings with the Russian leaders. But his predilections certainly did not include closer contacts with Continental nations if "sovereignty" was at stake.

The early mistakes Britain made concerning Europe left a difficult legacy for the politicians of the 1960's and 1970's. By not joining the Common Market at its inception (since it proved a success) Britain was bound to be asked to pay a substantial, and increasing, price as time went by if she later changed her mind. And if she remained adamantly opposed to joining she ran the risk of being isolated on the periphery of a rapidly uniting Europe.

Yet, despite pressing invitations from the Continent, and a debate in the Commons in which Edward Heath was one of the few to raise his voice in protest, Britain in 1951 adamantly refused to participate in the founding European Coal and Steel Community. She in effect killed the proposed European Defence Community which was to integrate European armies down to battalion level and end a thousand years of strife between Frank and Teuton. When the point of decision came in 1954 France could not face linking herself so closely with her historic enemy without the participation of Britain. Yet in the shambles which resulted from the rejection of the EDC in the French National

Assembly Britain had a change of heart. In an attempt to fill the European power vacuum Foreign Secretary Eden rushed round the European capitals and for the sake of creating the loose, ineffective, Western European Union (comprising the subsequent Six plus Britain), he gave precisely the guarantees, notably to keep two army divisions on the Continent for fifty years, for which the French had been asking for the EDC. Then, worst of all, there was the withdrawal of Britain's (low level) observer from the negotiations which led to the signature of the Treaty of Rome. Her European friends were desolated that she did not play a full part at Messina.

Most people in high places in Britain—notably the Foreign Office, the Treasury, the Board of Trade, and the Bank of England—apparently thought that the proposed customs union would not "get off the ground". And that if by some mischance they were proved to be wrong we could "always muscle in on our own terms later, with the leadership of Europe for the asking". But, alas, the sequel was the despatch of Reginald Maudling around Europe in a vain attempt to erect a free trade area scaffolding around the Market framework. He, or the Cabinet who briefed him, apparently had little idea that the founding fathers at Messina were attempting to build not merely a customs union, but a new and in the long run largely political, order in Europe.

Moreover, the two later attempts to join the Market were equally badly handled. The first by being too cautious and too detailed, with public opinion quite unprepared for such a remarkable volte-face (see Chapter Eleven): and the second in that it was attempted despite no apparent change of heart on the part of the French President, and in the naïve belief that he could be pressurised by the support of the Five into allowing Britain into the Market.

By chance, Britain's European mis-adventure, or rather non-adventure, at Messina almost coincided with another, more dramatic and more obviously disastrous mis-adventure. Perhaps the full story of Suez, of who colluded with whom for what reason, even when the Foreign Office vaults are opened in 1986, will never be told. If it is ever told it seems improbable that many of the participants will come out of it well. In history there can have seldom been such a sorry story of deception, self-deception, half-truths, lies, confused objectives and an outcome where the last state was worse than the first. But, from the point of view of British economic policy, and the lack of foresight which has often ruled it, the lessons were rather different.

There was the apparently immediate volte-face by the Treasury. It may be, of course, that senior officials there gave advice from the beginning to the effect that Britain could not go it alone, even in collusion with the French, without clear assurances from America that she would support the pound if necessary. If they did so, and their advice was rejected, that would be their problem—one of the disadvantages of working in a bureaucracy where secrecy is almost elevated into a virtue, and not least by the civil servants themselves (see Chapter Five). It seems at least as likely, however, and particularly so in view of the other monumental errors of judgement and of anticipation by British civil servants and their political masters in the last quarter century, that the Chancellor was advised that Britain's reserves were great enough to take the strain of a short war at Suez. It was indeed curious that Harold Macmillan was apparently, in the inner Cabinet cabal which directed the Suez operation, at first as enthusiastic as any for that ill- fated enterprise. And then, when it became apparent that "hot" volatile, short-term funds were pouring out of London, and that the enraged Americans, whose own record in this sorry affair was far from blameless, would give no support whatsoever to sterling, the Chancellor, it seems, was adamant for withdrawal.

Like the grand old Duke of York's, Eden's troops were first led smartly up the hill, and then down the other side in double-quick time. Surely some at least of this fiasco could have been foreseen?

For four and a half years after Suez there was relative calm on the economic front. Macmillan as Prime Minister brilliantly re-united a shattered Conservative party and rebuilt Britain's bridges to America. There were significant tax cuts in 1957 and 1958. In the famous pre-election Budget of 1959 Chancellor Amory "gave away" £360 million of revenue and in particular cut income tax from 8s 6d to 7s 9d in the pound. Even the April Budget after the October 1959 election, which returned Macmillan to power with an overall majority of 100 made some concessions, although the net effect was to increase the overall tax revenue slightly. The 1961 Budget also increased that revenue marginally but was notable for—in an act of remarkable political courage by Selwyn Lloyd, now

Speaker of the Commons, in the face of fierce opposition from
Labour, and especially from Harold Wilson—raising the starting point for surtax on earned income from £2,000 to £5,000 a
year. The background to these mild Tory Budgets had been
current balance of payments surpluses averaging over £200
million a year in 1956–59.

However, retribution was not long delayed. Economic
growth rates (in the gross domestic product) of 4.0 per cent in
1959 and 5.7 per cent in 1960, high by British standards, as so
often proved impossible to sustain without serious difficulties
on the external front. A current balance of payments deficit of
£265 million in 1960 was offset by a large inflow of "hot" and
not-so-hot money into London. But in 1961, although the
current deficit declined to almost nothing, the flow of short-
term and speculative money was out of London. Yet within
four months of the mild April 1961 Budget near-disaster struck.

The 1961 crisis measures were imposed with great rapidity
and with the appearance of some confusion, which was also
true of the dismissal by Macmillan of a third of his Cabinet a
year later. Selwyn Lloyd's main fault, it would seem, was to
have been more loyalist than the King, and to have stuck
rigidly to such unpopular aspects of the 1961 austerity
programme as the pay freeze for nurses. There is no doubt
(whatever Macmillan's deeply emotional memories of unemployment in the 1930's and his own honourable part as a back-bench
and unorthodox Conservative MP at that time in insisting that
"something must be done") that by 1961 Macmillan's thoughts
were already turning to the problem of winning re-election in
1964 at the latest, in tandem with a Chancellor apparently
devoted to financial rectitude at all costs, whatever the electoral
consequences. Yet the whole incident—the butchering at the
drop of a hat of so many Ministers and the dismissal of an
uninspired but undoubtedly loyal and diligent Chancellor—gave
an impression of short-term expediency in British politics which
lingers still.

These were the years, 1961–64, when discussion of the
"condition of England" question first became endemic, when
the quesion "what shall we do to be saved?" came to
dominate the thoughts of those who were concerned in this
country with political and economic issues. Britain's relatively
poor economic performance had been apparent well before
then, it is true. And certainly the exaggerated claims of the

Conservative Party in the 1959 election to have substantially improved the material condition of the people (whatever Macmillan's precise use of the phrase "you've never had it so good") grated even then on the ears of those who realised just how much needed to be changed in the economic field, in the taxation structure, in industrial relations, in creating a more competitive economy, in foreign and defence policy, if Britain was ever to hold her own again in world markets. In what countries after all had not living standards risen rapidly since 1945?

In the early 1960's thoughtful people became seriously worried that Britain could not continue indefinitely, with a low economic growth rate and an economic crisis almost every other summer, without becoming a backwater. There was a feeling that everything (except genuinely radical measures) had been tried and that nothing had worked. There was a sudden admiration of, and interest in, French indicative planning. Many came to believe that if Britain, too, could make businessmen more confident, more inclined to pledge their future by investing more, this in itself would engender a higher economic growth rate. A sort of "virtuous circle" of growth, a self-fulfilling prophecy of happier days, would ensue.

The Government only needed to tell people what the implications of an "x" per cent annual growth rate were for them personally, and they then only needed to work for it, for it to be achieved. The Government would at the same time actively intervene in its disposal of public sector contracts and would seek to influence the capital market in favour of "desirable" economic propositions (such as those which would lead to higher exports) in order to stimulate the growth rate. The apotheosis of this thesis was, of course, George Brown's 1965 ill-fated National Plan, which died the death of a thousand cuts in the 1966 crisis measures.

There was a danger of the British becoming uniquely introspective and depressed about their alleged inadequacies. The reaction was, of course, to espouse "planning", which had been out of favour since the disastrous end to the 1945–51 Labour Government. Prime Minister Macmillan himself, who had in his youth been an economic radical and had even described the then Tory front bench as "a row of burnt-out slag heaps", became in some respects a latter-day planner. His belief in the efficacy of State intervention in the economy had been spelt out in his book *The Middle Way,* published in 1938. His Chancellor, Selwyn Lloyd, Eden's Foreign Secretary at the time of Suez, initiated the "pay pause", and set up the National Incomes Commission, the "Three Wise Men" to take a longer view of incomes policy and the National Economic Development Council to foster a higher growth rate. It seemed as though these developments might herald a new beginning for Britain—even if, as it transpired, in fact everything remained the same.

Reginald Maudling, as intelligent a Chancellor as Britain has ever had, who (unlike Selwyn Lloyd or James Callaghan, for instance) could meet his senior officials on their own ground *did* try to change certain fundamentals. He did not, it is true, do anything very radical, such as recasting the tax system. No doubt he could not, in the time remaining to the Tories, do so, even if temperamentally he had had the urge to do so. But he was well aware of the fundamental fact that if the British could achieve a substantially higher growth rate almost all else economic would be given unto them. Unit labour costs would stabilise, exports would become relatively cheaper in world markets, eventually the balance of payments would improve, investment would pick up on businessmen's reviving confidence and so the capacity would be there for further growth.

It was not to be (at least not in the 1960's) and no doubt there will always be inconclusive controversy about what would have happened to the British economy had there not been a change of Government in October 1964. The defeat of Maudling's strategy of "accelerating into self-sustained growth", and the unscrupulous use Labour made in its propaganda of the resulting, probably temporary, large balance of payments deficit, are now part of history. Suffice to say here that it was clear, well before the election of October 1964, to anyone who did his homework on the trade figures and did not keep his ear cocked too closely to "guidance" from Whitehall, that things were not working out as planned. No doubt 1964 was an early stage of the upswing in the trade cycle; no doubt the longer-term benefits of a higher growth rate could not be expected to appear so soon; no doubt the *current* trade deficit was not unduly large at that stage of the trade cycle, when imports tend to increase more rapidly than exports as manufacturers re-stock; no doubt the facilities were available for Britain to borrow abroad well beyond October

1964 in order to test the thesis that higher growth in time would bring in its wake a stronger balance of payments.

Yet by the summer of 1964 at the latest it was clear that expanding imports of semi-manufactured and manufactured imports were contributing substantially to a yawning trade gap. In other words, it was not only higher imports of raw materials, many of which would eventually be re-exported in manufactured products, which were contributing to a deteriorating balance of payments. Maudling expected, and had prepared for, some deterioration and indeed it was inevitable. And he is thought to have urged Sir Alec Douglas-Home as Prime Minister not to "hang on" until the last minute but to call an election before this deterioration went very far. Yet the fact remains that the Treasury and Board of Trade during his Chancellorship gave the impression that all was well and going according to plan. It may be that pre-election pressures were too strong for this to have been otherwise. It may be that Maudling was not temperamentally willing or able to face unpleasant facts in time. But the facts were visible for those who had eyes to see.

But lack of foresight dominated economic policy even more obviously between 1964 and 1970 than it did before. Maudling was at least trying to do the right things in the right way and showed an intelligent assessment of the balance of risk. The same was true of Roy Jenkins. But not even their best friends could claim the same for that strange triumvirate of Messrs Wilson, Brown, and Callaghan, rivals in the 1968 contest for the Labour leadership, but by then "the crew of the Nancy Brig", who directed Labour's economic "policy" from the party's return to power in 1964 to the nemesis of devaluation in 1967.

At no stage did the triumvirate ever appear to be even remotely in control. "Every morning brought a gentle chance" but almost every morning also brought an unpleasant surprise. In Labour folk-myth their economic Ministers for the first time caught a glimpse of the other side, had a vision of total disaster, of Dante's Inferno when they took office in October 1964 and first examined the books. Yet, as has been pointed out, it was obvious well before then that things were not going as planned; the trade figures are after all published monthly. And as far as is known they are not deliberately "cooked" even in an election year. The "loss", the under-recording, of exports is quite a different matter. It may show carelessness on the part of the Board of Trade, on a par with the loss of Oscar Wilde's Earnest on the Worthing line—but it is a forgiveable carelessness in that it has exaggerated the apparent size of Britain's *current* balance of payments deficit (the error has made no difference to the overall outcome since it has been taken care of by an adjustment of the residual "balancing item").

The charade of the new Labour economic Ministers on taking office going into a huddle to battle with the powers of darkness in the shape of unexpected, looming, economic disasters is too absurd to dwell on. Wilson has "revealed" subsequently, for what motives it is not clear, that no solution was ruled out, not even the unthinkable one of devaluation (this though there have been reports from "usually well informed sources", and notably and commendably bravely by Peter Jay of The Times, that the Prime Minister at a later stage of the long-drawn-out devaluation saga gave orders that there should be no consideration in Whitehall of even the possibility of devaluation). As the world knows, and as in particular Britain's partners in the European Free Trade Area know, instead of devaluation (which, though inherently undesirable had probably become inevitable by then), the new Government decided on a surcharge on all imports except food and industrial raw materials.

Remarkably, the imposition of this import surcharge managed to break nine international trading agreements, including the General Agreement on Tariffs and Trade and the EFTA treaty. Labour Ministers appeared to be genuinely surprised by the international ill-will which the surcharge, imposed unilaterally without consultation, aroused. It was reduced from 15 to 10 per cent in April 1965, and abolished in November 1966, it is true, but the bitterness abroad it caused lingers yet. In November 1964 Callaghan also announced increased taxation designed to raise an extra £300 million of revenue in a full year—including 6d on petrol and 6d on income tax. Nevertheless, the import surcharge and the small export rebate together were equivalent, in so far as they made imports relatively more expensive and exports cheaper, to a small devaluation of the pound. They were a tacit, begrudging, and belated admission by the British authorities that the pound was over-valued.

If this had not been obvious in November 1964 it certainly was so by the summer of 1966 when the next major economic crisis broke. Labour had won the intervening election of March 1966 largely on the strength of as rapid a rate of wage inflation as had at that time been seen in peace time. Average hourly wage earnings had risen by 10 per cent in 1965 and were increasing at a similar rate in the first half of 1966 before the freeze. This was the time when Ministers spoke of a voluntary incomes policy taking twenty years to take effect, as often as not pointing vaguely in Nelsonian stance across the North Sea to "the Swedish example" (see Chapter Seven).

The way in which the wage freeze and unprecedentedly severe credit squeeze of July 1966 were introduced must rank, with the devaluation of sixteen months later, for all time as a classic example of lack of foresight. And the blame must largely rest with the economic Ministers of the time rather than with their official advisers. The Treasury, Department of Economic Affairs, and Bank of England officials most concerned were seriously worried about the rate of wage inflation and its implications for higher consumer spending and a bigger import bill. Yet at the beginning of March, before the election, Callaghan had said "I do not foresee the need for severe increases in taxation". At the beginning of May, after the election, he introduced the Selective Employment Tax (said to have been dreamt-up at three weeks' notice out of a dusty Kaldor dossier on "ideas for new taxes"), fixed the Corporation Tax at the relatively high rate of 40 per cent, introduced new gambling taxes, and put further curbs on overseas investment. These measures raised an extra £258 million in tax revenue.

Worse was to follow. Before his visit to Moscow on 16 July 1966, which was spent largely looking round the British Exhibition there, Wilson had given orders for a deflationary package of unprecedented severity to be prepared against his return. Money was pouring out of London and an immediate and substantial devaluation of the pound appeared possible, if not probable. It is now known that precisely such a measure was considered by the Cabinet and that George Brown, brought to the point of resignation (before his transfer to the Foreign Office) was a leading devaluationist, among other important Ministers. Unusually, the Prime Minister himself announced a financial measure, the deflationary package, on

20 July. It appeared that his Cabinet colleagues had insisted that he, rather than Chancellor Callaghan, should do this as a penance for his absurd over-optimism (a congenital weakness) about the economic situation.

As late as 12 July Wilson had been talking of "wet editorials" prophesying doom if action were not taken; and discounting talk of an economic crisis. This despite the manifest damage to exports of the protracted seamen's strike and the disruption to Britain's trade caused by the closing of the Suez Canal as a result of the Six-Day War in the Middle East in June. Wilson's penance for his sins of omission was as complete as any since King Henry II walked in sack cloth to Canterbury to prostrate himself before his Archbishop.

On top of the £258 million of extra tax revenue in a full year raised in the May Budget, the Wilson measures of July 1966 raised another £176 million. Many indirect taxes were increased, involving the use of the purchase tax "regulator" upwards to a maximum of 10 per cent; a 10 per cent surcharge on surtax was introduced for 1965–66; there were reductions in both Government and local authority spending plans and in the capital investment programmes of the nationalised industries, amounting to some £250 million; postal and telephone charges were increased; the foreign travel allowance was reduced to £50; and a total prices and incomes freeze was imposed until the end of 1966, followed by six months of "severe restraint". Some of these were announced after a delay of five days—an indication of the haste with which the "package" had been prepared. Britain's creditors, notably the International Monetary Fund, had been understandably pressing for some time for effective restraint on soaring incomes, and were rumoured to have been unimpressed by British Ministers talking of the need for a twenty-year view on the effectiveness of an incomes policy. The business of lending money to Britain, and more important and more difficult, getting it back was more urgent than that.

The official justification for these unexpected measures taken to meet an apparently totally unanticipated economic Armageddon was that the economy had suddenly been "blown off course". No doubt the protracted seamen's strike and the Six-Day War in the Middle East could not have been anticipated. Yet, when they did happen it was surely clear immediately that the results would be bad, if not disastrous, for Britain with its already over-valued currency. We shall never know, of course, to what extent senior officials reacted quickly, and urged action on their Ministers, to these untoward and unexpected events. It may be that, as so often in the past, they were too sanguine. But the whole sequence of events of July 1966 bears all the familiar signs of Wilsonian short-term expediency, a reluctance to look further ahead than next Monday, and ebullient unjustified over-optimism having little or no relation to the facts of life.

The July 1966 economic crisis, one of the worst of its kind even by post-war Britain's standards, and the forced devaluation of November 1967, did, however, illustrate a persistent trait of British official, or at least Ministerial, thinking in economic matters. At each successive post-war crisis, almost without exception, the unexpected has been bad for Britain. Seldom has any country had such consistent "bad luck" for so long. The seamen's strike and the Six-Day War, a slowing down in the rate of increase in world trade, overseas sterling area countries "unsportingly" diversifying their sterling balances into currencies other than the pound, endless disruptions caused by British labour troubles, the erosion of Commonwealth tariff preferences for British exports, even the formation of the Common Market itself have all, among other events, at different times been regarded in high places in Britain as in some way bad luck if not downright unfair. Yet the good things, like the improvement in Britain's terms of trade (largely reflecting lower commodity and raw material prices) in recent years, or the unexpectedly rapid expansion of world trade in 1968, 1969, and 1970 which did so much for British exports, are much less often mentioned—if at all.

When the balance of payments improved, as in the Autumn of 1967, or in 1969, according to Ministers in public and according to inspired "guidance" briefings in Whitehall to economic commentators, Britain had almost invariably turned the corner at last. Yet, almost equally invariably, unexpected disaster struck within months. British Chancellors came to resemble Sisyphus, the Greek God who wearily and eternally rolled his rock uphill, only to see it rolling down again on the other side of the hill.

The 1967 devaluation, carried out in conditions of near-panic, and in the utmost confusion, with almost no forethought, epitomises British economic policy in the last quarter century (see Appendix 1). It contrasted poignantly with the smoothness and deliberateness of the 1958 and 1969 French devaluations. There were, too, the deplorable official forecasts in November 1967 that the "benefits" to the balance of payments of a devaluation which the Treasury and the Bank of England had tried so hard and for so long to avoid would be £1,000 million a year in 1968. How wrong can one be? Why, when it had been obvious for years that the pound was seriously over-valued, was a planned devaluation apparently not considered in early 1967? Then the balance of payments was momentarily strong, before the "bad luck" of the summer. Done then or earlier it would rightly have been regarded as an act of economic statesmanship.

The French, it is true, do not have the problems and attendant obligations of maintaining a reserve currency. The fact remains that President Pompidou—with the important caveat that he did not consult his monetary allies—set a shining example of how these things should be done in August 1969, when the French had stolen away from their capital, as is their wont at that time of year, and most of Europe was on holiday and least expecting monetary coups, the French franc was devalued. And so far at least it has lived happily ever afterwards: French exports have increased, the balance of payments has greatly improved, and the reserves are no longer running down at an alarming rate. The French economy in fact has responded as the text books say an economy should react to devaluation: the British economy, which at times appears to obey no known economic laws, took nearly two years to do any such thing.

Yet it was not merely the British failure to devalue when it would have been relatively painless to do so which is so distressing. Even more remarkable, if possible, was the monolithic opposition of Britain's economic establishment to even the consideration of more flexible exchange rates. The City, predictably led by the Bank of England, the economic Ministries, and politicians of nearly every hue from Heath to Wilson, were almost to a man against the idea. Indeed, in the early days—which in this context means the early 1960's—only a few academic economists, widely regarded as eccentric, and a few brave economic journalists and commentators, such as Sam Brittan of the *Financial Times,* dared to mention the anti-

Christ. And even as late as the autumn of 1969, when more flexible exchange rates had become fashionable, and notably so in America, Britain's Treasury and Bank of England men went to the International Monetary Conference in Washington apparently prepared to defend to the last the semi-mystical concept of fixed exchange rates for currencies (since then the issue has unfortunately become mixed up with the even greater one of "Europe", with the Six showing marked signs of opposing greater flexibility; even though if Britain joins the Market there would be much to be said for dealing with the attendant balance of payments problems by letting sterling "float").

The objections to floating exchange rates are, of course, well-known. It would be surprising in view of the publicity they have received in recent years if they were not so. Almost no one who deals in currencies, or whose business involves exporting and importing, is in favour of them. They could, of course, all be wrong, and their worst fears be proved unjustified. It is often forgotten that the worst uncertainties of variable currencies can be offset by buying and selling them "forward" in the foreign exchange market. But clearly, other things being equal, practical men of business like to know, as closely as is possible, the probable price at which they buy and sell things.

It has also always been argued—albeit with decreasing force as world inflation accelerated—that fixed exchange rates provided feckless Governments with a degree of "discipline". In other words, if they over-spent and inflated faster than those of other countries, there would before long be an awful retribution in the shape of a devaluation, for which they would incur a just political odium. The British experience, however, suggests that, having incurred the odium, they go on inflating, if possible, even more rapidly than before, while mouthing platitudes about other countries inflating, too (ignoring the fact that most of those countries have a much more rapidly rising output over which to spread their increasing wage costs).

The main advantage of more flexible exchange rates is that they provide an automatic mechanism whereby currencies adjust their value in relation to each other. Gone are the absurdities, and sheer trauma, of the 1949 and 1967 British devaluations. They provide a self-balancing mechanism whereby if, for instance, Britain's exports become over-valued, as is their wont, sterling is correspondingly sold on the world's currency exchange markets, its value declines, and British exports again become more competitive. At the same time, imports become dearer relative to home-produced goods and the demand for them falls. Thus the balance of payments should remain automatically in equilibrium. It may be that that balance may be found at a low standard of living, however (as Keynes said, a nation can always balance its books at zero). For every time a currency declines in value, that country's terms of trade deteriorate and it has to export more to pay for a given volume of imports.

The world is almost certainly moving towards more flexible exchange rates in the long run, and it is encouraging that there are growing signs of a recognition of this fact even in Britain. One day we may see completely floating rates, unfettered by any kind of restriction. In the more immediate future we shall no doubt hear much of half-way-houses, such as "crawling pegs", "ratchets", and "wider bands", aimed at greater flexibility while avoiding the alleged worst excesses and volatility of total flexibility. It is unnatural that currencies should be the one good whose price cannot be varied without emotional heat and invocations of national pride.

No dissertation on the persistent lack of foresight and over-optimism which has dogged British economic policy these two decades and more would be complete without a genuflection towards the semi-official National Institute of Economic Research. Down all those weary years the NIESR, which has close links with the Treasury, and receives large sums from the Government, has been consistent in urging on successive Governments expansionist economic policies (and in a sense it has been right, for without economic growth this country's future is bleak indeed). It has also, however, been almost as consistently wrong in forecasting what would, as opposed to what should, happen to the balance of payments. And its views, nevertheless, still carry much weight.

Economic forecasting is an inexact science, it is true. But would it not be better to admit this and desist from making detailed "guesstimates" of the probable future course of events which depend on so many uncertain assumptions and inter-linked variables? By so doing forecasters, like public opinion polls, are in danger of giving an impression of spurious accuracy which their work does not, and cannot, have.

Thus in November 1969 the NIESR was predicting an incredible overall British balance of payments surplus of £850 million for 1970: by May 1970 their forecast was down to £650 million; by August to £475 million (which in the event was for once an under-estimate). Such revisions, nearly always in a downwards direction, have happened so often that the layman could be forgiven for assuming despite the large overseas trade surplus for 1970 that, as usual, things would soon once more deteriorate rapidly and "unexpectedly". Wherein lies a tale which has still to be told. . . .

CHAPTER FIVE

Bureaucrats as Well as Politicians

Major errors of economic policy over a long period (indeed for as long as most people can remember), almost invariably erring on the side of over-optimism, raise, of course, important questions about the quality of Britain's politicians and the institutions through which they operate. They raise similar questions, however, about the officials who advise Ministers.

In that Ministers cannot possibly know all, or even most, of what is going on in their swollen Departments—Ministerial responsibility perforce flew out of the window many moons ago—senior civil servants must inevitably take some of the responsibility for the errors of British economic policy in the quarter century since the 1939–45 war. Those senior officials would no doubt argue that, even if they had tendered the right advice, it is doubtful, to say the least, whether it would have been accepted. Yet this is in a sense a circular argument. For if politicians will not face harsh decisions and difficult choices; and officials, knowing this, will not tell them what needs to be done, how is Britain ever to get out of her difficulties?

To take a small example, the author remembers in his short time at the Treasury as a junior civil servant on secondment from industry, suggesting that a meeting which had been called to consider the long-term finances of the Post Office might ask for a paper on the possibility of denationalising telecommunications. Such a move would relieve the taxpayer of part of the burden, via a swollen gilt-edged market, of financing the large telephone capital investment programme, now running at £540 million a year. This straightforward suggestion was, as if by reflex action, rejected at once on the grounds that at that time (1966) no political party would look at such a radical idea within the foreseeable future. Yet within two years such prominent Tories as Ernest Marples and Enoch Powell were suggesting just such a move.

On the wider front, Treasury officials would no doubt be reluctant to take much responsibility for optimistic and highly inaccurate balance of payments forecasts in the past. They give advice on the basis of a range of forecasts—for example, it might be a surplus of £100 million to £500 million for 1969—and the Chancellor takes his pick within that range. He could of course in theory go outside that range if he felt sufficiently sure of himself. But in practice he would seldom, if ever, do that, if for no other reason than that, under the British tradition of moving politicians around between Departments fairly frequently so that they are usually far from being expert in the problems of the Ministries over which they briefly preside, he would not feel himself sufficiently well informed to fly in the face of ostensibly expert advice. Yet some balance of payments forecasts, such as those for 1968 after the 1967 devaluation, have been so seriously out as to suggest that the outcome did not remotely resemble *any* of the figures within the Treasury range of forecasts.

There have been many other similar, although fortunately often less dramatic, mistakes. Politicians are, of course, perennial optimists. If they were not so inclined, no doubt they would have chosen other, less extrovert, jobs. To that extent civil servants can certainly claim, with some justice, that their political masters tend to work on, and indeed to stimulate, the most optimistic advice possible. Yet it is difficult, if not impossible, to believe that some of the mistakes of British economic policy since 1945 have not in part originated in the over-optimistic advice of officials themselves. Some of the errors of earlier post-war Conservative and Labour Governments have been mentioned in Chapter Four. Those since 1964 have been, if possible, even more serious.

Thus in May 1965, seven months after Labour took office, James Callaghan, then Chancellor of the Exchequer, said: "I expect to see us well on the way towards balancing our payments in 1965 and completing the process in 1966." The outcome for 1965 was a current account balance of payments deficit of £81 million.

In July 1966, at the time of the imposition of the wage freeze and a credit squeeze of unprecedented severity, Callaghan at least admitted his error. In contrast Wilson referred to "jeremiahs and wet editorials" creating an unjustified air of gloom only a fortnight before this particular economic Armageddon—and never subsequently admitted that he had been wrong. The Chancellor said: "It was the intention of the Government to reduce the (balance of payments) deficit to nil by the end of the current year, but it had become clear that we were not making sufficient progress towards that goal." The outcome for 1966 was a surplus of only £40 million.

In September 1966 Callaghan said: "As for 1967, on the basis of our revised policies I am looking forward not merely to a bare balance but, in fact, I hope for a surplus." The outcome for 1967 was a deficit of £322 million. With a forced devaluation came a new Chancellor—but not a new theme. Roy Jenkins said in March 1968: "I certainly hope and expect that we shall be in surplus in the second half (of 1968). For the future we need, as I have said, to achieve a continuing balance of payments surplus of the order of £500 million a year as soon as we can and to sustain it for as far ahead as we can see." The outcome for 1968 was a deficit of £309 million.

A balance of payments surplus somehow still receded like the mirage it had so far proved. But Jenkins was at least more modest by October 1968: "I cannot predict the exact time at which we shall break even and cross the line from deficit into surplus. It should come in the first half of next year (1969)." Then under the shadow of the bailiffs, impatient men from the International Monetary Fund, Jenkins said in June 1969: "I am stating an objective of a £300 million balance of payments surplus for the current financial year." The outcome for that year, April 1969 to March 1970 (the relevant year was for some reason changed) was a surplus of £387 million.

At last, at a grave cost in terms of a low economic growth rate, increases in national output lost for ever, and a relatively poor level of investment, Britain had reached the promised land of external viability.

What then is to be done? How far have our economic difficulties reflected institutional factors, such as the remoteness of the economic Departments, and in particular of the Treasury, from the day-to-day life of industry? Such as the lack of trained economists as administrators in the economic departments? Such as the lack of civil servants who have the time—and perhaps as they grow older the inclination—to think?

Such as the obvious disadvantages of a hierarchy which has

seldom promoted people to the Administrative Grade (the top policy-making cadre which advised Ministers) much before the threshold of middle age—by which time they have lost a good deal of whatever dynamism and originality they may have ever had? Such as a system which, at least until the 1968 Fulton Report urging radical changes in the organisation of Whitehall, moved officials between the economic and management wings of the Treasury almost at random, although these demand different skills? A system which discouraged (or at the least did not encourage) officials from expressing a preference for their next job even though, other things being equal, it might be thought that people tend to perform best at jobs which they most want to do?

Such as an approach to government which for five recent years—albeit on political orders—sought "creative tension" between the Treasury and the ill-fated Department of Economic Affairs which seldom had much time, or perhaps even inclination, to consider the longer-term prospects of the economy? Which has re-arranged the functions of the economic Departments (and particularly those of the former Board of Trade) endlessly so that some officials can scarcely remember when they last did what job, where, or in what Department?

A good deal of this should change as a result of the implementation, which is already under way, of the Fulton recommendations. And it ignores the many good aspects of the Whitehall machine which is widely regarded as among the finest in the world. It also ignores the sheer brain-power and almost unbelievable dedication of so many civil servants—an aspect little enough appreciated by so many who inveigh indiscriminately against "faceless bureaucrats" (although a dedicated civil servant pointing in the wrong direction can do more harm than good). It also ignores the great difficulties that senior officials often work under: in particular of administering policies which may be inconsistent with each other and even with themselves over a period of time. Thus, for instance, "planning", one year all the rage among politicians of all parties, the next year is abhorred across a wide range of the political spectrum.

Clearly institutional factors have played at least some part in Britain's poor economic performance. And if sheer over-work comprises an institution in this context, then it must be rated a most important one. How hard—too hard—the average Administrative Grade official works! And Executive Grade officials (the next rung down Whitehall's until recently carefully graded ladder, ostensibly the executors rather than the makers of policy) are often just as over-burdened.

Senior Treasury men, for instance, unquestioningly regard it as part of their lot to work regularly nine hours or more a day at the office with barely time for a sandwich lunch; to have to produce Briefs for Ministers at an hour or two's notice despite continuous interruptions; to read office papers—of low secrecy classification!—on their commuter trains both mornings and evenings; and on occasion to sit up at home until far into the night preparing yet more Briefs for early the following morning. It is hardly surprising that in these conditions officials often find it difficult to read the newspapers properly, and so to relate their own work to a wider world—let alone to think deeply about the significance of their work and its longer-term potential.

Such historic mistakes in economic and foreign policy, for instance, as the British failure to take part in the negotiations at Messina which set up the Common Market, are more explicable in this context—although only just. The tradition of secrecy in Whitehall makes it difficult to be certain. But the evidence is that the Departments most concerned were almost uniformly opposed to even exploring the possibility of signing the Treaty of Rome. At the time no doubt those most concerned, or those who should have been concerned, were barely aware of, let alone equipped with a view on, the proposed Common Market owing to the pressure of more immediate problems.

It is true that Permanent Secretaries and their immediate subordinates are paid to think about broader national issues. But they tend to be older men well past their physical—and it may well often be mental—prime, bogged down by an enormous weight of papers to read and telephone calls to make and answer, many requiring instant action. Thus when the author saw one of the then Joint Permanent Secretaries at the Treasury for what was to be ostensibly a half-hour's talk about "my job and how I see it" consecutive conversation was barely possible owing to constant telephone calls (including one from the Prime Minister), and the endless comings and goings of underlings bearing urgent messages or papers.

An outsider inevitably notices how little contact all but the most senior Whitehall officials have with people in jobs elsewhere. The problem is particularly acute in the Treasury which works on the whole *through* other Departments. Brief and unpredictable lunch breaks; the lack of expense accounts which make it virtually impossible for officials to reciprocate hospitality (and therefore often reluctant to accept it); the difficulty of taking even a day off to visit a factory, important though it may be to one's job—all these factors combine to make the average junior and medium-grade official too out of touch with the big outside world with which he is dealing and in a real sense controlling.

This out-of-touchness at a personal level makes it difficult for officials concerned with, for instance, monetary policy to assess such intangible but germane factors as "businessmen's confidence". Thus an 8 per cent Bank Rate, although ostensibly good for encouraging "hot" (that is short-term, liquid, foot-loose, even speculative) funds to come to, or to stay in, London, may have a discouraging, if unquantifiable, effect on businessmen's plans, and indeed on their view of the whole future economic climate.

Perhaps few things, for instance, have been more misleading than the divining by the former Board of Trade and by the Confederation of British Industry, by questionnaire, of business-men's plans, and in particular of their assessment of export prospects, and capital investment levels. A sort of vicious circle has emerged whereby politicians make optimistic speeches, busin-essmen at least half-believe them, fill in their questionnaire forms optimistically; and the Ministers of the economic Departments then interpret these findings as "evidence" of better times ahead.

The Fulton Report is a useful start to reform. Most of its recommendations were being implemented in 1970–71 by Sir William Armstrong, brilliant former Joint Permanent Secretary of the Treasury at the new Civil Service Department. It should lead in time to a much more flexible and less "caste-conscious" civil service hierarchy. All-round suitability for the job, rather than one's educational qualifications—often earned a long time ago—will increasingly be the main criterion for the Whitehall career structure. In January 1971 the Administrative, Executive, and Clerical classes of the civil service were merged into a single unified Administration Group.

It was sensible, too, to take away the management of the civil service from the Treasury and give it to a new Department reporting directly to the Prime Minister. There was no particular reason, except largely historical accident and a certain ad hoc convenience, why the Treasury should plan the careers of senior civil servants throughout Whitehall (except in so far as there is an organic and obvious link between the control of public expenditure and the control of the people who spend it). Sound "economic" Treasury officials are not necessarily well qualified to deal with personnel problems, and vice versa.

Fulton's emphasis on the value of some economic training for all Administrative Grade civil servants, on the extension of the excellent courses now run by the Civil Service Administrative Centre, was sound, on balance, though it put too much emphasis on the importance of economics as a training for the administrative art (or science). Good economists do not necessarily make good administrators: the skills involved are different.

Probably the least controversial observation of Fulton was that many civil servants work in deplorable conditions—quite apart from the overall pressure on their working lives. The Report rightly commented on the absurdity of, for instance, highly-paid officials walking up and down long, bleak corridors, clutching their own individual do-it-yourself towels and soap. The saving to the Exchequer, dictated no doubt by the ubiquitous Ministry of Works, from such "economy measures" is difficult to justify, or indeed to discern. Indeed, *could* anyone, even if they were so minded, have a bright, original, epoch-making idea about Britain's long-term economic future (or anything else, for that matter), while working in the Treasury's bleak, rambling, "temporary", scheduled-to-be-replaced-by-the-end-of-the-century quarters in Great George Street?

Most junior officials, and many more senior ones, work in conditions of considerable (to the outsider) chaos. Secretarial help is often spasmodic, if not downright inefficient: Whitehall secretaries are paid relatively badly, on the "candle ends" principle. "Non-urgent" documents are usually sent to the Government's typing pool, "somewhere in the home counties", and may be unduly delayed there, or in transit. Telephones often ring continuously, frequently demanding instant action. Vast piles of paper, maily "for information", tend to accumulate in the average official's In Tray each day—unsorted and often peripheral, if not irrelevant, to his actual job. The papers would probably be sorted, it is true, if he was an Assistant Secretary in the élitist Administrative Grade before the Fulton reforms because by then he would have a Personal Assistant—maybe a middle-aged "queen bee", who had made the Service her career. But by then he would also usually be on the threshold of middle-age himself, having laboured often for nearly two decades for his substantive promotion from the basic rank of Principal.

Much of this unplanned pressure is an inevitable aspect of almost any administrative job, of course. But industry, for instance, will usually not spare expense to ensure that able and highly trained people can meet the demands of their job. But in the Treasury, and in many other Departments, Assistant Principals and Principals must fend for themselves with no one even to take their telephone calls. Yet they may be at the time under desperate pressure to produce, say, the answer to a Parliamentary Question, or even a Brief for a Minister, often required at only an hour or two's notice.

All this takes place behind firmly closed doors, and especially so in the Treasury and the Ministry of Defence, where passes are required before the draw-bridge is even raised an inch to a stranger, who is escorted everywhere as if under house arrest. Fulton was right to deplore the quite unnecessary secrecy in which most officials work; and to suggest that no harm would be done to the nation's vital interests—except perhaps in "Defence"—if some nine-tenths of all official docunents were "declassified". At present the revelation of the contents of *any* document which an official may see in the course of his work is in breach of the Official Secrets Act. This he signs on joining the Service. So, although all documents are by definition secret, some are more secret than others. "Secret" documents come in two envelopes, one within the other; other, "Confidential", ones are spared this dramatic treatment.

So much secretiveness, in the civil service as in industry (see Chapter Eight), seems to be a particularly British characteristic, and a peculiarly unattractive one to boot. Most of the documents which civil servants read and most of the discussions in which they take part, would be ineffably boring to the man-in-the-street, let alone to the intelligent layman, were they to be made public. The author remembers a civil servant remarking that it was not the public, but the other Departments, from whom the Treasury wished to keep its secrets.

Washington works in a far more "gold-fish bowl" atmosphere than does Whitehall, with no obviously disastrous results. And in Sweden, another unusually successful economy, all official documents are public property unless stated otherwise, which is a relatively rare event. There seems to be no good reason, if a lot of predictable objections, why the same rule should not apply in Britain. Within the British civil service far more material is classified than can be justified on security grounds. Officials, particularly junior ones, tend to err on the side of caution; this can cover up incompetence.

The working of the Official Secrets Act, for long suspect, came in for severe criticism in early 1971 after the acquittal of the *Sunday Telegraph*, its Editor, Brian Roberts, Col Douglas Cairns and Jonathan Aitken on charges brought under that Act. In his summing up at the end of the trial Mr Justice Caulfield suggested that Section 2 of the Act should be "pensioned off".

The Prime Minister was expected to appoint, partly as a result of the protracted and costly trial a high level committee of inquiry to review the working of the Act. If the inquiry was to achieve anything its terms of reference seemed bound to go far beyond the working of the Act itself. Among other things, it would have to consider the attitude of civil servants themselves towards information; and attempts to define more exactly legitimate areas of security. What should the Government be allowed to keep secret and how should it do it?

Such an inquiry would almost certainly be politically uncontroversial. In 1970 the Labour Government had decided on a similar inquiry but had awaited the outcome of pending prosecutions under the Act of the former Labour MP, Will Owen (eventually acquitted), and of the *Sunday Telegraph*. Such "postponements" of successive proposals to review the working of an Act passed hurriedly during a spy scare in 1911 had been not uncommon over the years.

The path of reform seemed unlikely to be smooth. Parliamentary privilege, as well as the Act itself, was a dyke against the free flow of information. In Opposition the Conservatives' law review committee had come to some tentative conclusions on the problems involved. These were notably: that of definition (what is a State secret? does it involve only security?); weak disciplinary sanctions within Whitehall and the difficulty of dismissing a civil servant; the inherent penchant for secrecy of officials and often of politicians when it suited them; whether or not the sanctions which a private company or individual can use against a breach of confidentiality were applicable or adequate in the case of government.

Some members of the committee concluded tentatively that the whole of the Act needed to be redrafted more explicitly; the repeal of Section 2 would not be enough.

Any reforms of the civil service must involve its relationship with Parliament, if for no other reason than that the British tradition of Ministerial responsibility has become largely a myth. The vast, sprawling Departments which Ministers now nominally control, like juggernauts inevitably have a volition of their own. This was never more clear than in the summer of 1970, when before and after the surprise Tory election victory, and despite two changes of Chancellorship on account of the tragic death of Iain Macleod, the Treasury went on giving the same (as it happens, correct) economic advice that there was no case for expansionary measures in the short-term.

But in a more detailed and specific way Ministers cannot possibly control, or even know about, everything which is going on in their Departments. Most Ministries are quite simply too big for that to be possible. There is, therefore, a strong case for making officials, and particularly senior ones, more immediately responsible, more directly accountable to the great British public, for their decisions. This is, of course, part and parcel of their being less secretive.

Some modest progress has already been made in this direction. Roy Jenkins, when Chancellor, persuaded the Treasury—or, conceivably it persuaded him—to publish the basis, the assumptions, on which its economic forecasts are made. Moreover, senior officials are now accustomed to being questioned by the Estimates Committee, the Public Accounts Committee, and the Select Committee for the Nationalised Industries. They were becoming used, too, to the idea that they would be increasingly questioned in future by Parliamentary Specialist Committees "shadowing" the great Departments of State. But now the whole concept of such committees is being questioned. No Executive, no great political party, and certainly no ex-Chief Whip turned Prime Minister, takes kindly to the idea that Parliament (and therefore, indirectly, the public) should have a greater say in the decision-making process, and be brought into it at an earlier stage.

Yet that is precisely what needs to be done. In the glad confident morning of Labour's return to power in 1964, and especially after Richard Crossman became Leader of the

House, it seemed conceivable there might be rapid progress in this direction. But Whitehall, and notably the Treasury (on the grounds of their cost?), were apparently never keen on the new "experimental" Specialist Committees which Labour set up. This was hardly surprising, and entirely predictable, in that they make heavy demands on the time of those same already over-loaded officials.

Yet the answer is surely to unload them in other ways— such as delegation of less important work where possible and, more fundamentally, reducing the activities of the State—rather than to disband the committees. Time spent in discovering what Ministers are hatching is indeed time well spent. There is a well-justified feeling among back-bench MPs that they are not consulted often enough or early enough about Government policies; and that they are then confronted with *faits accomplis*.

A classic example was the absurd decision to decimalise on the pound rather than ten shillings. Consideration, consultation and indeed decision-taking in the Treasury and the Bank of England were far advanced before MPs were consulted on this important issue; and even then Labour MPs were "whipped" to vote for the pound, against the advice of almost every interested organisation and almost every informed citizen in the country. Now we reap the whirl-wind in the shape of avoidable price increases and endless problems over coin-operated machines.

Airey Neave, MP, an expert on the machinery of Government, suggested in a pamphlet which he wrote in 1968, that there should be Specialist Committees on: Science and Technology, Industry and Trade (including Agriculture), Regional Development (including Housing and Transport), Home Affairs, Social Security, Education, and Foreign and Commonwealth Affairs and Defence.

MPs on such committees can inform themselves on policy-making in their fields and become real experts therein. Officials ideally have to justify their actions and inform MPs of what they were doing and the reasons for them. A concomitant in the longer run should be that civil servants will be less secure in their jobs. Heads should roll (metaphorically) when there are major blunders. Ministers should continue to feel obliged to resign on occasion but it should not only be they who feel thus. On occasion, where the Minister concerned could not be held remotely responsible for a débâcle, except under the myth of Ministerial responsibility, the official and only he should go.

It is a truism that now in practice, whatever Whitehall standing orders may stipulate, civil servants can only be fired for such unusual things as gross indecency or peculation. Incompetence or idleness, which to be fair are rare, are not thought to be sufficient reasons. Administrative Grade people, for instance, have been promoted almost automatically to the rank of Assistant Secretary—albeit at varying ages, reflecting their performance and the needs of their Department.

Westminster and Whitehall in *some* respects have much to learn from Washington. American Congressmen and Senators, through their work on House Committees, which brings them closely into contact with senior officials, have a much clearer idea than do their opposite numbers here of what is going on and why—before it happens, as it were. There are historical reasons for this, mainly concerned with the delicate balance of power in the American constitution; but there is no doubt that the British Parliament could move some way in the same direction if the political will to do so was there. There is the practical point, too, of course, that American legislators have far better working and research facilities. A small start has been made at Westminster, but the lot of British MPs must be improved substantially in this respect if they are to play a more effective part in policy-making. Those MPs who need them should certainly have their own office, a secretary, and a research assistant to "devil" for the facts and figures which can be used to harry constructively the Government of the day.

To make more time for committee work, it would be necessary, as is in any case intrinsically desirable, that more of the Commons work should be done off the floor of the House in committee. Recent experiences in this respect with Finance Bills may not have been altogether happy, for particular reasons, but the long-term trend must be in that direction.

What of the Conservatives' long-promised review of the machinery of Government? What of the hope of more "cost-effectiveness" in Whitehall? The guide-lines for the Tory bureaucratic millenium were laid down in David Howell's *A New Style of Government*, published just before the 1970 election. The Conservatives came to power intending to carve up the vast, cumbersome Ministry of Technology. It was to be merged with the Board of Trade, but the combined Ministry would be shorn of responsibility for particular industries, with one or two exceptions. Certain functions, such as purchasing, would be delegated to various agencies and Boards.

Yet this was easier said than done, as the Government soon discovered. In the summer of 1970 there were many anxious comings and goings between the Ministers concerned. The Prime Minister took personal control of the whole review of the structure of Government. The new Chancellor of the Exchequer, Anthony Barber, and his Chief Secretary, Maurice Macmillan, were closely involved. So, too, were Lord Jellicoe, the Civil Service Minister, and the Leader of the House of Commons, William Whitelaw.

In particular, the procurement function proved hard to farm out. It may now take years before there is an entirely new structure to sponsor and finance the nationalised industries. Meanwhile, although a number of functions might eventually be redistributed between them, the Conservatives' two new super-Ministries, of the Environment and of Trade and Industry, seemed safe for at least some way ahead; their creation raised no violent objections from Labour. Even so it might be doubted whether any one man, however brilliant, could cope satisfactorily with such Herculean administrative jobs. There was also the danger that good ideas, which once got a hearing in (an admittedly larger and more cumbersome) Cabinet would now go by default.

Not surprisingly, the core of the dilemma lies in the position of the Treasury. And the problem is almost as old as democracy itself: how to spread power while retaining control and remaining reasonably efficient. The Tories like strong government and when they were in opposition they had teased Harold Wilson—as indeed does this book—for aiming at "creative tension" between a new Department of Economic Affairs and a truncated Treasury. After the demise of the DEA Anthony Crosland, then President, had sought, unsuccessfully, to make the Board of Trade the new power-house pushing for economic growth. So, *faut de mieux*, Sir Frederick Catherwood, head of the National Economic Development Council, became the main exponent in Whitehall of "why growth matters".

In essence, the Conservatives wish to increase the central government's ability to control public expenditure; and to choose between the priorities from which public expenditure flows. They wish to graft on the techniques of modern industrial management and expenditure control developed in North America to the Whitehall machine, to create a "capability" at the centre of the government machine for analysing programmes, monitoring efficiency, and organising resources.

Such a "capability"—a nebulous concept—could be attached to the Treasury, repository of the time-hallowed function of controlling public expenditure. But there are many, not least on the Tory benches, who believe that the power of the Treasury, like that of the State itself, has in any case increased too much and ought henceforth to be diminished. They ask: what is the meat upon which this, our Caesar, has grown so great? Would not such a move make the Chief Secretary, or whoever else was put in charge of the expenditure division, even more powerful? There would, of course, be the right of appeal against him, to the Cabinet, but past experience would not suggest that the chances of the appellants would be very good.

An alternative, much favoured by some Conservatives when in opposition, would be to copy the Americans and create a Bureau of the Budget. But if the Bureau had no sponsor, no powerful patron, it would be a headless monster. Much better in terms of sheer efficiency, that it should report direct to the Prime Minister. But his colleagues, let alone Wilkes-like back-bench guardians of freedom such as Michael Foot and certain influential senior Conservatives, could hardly be expected to welcome such a significant increase in the powers of the Prime Minister. It would amount, indeed, to a radical "unwritten" change in that famous unwritten constitution.

The dilemma, therefore has all the makings of a British compromise. The Treasury could be encouraged to expand its public expenditure function and to take an even larger part in the policy-making of the individual spending Ministries. Meanwhile, back in Downing Street, this enhanced power could be offset by a new Cabinet public expenditure committee, presided over by the Prime Minister himself. Unlike the old Department of Economic Affairs, this would approach problems from a non-departmental stance. It could work, and in time would probably prove to be an improvement on the traditional situation, where in practice no one was able to say "nay" to the Treasury. And it would closely resemble President Nixon's new balance between an Office of Management and Budget, corresponding to the Treasury expenditure divisions, and a Domestic Council which is in effect a "think-tank" for new ideas and for setting priorities.

But in the British context such a compromise, would look, if it materialised, like "creative tension" re-born—this time between the two sides of Downing Street.

CHAPTER SIX

A Miasma of Consensus

Institutional factors and national characteristics have certainly played a major, if not key, role in the many economic débâcles of the last quarter century. Fiascos, such as failing to join the Common Market when it would have been so easy to do so, the 1961 and 1966 financial crises which apparently blew up out of an almost cloudless sky, and the 1949 and 1967 forced devaluations, must in part be put down to a British tendency to get the worst of all possible worlds.

This characteristic of complacency has its advantages, of course. It makes for stability and continuity in that although, or perhaps because, there have been so many blows to morale since 1945, people in this country have on the whole just carried on as if nothing much had happened. To this extent the "Dunkirk spirit" does have its good side—although it is unfortunate that the country ever gets into a situation where it is needed or has to be invoked. Still, morale has never in Britain, despite all the avoidable post-war crises and all the inevitable vicissitudes of imperial withdrawal, deteriorated alarmingly.

Yet there is another characteristic—and this is more than relevant in the civil service context—which makes it difficult for Cassandras pointing to the wrath to come to gain attention if changes are not soon made. An obvious analogy is Churchill in the 1930's, although then there were special factors, such as his monumental misjudgement over the Baldwin Government's proposals to give India limited internal self-government, which condone if they do not excuse the way his warnings about Germany's manifest rapid re-armament were ignored. Britishers tend to agree with each other; and they have an immense capacity for self-deception. In particular, they live in an ancient and homogeneous society where members of the educated élite, which "influences" and has power, often know each other well— frequently from school or university days, or from both. Hence they tend to think in the same way and to reach the same conclusions. When two or three Englishmen are gathered together the phrase most often heard will tend to be "I agree". Or, as Adam Smith said "They make a conspiracy".

This will to "consensus", of which so much has been heard in recent years, is, moreover, carefully fostered by the policy-makers. Background briefings for "reputable" journalists, "not for attribution", are an intrinsic part of the Whitehall scene. Such briefings are not, of course, unique to Britain, but they seem to be a particular fetish here, and some of their results are particularly unattractive. The theory behind them, of course, is sound enough. It is better that commentators should be well informed on what is really going on than that they should write or talk "off the top of their heads", other things being equal. Anyone who has had even the most cursory contact with the process of Government will realise that the gulf between what is actually happening in policy-making in Whitehall, or its equivalent, and what the public believe to be happening, is a yawning chasm. The gulf is no doubt unusually wide in Britain because of the tradition of secrecy which pervades Whitehall (see Chapter Five). But the gulf exists, and short of doing away with the secrecy (which is unlikely to happen overnight), an obvious solution is to tell the opinion-makers "off the record" what is actually happening.

What are the results? The most apparent is a tendency towards a general miasma of agreement on the desirable ends of policy-making between the "doers" and the "watchers". "Guidance about the PM's (or Chancellor's) thinking" can become indistinguishable from journalists' own thinking. The process is imperceptible, insidious, and difficult for even the most honourable and "aware" commentator to resist. Naturally he wishes to know as much as possible about what is going on. And he is indeed often told a great deal on condition that he does not use it directly (or even at all) in his articles or programmes. As a result, though the iceberg may be large, the tip visible from the deck of the metaphorical *Titanic* is often small. Hence the disaster, if that is what ensues, is the more surprising and the greater.

This is, of course, to paint the picture at its blackest. Often, even for quite long periods, the results of confidential briefings and the whole consensus approach to government are not obviously bad at all. The two main political parties alternate in power and provide a stability and continuity which is widely admired elsewhere. Backing them are able, hard-working, dedicated, incorruptible civil servants who in many ways have few peers. Commentating on this ostensibly Elysian scene are some of the best-informed, and certainly best-written newspapers in the world (what paper can better, for instance, the *Financial Times* in its own sphere?).

And yet, and yet . . . when the mistakes *are* made they are monumental. Thus it was clear in any number of postwar financial crises, such as those of 1961, 1964, 1966 and 1967, that the situation was becoming much worse than either the authorities or most economic commentators would admit, at least in public, or indeed in some cases realised themselves. There are, of course, reasons for this—not all bad ones by any means. In the exposed position of sterling since 1945 it was almost a patriotic necessity, at least until the remarkable improvement in the balance of payments in 1969–70, for all concerned to make the pound appear to the world as strong as possible. To emphasise that "it was all done by mirrors"; that one of the two reserve currencies, in which half the world's trade was done, had little but borrowed money to back it; that Britain's trading position was in "fundamental disequilibrium" owing to her over-valued currency—all this was to "rock the boat", than which there are few worse crimes in the British public school élitist book. And again not entirely without reason. Thus *the Economist*, which had long been an advocate of devaluation, found it almost impossible to say so in so many words.

The events which led up to the fiasco of the forced devaluation of November 1967 are a good, albeit unusually graphic, example of the dilemma. The tragi-comedy sequence of events in 1967 was almost a caricature of "why England sleeps" (see Appendix 1). Even those who believed that the pound's parity must be reduced to a more realistic level hoped that it could be done in rational conditions, without the uncertainty, expensive speculation, panic, and glaringly broken promises which in the event were the hall-marks of the 1967 British devaluation. Although it would have been more difficult (but not impossible) for Britain, because of the reserve currency status of sterling and because of her greater world-wide commitments, the model for the 1967 sterling devaluation should have been the way the French subsequently devalued the franc in 1969 (see Chapter Four). The French lack of consultation with her monetary allies on that occasion is to be deplored; the forethought, aplomb and smoothness with which the exercise was carried out is to be wholly admired.

But 1967 was merely one of the more dramatic stories of lost opportunities, of not facing a problem until it explodes, and as such is worth chronicling in some detail; there have been many others. The mistake was not to devalue earlier in 1967 or preferably in 1964, when Labour came to power, or even in 1966 at the time of the wage "freeze" when, it transpired later, about half the Cabinet were, in fact, for devaluing. But how could such a sensitive issue be considered objectively when, it seems, the Prime Minister gave specific instructions that it should not be so considered? And even if he had not done this, how many of the Government's advisers would have urged that devaluation should be debated as one of the possible options open to an ailing Britain? Or did so before Wilson's diktat?

This is not to argue that devaluation would have been an unmitigated good even if it had been done earlier and had been handled competently. By definition it involves breaking faith with foreigners, both individuals and Governments, who have been foolhardy enough to hold their money in one's currency. And it involves shifting the terms of trade, that is the amount a country has to export to pay for a given volume of imports, adversely against oneself. And it usually involves going back on a number of previous pledges that no such thing is contemplated. But it is at least an option which should be considered as such: and one, moreover, which in the short term at least (as Britain saw in 1969 and 1970) can produce a big improvement in the balance of payments. To rule it out, on principle, in advance is ludicrous.

But this type of patriotism can be carried too far. The

author remembers going to a private dinner given by a man prominent in the British export trade only three weeks before the 1967 devaluation. The object of the meeting was, it seemed, to discuss a far-from-promising economic outlook and what might be done to improve it. Yet—with no disrespect to our charming host who was obviously, and rightly so, well liked by his journalist guests—it is a remarkable fact that at no stage of the evening was the possibility of devaluation even mentioned, en passant. Almost everything else but the unspeakable was discussed: export prices, credit terms for exporters, the dock strike, the Six-Day War, the alarming level of imports. Yet when six or eight are gathered together to eat good food and bib fine wine, can it be a crime to mention in private what is uppermost in everyone's mind?

It was clear then that things were not going as well as they were said to be, to the objective observer who merely did his home-work on the economic indicators, and in particular on the balance of payments figures (for which a three-dimensional, water-cooled, slide-rule is an optional extra), but did not necessarily inhabit the corridors of power and of "influencing". Similarly, in 1964, whatever the merits or otherwise of Reginald Maudling's attempt to "accelerate into self-sustained growth", it became clear at a fairly early stage that the exercise (which will be tried again in one shape or other when the necessary structural reforms of the economy have been carried out) was not going according to plan.

If the follies of the consensus approach to government, where most people are wrong for so much of the time, are to be avoided in the future there would be much to be said for discouraging officials and even Ministers from frequently seeking out certain favoured journalists for this "briefing" treatment. The journalist who does his home-work—such as the excellent "fourth estate" independent, free-wheeling, outspoken columnists in America—should not need endless background briefings. Before writing he should make up his own mind what needs to be done; and about what is happening, and is likely to happen in the future, if present policies continue.

As a corollary of this, "hard" news should be given with a

minimum of "interpretation" and embellishment. And economic commentators from all newspapers, from The *Times* to the *Mirror*, should be treated on equal terms with no inner circle of those who can be "trusted" to draw the right conclusions. There would, of course, be less possibility of serious error all round, for officials and journalists alike, if the suggestion in Chapter Five and in the Fulton Report that there should be a much more "open", less secretive, civil service were adopted.

It is a mistake, however, to blame too many past mistakes and too much of Britain's present poor economic health on government alone. The sheer conservatism of much of British industry, the parochialism and irresponsibility of many trade union leaders, the "couldn't-care-less-I'm-all-right-Jack" attitude of many people, have also played their part. So, too, has the unenterprising approach of the mass media: television, radio, and newspapers. In the context of consensus government, the Press Lords and their editors should surely insist that journalists covering financial, economic and industrial topics do their home-work more thoroughly. If that means spending more time in factories talking to businessmen and workers and less time in Whitehall being *told* what is happening, both at the summit and at the grass-roots, then so much the better. And if it means employing more journalists and leader-writers with the inclination and the time to think and to "devil" out facts for themselves, then so much the worse for newspapers profits in the short term. But so much the better for their own reputations as independent organs of news and opinion, as countervailing centres of influence to the ever-growing power of the State. So much the better for the health of democracy. And so much the better in the long run it might well be—as educational standards rise and people become more discerning and exacting in what they demand of the mass media—for their circulations, or "TAM ratings", and hence eventually for their profits.

Less bias in the presentation of actual hard news by the mass media, and more separate, genuinely independent, comment would do much to reduce the dangers of consensus government. At the moment there is too great a tendency, owing in part to the pressure of events, to accept so-called hard news in leader columns and on city pages as presented by the Government without enough critical analysis and com-

ment. Thus in the run-ups to the various financial crises
which have beset this country in the last quarter century
there have been some commentators who have not accepted,
for instance, the Board of Trade's (now absorbed into the
Ministry of Trade and Industry) interpretation of the latest
month's balance of payment figures, but too many who have
done so—uncritically. Strikes, both at home and abroad,
"seasonal" distortions, acts of God or the Devil such as the
Six-Day War, unforeseen and by implication unforeseeable
events like a slackening in the rate of growth of world
trade—all these and many others have been given as reasons,
or rather excuses, at different times for a weak British
balance of payments, and for a steadily declining share of
world trade.

A corollary of civil servants seeing less of "media men"
from the Press, television and radio is that they should instead
see more of other people and, more important, see their point of
view. Officials, especially the more senior ones, tend to be grossly
over-worked (see Chapter Five) but a way must be found of
getting them out more into the factories, offices, shops and small
businesses which many of them watch over and whose fortunes
they influence, if not control. For instance, the officials at the
Confederation of British Industry who prepare and collate the
questions about the state of businessmen's "confidence" concerning trading conditions might treat their questionnaires with
much more circumspection and realism if they knew more about
what makes industry tick. They might then appreciate more, for
instance, that successful businessmen are and need to be profes-
sionally optimistic to get ahead of their rivals. But it is a very
different matter to add up all their largely optimistic answers and
say that therefore the prospects, for, say, agricultural machinery
(in fact a great British post-war export success story) in the
aggregate are necessarily good. Such questionnaires may detect a
change in the aggregate mood of a certain industry and yet still
contain a built-in bias towards optimism.

No doubt it will take time to bring over-burdened civil
servants more into touch with "the people" by, for instance,
giving them the wherewithal to entertain, insisting that they
spend more time on business courses and in factories, and
re-allocating senior jobs so that seeing the bottom of one's
In-tray is not a major daily achievement. But it should be
possible to extend the present exchange scheme whereby young

men are lent to Whitehall by industry and, to a lesser extent, by banks and universities. This scheme was started in 1965 with the commendable objective of increasing "cross-fertilisation" between Whitehall and the big wide world outside. It also so happened that the Civil Service Commissioners—they were not to foresee the remarkable increase in the scope of government in recent years—for years seriously under-recruited into the élitist Administrative Grade. In part this was because they refused to lower their standards. They insisted on an absolute standard for the home service and diplomatic corps. If there were not enough bright young men among so many candidates of that standard— then *tant pis*, Departments would have to do with fewer recruits.

But now time has largely caught up with this error and as a result there is at last a great opportunity to get civil servants out into "the field" to learn how the world goes round. The exchange scheme is regarded as only a moderate success by Whitehall. Some recruits have been judged to have done well in their two years there, others have been returned to their companies without a "cum laude" commendation. No doubt this is to some extent inevitable. Companies have sometimes off-loaded men whom they were glad to see the last of for a while; the civil service is a strange environment to the outsider, whose mores take some getting used to; running a factory is very different, and much more genuinely an administrative job, than shifting piles of paper "for urgent action"; and in some cases Whitehall has probably been too busy or too insensitive to spare the time to train, however briefly, the "green" outsider. It has also been most loath to spare its young men for a comparable stint of two years or more in industry, akadëmeia or the City (with a shortage of able people this is understandable, if not commendable). There would need to be an edict from on high *insisting* that Departments make people available for industry.

From industry's side there are problems of absorption, of course. Running even the smallest manufacturing unit is different in kind from, for instance, controlling the endeavours of several executive officers. But the problems are not insuperable. Men loaned from Whitehall might be placed in, say, the accounts, or market research, or economic advisory department of their host firm and still learn a great deal about the environment of what is to many of them otherwise virtually another planet. It would be an excellent thing, too, if older and more senior people from industry were loaned to Whitehall, at Assistant Secretary level or higher, instead of merely at Principal level.

Again the problems of absorption would be considerable, and there would be a predictable outcry from the civil service unions for threatening the promotion prospects of the "regulars". But again they would not be insuperable and would be worth overcoming for the injection of outside expertise it would give Whitehall. The Conservatives have talked for some time about bringing more businessmen through those sacred portals, in order, *inter alia*, to increase Whitehall's "cost-effectiveness" (see Chapter Five).

Heath made a start in 1970 with his "think-tank" of pundits, under Lord Rothschild, commissioned to produce radical ideas for the enlightenment of "No. 10" and of the Cabinet and with his handful of high-powered businessmen seconded from industry to the civil service. But it was not overwhelmingly clear what they would actually *do*. They needed to be given specific, concrete tasks if they were not to be excluded by the "regulars" from the centres of policy-making.

Cross-fertilisation at such senior levels of the bureaucracy is more common in certain other countries, such as America and Australia. And, to be fair, Whitehall is making a start by advertising, albeit on a limited and cautious scale, for men who have had experience of other walks of life to enter the civil service years after they have left the university, or its equivalent, by competitive examination. The problems of absorption of men of such relative seniority cannot be insuperable in principle, for they include jobs of Assistant Secretary level.

CHAPTER SEVEN

Incomes Holy Grail

The incomes policy saga has in many ways epitomised Britain's relative economic failure in the last quarter century. The results have been almost totally negative (and certainly invisible to the naked eye) if not actually harmful, but there are still many in Britain who mutter, like some primordial religious incantation, about the need for such a policy: "the ultimate test of a free society", "the need for discipline in peace as in war", "the spirit of Dunkirk...all pulling together", "must put one's house in order at last", "these people need to show some self-restraint...need cracking down on", and so on.

Every cliché has been used, and sometimes still is, to justify the futile search for the Holy Grail of an incomes non-policy. It has, of course, long, if unrespectable, antecedents. Sir Stafford Cripps during the first post-war Labour Government achieved some appreciable, if transitory, success in persuading the trade unions—if only in the interests of the solidarity of the "Labour Movement"—to moderate their wage claims. And in 1956 Harold Macmillan in his brief tenure of the Exchequer, underwent a transitory aberration in appealing for a "price plateau". This achieved little more than a fortunately short-lived distortion of national resources through the artificial restraint of prices, and therefore the artificial stimulation of demand, for the products of the nationalised industries.

Five years went by before Selwyn Lloyd, a Conservative Chancellor, asked for a temporary pause in the rise in incomes "until productivity has caught up and there is room for further advance". The pause lasted for eight months, and did little more than earn the opprobrium of the nurses, civil servants, teachers, railwaymen and others in the public sector who suffered most from it—although they did, nevertheless, receive appreciable pay increases during the "pause" or shortly after it had ended.

The Macmillan Government even so persevered. Early in 1962 it published its White Paper "Incomes Policy: The Next Step". Three to 3½ per cent was set as the famous "guiding light" for an average annual increase in money incomes, assuming an average annual expansion of the economy of 4 per cent. Subsequently the National Incomes Commission, known irreverently as "the Three Wise Men", was set up with no visible effect, for better or worse, on the upward march of man.

Undeterred by this relative failure of incomes policy (a so-called policy in which Maudling, in particular, strongly believed during his tenure of the Exchequer in 1963–64), Labour made it a corner-stone of its 1964 election platform, with its gobbledegook about a "planned growth of incomes". Wilson said then: "We shall not as a matter of policy hold production down, cripple productivity, and then try to cut the wages system to fit it. Nor shall we use unemployment and family hardship as the sanction to enforce a wage increase."

In the (Labour) beginning there was the Prices and Incomes Board, presided over by Aubrey Jones, former Conservative Minister and businessman with a varied industrial career. Intellectually brilliant, a poor boy made good, an exponent of the "now-you-see-me-now-you-don't" approach to business with several boardroom appointments, his recruitment to the PIB was regarded by George Brown and his nascent Department of Economic Affairs as a major coup. The thought was, *inter alia*, that such a gifted radical Tory was the very man to bind the nation's wounds: businessman would speak truth unto trade unionist when the PIB chairman waved his magic wand. In high excitement Brown persuaded both sides of industry to sign the famous Declaration of Intent on incomes policy, the PIB was given "guidelines" for discriminating Good pay claims from Bad ones, and the economic millenium seemed to be at hand.

It was not to be. Almost from the beginning things went badly wrong and before long Jones himself was saying that an incomes policy made only a marginal difference—less than 1 per cent a year—to the rate of wage inflation. Meanwhile, back in Whitehall George Brown was making noises in loyal but ineffective support. Endless investigations, probes, homilies, exhortations, lectures poured out from the busybody PIB as if from some conveyor belt. The Board's rate of increase in staff employed and money spent indeed seemed to be at least the cube of Britain's economic growth rate. Yet it may be unfair to dub this relationship Aubrey's law, with apologies to Professor Parkinson, because it embraces other State and para-State bodies besides the PIB. Undoubtedly, however, the Board consumed in its heyday an exceptional amount of its own and of other people's valuable time.

Labour's incomes policy was indeed ill-fated from its inception. James Callaghan, then Chancellor, was soon complaining, as well he might, of its manifest failure. And Frank Cousins, on loan from the Transport and General Workers' Union and then Minister of Technology, acted as an effective Trojan Horse within the Cabinet in undermining the policy. Even George Brown, high priest of the policy, was soon attacking the trade unions for their non-cooperation and announced his intention of legislating for compulsory "early warning" of proposed wage and price increases and their deferment for examination by the Prices and Incomes Board. There was also a lot of talk, as wages rose more rapidly than was their wont, of such a policy taking a decade or two to become effective in a free society, with obscure references to Sweden, always regarded as a Socialist Mecca, thrown in for good measure.

All to no avail. It is true that during the March 1966 election campaign Harold Wilson gave the impression that all was well. He even said "I do not think you can ever legislate for wage increases . . . once you have a law prescribing wages I think you are on a very slippery slope." Meanwhile Edward Heath warned of the dangers of earnings, prices and production expanding in the ratio of 9 to 5 to 1.

When the inevitable reckoning came and the economy was "blown off course"—ostensibly as a result only of the Six-Day War in the Middle East and the protracted seamen's strike, as Ministers were quick to claim—there were some revealing admissions. Wilson said that ever since the "great landmark" of the Declaration of Intent "wage increases have outrun the figure allowed for". And a year later Michael Stewart, then—remarkably—Secretary of State for Economic Affairs, said that "runaway inflation" had threatened Britain. There is no doubt that this almost unprecedentedly rapid wage inflation exacerbated the long-standing over-valuation of the pound, made

British exports even less competitive in world markets, and so contributed much to the July 1966 economic crisis. The Prime Minister, having spoken disparagingly of "wet editorials" needlessly prophesying disaster, on 20 July said that no "elaborate statutory controls" were necessary or intended. Ten days later legislation for such controls was introduced in the shape of "Part IV" tacked on to the 1966 Prices and Incomes Act already before Parliament.

These unprecedented powers involved a six-month freeze on any wage or price increases—even including those resulting from arbitration or Wage Council awards, and those due to be paid under existing agreements, which employers were exempted from breaking. They also forbade back-payment of frozen increases. Penalties for infringing freeze orders or striking in support of a frozen increase went up to £100 on summary conviction or £500 on indictment. For good measure, unlimited fines were thrown in for corporate bodies, such as companies or trade unions.

The subsequent story was one of steady retreat from such futile Draconian powers to the 1970 and 1971 situation of wages increasing, if possible, even more rapidly than in the early part of 1966 before the "freeze". Yet, even though the incomes policy was effectively allowed to lapse, legislation continued and the Labour Government produced seven White Papers, three Acts of Parliament, and many statutory orders on incomes policy. In addition a great deal of heat was generated within the Labour Party and between the Government and the trade unions—time, energy and bitterness all completely wasted.

The message of the incomes policy fiasco—seldom have so many for so long achieved so little—is so important and so depressing that it cannot be swept lightly aside. For that reason the events of recent years are worth recapitulating in some detail.

For it was not only the PIB and its prey which wasted so much time, money, and effort. In addition large numbers of people were tied up administering the so-called policy. General responsibility for incomes policy rested with the Department of Economic Affairs from 1964 until 1968, when it was moved to the Department of Employment and Productivity (the old Ministry of Labour, writ large). But other Ministries were also involved in the "vetting" of prices in their own fields—for instance the Ministry of Agriculture of food prices.

Yet the last state was worse than the first. It was clear, indeed, by the summer of 1967, when "severe restraint" ended, that incomes policy was as much a failure then as it had been a year earlier when the freeze was imposed. The author said as much in an article on the leader-page of the *Daily Telegraph* (at a time when it was regarded in some quarters as vaguely unpatriotic, un-Dunkirk-like, to question the efficacy of the incomes policy) and implied that the pound was over-valued. It was not at that time possible, or at least not desirable, to say that devaluation was by then inevitable. To have done so might, without exaggerating the influence of the Press, have made even more likely an event which there was much to be said for avoiding if at all possible. It was desirable to avoid a *forced* devaluation in the conditions of confusion and humiliation which in the event prevailed in November 1967.

It is true that the 1966–67 period of freeze followed by severe restraint had *some* effect: it would have been remarkable if it had not done so. But was this effect desirable? That semi-official body, the National Institute of Economic and Social Research, said in its Economic Review of February 1968 that the increase in average weekly earnings from July 1966 to October 1967 was "if anything fractionally higher than the rise during previous roughly comparable periods of rising unemployment and low economic activity". The PIB itself made the topical and shrewd (but perhaps surprising, from such a source) point that a freeze could actually lead to greater trade union militancy by increasing anomalies, so exacerbating the inflation it was supposed to mitigate!

In some cases, such as for instance the probe into Fleet Street, and apparently into Courtaulds, silly questions inevitably got silly ripostes and the answer was a lemon. The PIB reports on such mundane topics as bakers' pay will always be of interest to the social historians, if to few others. But they were introduced with great panache at the Chairman's press conference. Aubrey Jones seemed to have a word for everyone, and appeared frequently on television enlarging on the British people's manifold sins and wickednesses. Such was his self-confidence it seemed that there had been nothing like it since the elder Pitt's assumption of power: "I know that I can save England, and no one else can."

There was certainly a temporary slowing-down in the rate of increase in earnings during the six months freeze—and even during the subsequent six months of "severe restraint". But after that—the deluge. Price and wage inflation soon reached, and then overtook, their former rates, and by early 1970 were proceeding at an annual rate of at least 7 and 10 per cent respectively. And worse was to follow in 1971 with respective figures of 8 and 13 per cent or more. Such inflation in peace-time was undoubtedly in part a delayed action response to the freeze and squeeze during which people felt worse off than in fact they were. Enormous wage claims, ranging exceptionally up to 50 per cent, gave the lie to those who argued that growth does not matter and that the British do not pine for material things. They also gave the lie to the philosophical basis, such as it was, on which the incomes policy had been based, and to the Wilson Government's claim to have achieved something new in human engineering.

Many Socialists saw—and still see—an incomes policy as an instrument of social justice. The PIB was specifically enjoined to do what it could for the lower-paid workers. This objective, too, proved to be a chimera. Indeed, the evidence is that low-earners have fared relatively badly in recent years. Unions such as the Transport and General Workers' Union tend to be too unwieldy, cumbersome and dispersed among a number of industries to put the maximum pressure on employers. In contrast, the so-called white-collar workers and professional classes, of the ilk represented by Clive Jenkins, became increasingly militant and successful in winning king-sized wage settlements. That "the strong" should gain most from a "free-for-all" was, of course, an aspect of capitalism which the Left in theory most deplored.

It was reported in the Press in 1969 that an unpublished (of course!) report for the Government by Richard Lipsey and Michael Parkin of Essex University showed that Labour's incomes policy had been, as Wilson would say, counter-productive. They apparently concluded, in examining wage rates rather than earnings, that wage inflation becomes virtually insensitive to the level of unemployment when such a policy is ostensibly operating. And that it tends actually to aggravate wage inflation, rather than mitigate it, except when unemployment is relatively low, that is below 1.8 per cent.

The objection to an incomes policy, except for very short periods in conditions of emergency, are, of course, several and powerful. The evidence of both Conservative and Labour post-war years indicates that a so-called "norm" (the average permitted annual increase in wage rates) almost immediately becomes a minimum below which no self-respecting trade union leader can allow himself to fall. This seems to apply particularly in circumstances where fears of unemployment would otherwise have dampened down wage demands. An incomes policy also, in so far as it diverts the course of events at all, must add an extra rigidity to (in the case of Britain) an already arthritic and relatively inflexible economy. Since it cannot, in an imperfect world, be evenly applied it inevitably creates injustices and anomalies. Equally inevitably, these multiply for as long as the policy is maintained.

The case of the nurses under Selwyn Lloyd's incomes policy is notorious—perhaps unduly so in the light of subsequent events (public employees tend to fare relatively badly in such a situation as the State sets an "example" in restraint to the private sector). There were inevitably more similar, but worse, cases under the Labour freeze of 1966–67: those who had just had a pay increase when it started fared relatively well compared with those whose annual pay claim was just coming up for settlement.

There is, however, a caveat: during that freeze back-payment of frozen increases was allowed. Thus if workers could eventually extract such back-payment from their employers they fared well compared with those who were less fortunate. Moreover, some people were able to claim productivity increases, thereby escaping the worst rigours of the freeze. While others, owing often to the nature of their jobs (they might be night-watchmen), could not plead higher productivity. There were also the absurdities during the freeze of, for example, four freeze orders having to be withdrawn when the Court of Appeal found that the Government had misapplied the law.

Yet the fundamental weaknesses of an incomes policy lie elsewhere. Its application, at least at first, tends to persuade people that this is "a new beginning", a new *démarche* in economic policy; that a fundamental change from the unsuccessful past has occurred; that someone "up there" (it may be Aubrey Jones of the PIB in Kingsgate House or Sir Frederick Catherwood of the National Economic Development Council in Vickers Tower) is "doing it all for us", so do let's all relax.

It is also obvious that certain countries, which have highly successful economies, such as Japan, do not dally with incomes policies at all. They put their faith in rapid economic growth, in change, in innovation, in advanced technology, in many of the things which have been too much strangers to the British scene in the last quarter century. It does not follow, of course, that all incomes policies are therefore by definition *necessarily* futile, but it does suggest that they are probably irrelevant, to say the least, to the fundamentals of economic success.

The absolute level of wages is never the most important factor in a country's economic success or failure. How else could America, with wages twice as high as those of Britain, compete effectively at all in world markets with her? Indeed, though it may be almost tautological to say so, a major cause of American prosperity—as well as her vast tailor-made home market and enormous natural resources—has been her relatively high labour costs. As long ago as the last century those high wages were encouraging, even forcing, employers to put in capital-intensive, labour-saving machinery.

Productivity has, alas, become a somewhat discredited word of late in Britain, if only because of its connection in the public mind with the ill-starred incomes policy. But there can be no doubt that in higher productivity, and not in relatively stagnant real wages, lies Britain's economic salvation. And that greater output per man-hour will only be achieved by such overdue radical changes as much less Government expenditure, a recast taxation system to encourage incentives, trade union and industrial relation reforms, a sustained higher level of investment, and more "competition" (which ideally would include entry into the Common Market).

The danger is that both major political parties will continue to flirt with the chimera of an incomes policy, despite its manifest failures. They can always persuade themselves that it has not been the king, but his advisers, who have been at fault; that the so-called policy is right in principle but has been badly administered!

The PIB saga effectively ended by Aubrey Jones bailing out in the nick of time within a month of the unexpected Tory election victory. To be fair, he had offered his services to the Heath Government within days of 18 June, stressing on television the paramount and continuing need for an incomes policy: but answer came there none. And long before that, when it was assumed that Labour could not possibly recover in time from its many by-election reverses to go on and win the General Election, Jones had lined up a job on the Board of International Publishing Corporation. This had collapsed with the take-over of IPC by the Reed Paper Group. Whereupon Barbara Castle had offered him—apparently after prolonged haggling about terms—the £18,000 a year job of chairmanship of the nascent Commission for Incomes and Manpower (of which more anon). Jones's return to private industry as £9,000 a year part-time chairman of Laporte Industries was a come-down from such lofty heights (the PIB paid £16,000 a year), but it would at least allow him time to do other things.

There was some discussion in the early months of the new Government of a possible remaining, residual role for the PIB under the Conservatives. On one Sunday in August 1970 indeed, two "high-brow Sundays" had stories prophesying respectively the death of, and a reprieve for, the PIB. Received wisdom from Whitehall was that it might be retained as a review body for the salaries of certain State employees, like the Chairmen of nationalised industries, and National Health Service doctors. Robert Carr was thought to be arguing in Cabinet committee for some such role, backed by Reginald Maudling, ever a believer in some sort of do-it-yourself incomes policy. The word was that Sir Keith Joseph was for sending the PIB packing—as eventually it was.

The Prime Minister, who during the summer 1970 Parliamentary recess was criticised for not spending more time on dry land well away from his yacht, was apparently inclined to agree with Joseph. Much turned, indeed in a sense the Government's whole economic strategy turned, on Ministers' success or otherwise in decelerating the rate of wage inflation.

Most of those who urged Heath, potentially one of the most conscientious Prime Ministers this country has ever had, to *do* something seemed to have little idea what it should be. They had in mind, mainly, however, and understandably, the alarming rate of wage inflation and the repeated crippling of major industries, and in particular of the car manufacturers, by "wild-cat" strikes. Long years of political gimmickry, of endless rabbits out of the metaphorical hat, had still not convinced many people that the solution of Britain's long-term problems, such as carefully-thought-out industrial relations legislation against bitter opposition, was essentially a *long*-term problem. They believed strongly that it was essential for a Prime Minister to be *seen* to be doing something, however futile. The ghost of Harold Wilson's first "Hundred Days" despite its disastrous sequel, still lingered six years later. Public relations had triumphed.

Heath ignored that victory and remained on "Morning Cloud", while instructing his Ministers to get the firmest possible grip on the wages situation, pending the introduction of more fundamental structural reforms in the autumn when Parliament reassembled. At the same time, many economic commentators urged from the side-lines that an incomes policy was the only answer to Britain's predicament of rapid inflation, high unemployment, little growth, low investment, and a weakening balance of payments. They even pointed once more, if more hesitantly than in the past, to certain other countries, notably France and Sweden and Holland (America was sometimes included for good measure) as "examples" of where such a policy had succeeded.

Ministers rightly eschewed such a deadly chalice and remained committed to the view that a formal incomes policy with all its attendant nonsense of ineffective, complex "guide-lines" to good behaviour and so on, did more harm than good. Instead, they began to "lean" heavily on the State industries to stand out against outrageous wage demands and showed every sign of encouraging private employers to do the same, even at the risk of, in the short-term, damaging strikes. Meanwhile, the money supply remained under fairly tight control, with the aim of ensuring that the wherewithal would not be there to pay higher wages (there did, however, seem to be scope for some minor tax-cutting, if only to encourage morale).

The "expansionists", which as usual included the influential National Institute of Economic Research, and certain notable "quality" newspapers, predictably lambasted this as a totally negative policy, a formula for economic decline. They pointed to the (small) margin of unused capacity in the economy. They never explained, however, because they could not do so, how a policy of full-steam-ahead expansion could be undertaken safely when it had been so disastrous in the past (there were some, of course, who argued that the balance of payments did not matter anyway—for as long as, presumably, other countries were content to go on lending Britain money if a yawning balance of payments deficit reappeared).

The expansionist argument was beguiling and particularly so to anyone, such as the author of this book, who believed that fairly rapid economic growth was in the long run essential to Britain's salvation. But Conservative Ministers, and in particular Heath, seemed to have grasped the point, to have learnt by hard experience, that a pre-requisite of respectable, sustainable growth must be overdue, radical reforms to make the British economy fundamentally more competitive and efficient.

Success in the Conservative Government's fight against the almost unprecedentedly rapid wage inflation which had developed in the twilight of the Wilson era was slow in coming—which should have surprised no one. It would be fanciful to suggest that the pound was ever likely to go the way of the German Weimar Republic's Mark, when for a short time a suitcase of notes was needed to pay for a restaurant meal; or of the Brazilian cruzeiro, which depreciates by a third in a relatively good year. But the warning signs were there, flashing amber for all to see. *The Times*, in a brilliant first leader, pointed out the implications of price inflation at 10 per cent a year: the value of the currency halved in a few short years, the social fabric disrupted and so on. A generation ago the great economist Keynes had warned of the social evils of runaway inflation, and how right—in this as in so much else—he had been. Even the 1970 rate of an 8 per cent rise in retail prices, if for long maintained, threatened the virtual extinction of the rentier (unfashionable word), the widows, non-State pensioners and others living on fixed incomes.

Once they get a grip, inflationary expectations are extraordinarily difficult to rein back, as Heath's Ministers discovered to their cost in the winter of 1970-71. The money supply was allowed to rise by about a tenth in 1970, against a background of wage earnings increasing by about half as much again by the end of the year. Some economists argued that this was not enough: the money supply should be squeezed "until the pips squeaked", until substantial companies were forced into bankruptcy or at least into shedding their redundant labour.

But the Governor of the Bank of England, reappointed to a second term early in 1971, among others showed signs of rebelling against such a harsh, almost Calvinistic, doctrine. He

had the problem of maintaining the semblance of an orderly
gilt-edged market (selling Government stock at even nominal
interest rates of around 10 per cent was no easy task in such
inflationary conditions, and yet this had to be done if surplus
liquidity was to be mopped up). Bank governors had for long
regarded, with some reason, successive Governments of whatever political hue as much too inflationary in their fiscal policy,
in that in particular Government expenditure was allowed to
grow remorselessly.

It seemed unfair to the Bank that monetary policy should
be asked to bear the brunt of re-corking the inflationary genie.
Moreover, in early 1971 "hot" and other footloose money was
pouring into London, attracted by the relatively high interest
rates prevailing there, and by the sheer size of Britain's
unwonted balance of payments surplus. Although an unfamiliar
problem, and one which would not last long unless wage
inflation was controlled, this money from abroad added to the
Bank's problems in that it increased the money supply in the
short term.

Yet there was another major weapon in the Chancellor's
armoury. In January 1971 he publicly rejected too harsh a use
of monetary policy on the grounds that it was not necessarily
less painful than fiscal measures, or more effective. Certainly
looking across the Atlantic, where ("I am now a Keynesian")
Nixon had perforce gone sharply into reverse in expanding the
money supply, it was difficult to argue that the Friedman
approach of monetary restraint, in order to restrain inflation,
had been an unqualified success.

To the derision of those who believed in a so-called
incomes policy, or in another total wage freeze, as the key to
Britain's economic salvation, Conservative Ministers evolved
the "x—1" doctrine of de-escalating wage awards. Infuriated
by the Scamp Award of a 15 per cent pay rise in October
1971 to dustmen, who a year earlier had been bought off by
similar generosity, they were determined "never again". Wages
awards must henceforth be progressively reduced to a level—
age-old dream—which corresponded to the annual growth of
productivity, or at least did not threaten to price British exports
out of world markets.

When 1971 opened 10 per cent wage increases appeared to
be the immediate "norm" at which Ministers were aiming,
reducing eventually to perhaps half that amount. Critics argued

that this was in effect an incomes policy, often not mentioning that in the past such a concept had been associated with complicated guide-lines for good behaviour, pontification from "on high", and much talk of social justice (ironically since the poorer-paid workers seemed to fare worst from such an alleged policy). A more valid criticism was that Ministers should do their "dirty work" themselves and not despatch officials to define the "national interest" as they did before the Wilberforce Inquiry on the power workers' claim.

The calling-off of the power workers disruptive go-slow in December 1970 had been an undoubted, if limited, success for the Government's approach. Public opinion had been firmly against a group of not obviously under-paid workers, who had certainly not fallen behind in the so-called wages free-for-all: on the contrary. Thus emboldened, Ministers gave no encouragement whatsoever to the Post Office to improve on its 8 per cent wage offer, despite a costly and protracted strike in early 1971, and the 25 per cent pay claim of the railwaymen, among many others, seemed certain to be similarly laughed out of court—but probably at the cost of some disruption.

It was difficult, if not impossible, to see any alternative to this combination of monetary policy and "leaning on" State expected miracles from such an approach: reducing the rate of employers in the expectation that those in the private sector would eventually follow suit. No one expected miracles from such an approach: reducing the rate of wage inflation by a half or even two-thirds would not in itself solve Britain's endemic problems of under-investment, sluggish productivity, a heavily protected and often State-subsidised, home market, and chaotic industrial relations. But even a limited success on the wages front would buy time for the radical structural reforms of the Heath "quiet revolution" to take effect.

CHAPTER EIGHT

Why Not Compete?

The Conservative Government's aim should be to ensure that Britain's scarce resources are used in the most economical way to sort out the industrial wheat from the chaff. In many industries more "competition"—defined in the broadest way—would surely do the trick over a period of time. Market forces will ensure that this country's capital and human assets are deployed where and how they are most needed. In the longer run this will produce higher living standards for the country as a whole, and greater resources to cushion the shock of redeployment for those caught in declining industries.

Competition in this sense can take a number of forms. It can, for instance, take the form of tariff cuts. It is not generally realised that for years (and certainly since Imperial Preference was introduced nearly three decades ago) Britain has had a relatively heavily protected economy. In all the talk of the Common Market being an "inward-looking community" it is often forgotten that the average level of its Common External Tariff is actually lower than the average British tariff on manufactured goods. It can be argued that this matters less than it did in so far as Britain, like other industrialised countries, is committed to a phased reduction of tariffs under the Kennedy Round of the General Agreement on Tariffs and Trade. And this country already belongs to the European Free Trade Area, within which there are now no tariffs between members. This area of free trade would, of course, be enormously expanded if Britain joined the Common Market. If she did not do so then instead of chasing will-o'-the-wisps such as the so-called North Atlantic Free Trade Area, she would surely be well advised to consider reducing tariffs unilaterally.

There is, of course, never a good time to do such a thing; the balance of payments is allegedly never strong enough, and the Foreign Office is apparently always opposed to "concessions" for which no *quid pro quos* are offered by other countries. Yet the Germans did it and unilateral tariff cuts almost certainly contributed to the Erhard "economic miracle" by stimulating German industry to greater efforts. The effect should be the same in Britain, where feather-bedding of some British industries has at times reached absurd levels. There was a time not so long ago, for instance, when the price of certain British-produced fertilisers was higher than that of those available for purchase abroad by more than the value of the fertiliser subsidy. In other words, the British manufacturers did well, the British farmers bought their fertilisers relatively cheaply, and the British taxpayer was left footing the difference!

Competition can take the form, too, of lower company taxation. That ever-willing but over-burdened milch cow has been brought almost to its knees by successive, and deliberate increases in the tax burden it bears. Corporation Tax was successively increased by Labour far above the level equivalent to the old income tax and profits tax on companies. Corporation Tax was devised in part with the object of persuading companies to retain more of their earnings for investment rather than "wastefully" paying them out in dividends to shareholders. The results have not been encouraging. Britain's investment rate, the seed corn of future growth, still jogs along at only a half or two-thirds of the level of its main international competitors. As a result when Chancellors attempt to expand the economy and make "a dash for growth" the productive capacity which is needed to sustain the additional output just is not there. The economy then develops all the familiar symptoms of "over-heating" and inflationary pressures.

Cause and effect in economics are always difficult to prove; usually there are so many factors involved in a situation that it is virtually impossible to "isolate the variables" involved. Because direct taxation of large incomes and company taxation are heavy here and at the same time Britain has such a sluggish economy it does not *necessarily* follow, as night the day, that the one is the cause of, or a contributor to, the other. The proposition cannot possibly be proved but it seems "common sense" to believe that there is probably some connection.

It is true that the widely-held idea that Britain is more

heavily taxed than, for instance, the Common Market countries is erroneous—as is the assumption that she has a higher level of public expenditure, particularly on the social services. In fact, the total burden of taxation as a proportion of the gross national product in this country is only about the average of the Six—and actually behind that for France, Holland, and West Germany.

Yet where the shoe pinches, as in the higher reaches of surtax and the taxation of certain "closed" (usually family-owned) companies, it pinches exceedingly. And, whatever the precise incidence of taxation here compared with other countries, it is surely reasonable to assume that Britain's poor economic performance would be better if her taxes were lower. Much was heard of this in the 1970 election and no doubt much will be heard at future elections about it—unless and until radical changes are made. The Conservatives had their chance in their thirteen years of power and did nothing radical; only their non-economist Chancellor Selwyn Lloyd showed any real initiative, imagination and courage in raising substantially the starting point for surtax on earned incomes. For the rest, although the Tories reduced income tax along with other tax cuts, from 8s 6d to 7s 9d in the pound during their long period of office, they did little indeed to mitigate the remarkably high marginal rates of taxation (among the highest in the world) introduced in the exceptional conditions of the 1939–45 war. Labour had their chance, too, and did much worse than nothing in 1964–70 with, among a host of other tax increases, 6d on income tax and even a surcharge on surtax, which was itself originally regarded as a surcharge on income tax!

The Conservatives' failure on the tax front, for which they have had time to repent at leisure, was all the more remarkable in that one of the few consistent, endemic, aspects of their philosophy over the decades has been their belief in the virtues of low taxation. It is true that at times, as in the war-time Coalition Government with Labour, they have presided over some of the biggest increases in taxation Britain has ever known. But at least they have continued to pay lip-service to the need to reduce it and usually when they have had the chance they have done something in that direction.

Yet that something has been small compared with what might have been. The Conservatives' failure must be put down in part to sheer inertia, the abiding British disease, plus a calculation (in the event wholly unjustified) that "equality of sacrifice" would somehow deter the trade unions from such dreadful things as making enormous wage claims. The following table shows the remarkable difference between top tax rates in Britain and in comparable countries (reducing surtax by a half would cost only about £140 million a year, equivalent to about a tenth of the revenue from the tobacco tax) before the 1971 Budget:

MAXIMUM MARGINAL TAX RATE ON EARNED INCOME
Married Man with Two Children Under Eleven Years Old

Country	At maximum tax rate: income remaining from extra £100 earned			Income level at which maximum tax rate is reached
	%	£	s d	£ a year
Britain	91.25	8	15 0	18,900
Canada[1]	84.20	15	16 0	155,038
Holland	70.50	29	10 0	18,992
America[2]	70.00	30	0 0	84,750
Australia	68.37	31	12 7	15,248
New Zealand	67.50	32	10 0	4,088
West Germany[3]	54.59	45	8 2	23,225
France	43.20	56	16 0	25,316

[1] Ontario, including a 3% tax surcharge.
[2] Excluding the 10% tax surcharge
[3] Including a 3% tax surcharge
Source: Industrial Policy Group Study No. 3: "Taxation", Table VIII

Does it matter that Britain's marginal tax rates in the upper income brackets are the highest in the world among comparable countries? It is significant that this question is posed at all. The fact that it is disputed—seriously—in Britain, and is even an issue between the political parties (although Roy Jenkins paid lip-service as Chancellor to the need to reduce direct taxation), reveals as much about morale in Britain today as it does about the tax system itself. Learned academic economists bend their efforts to showing ostensibly that earning more money after tax is not a—and certainly not the—major factor in persuading people to work harder. Certain surveys of "what makes executives tick" purport to show the same thing.

In the 1970 election campaign the Labour election manifesto claimed that there was much more to do to achieve a fairer distribution of wealth in our community: "we shall ensure that tax burdens are progressively eased from those least able to bear them and that there is a greater contribution to the national revenue from the rich". The phrasing was suitably Wilsonian and Delphic but could be taken to mean that more taxes should be piled on the existing plethora of taxes on both capital and income. It appears, indeed, that on the Labour side Roy Jenkins is almost the sole bulwark against even steeper taxation of incomes if Labour is returned to power.

Yet elsewhere it is usually regarded as axiomatic that financial gain is a powerful incentive to harder work and more initiative. But there are even those in Britain who argue that the heavier direct taxes are the harder people work in order to maintain their standard of living. This may be true in certain special cases (it might be in the case of a journalist writing a hurried free-lance article or even a book to meet an unexpected tax bill) but it can scarcely be considered to have a universal validity. If it did presumably people in Britain and India would be among the hardest workers in the world, and enjoy two of the highest standards of living.

A certain amount has to be taken on trust in life and it does seem obvious that, other things being equal, a man works harder if he has a powerful financial incentive to do so. It may not be possible to prove this conclusively and no doubt the extent to which it is true or otherwise will provide a rich vein of controversy for academics and politicians for the rest of time. And perhaps particularly so in Britain where, at the drop of a metaphorical hat, a thousand and one reasons can usually be conjured up in order to "prove" that any radical change, such as a big cut in direct taxation, is impossible, or undesirable—or preferably both. There are many matters which it is not possible to prove conclusively but which seem plain common sense and which it is best to accept as such. Which is not to say, of course, that there are not many other factors which influence how hard and how well a man works: such as the satisfaction which his job gives him, the happiness or otherwise of his private life, how ambitious he is, and so on.

It is difficult to believe, nevertheless, that the contrast between, for instance, Wall Street and *parts* of the City has nothing to do with the British tax structure. In New York brokers and lawyers working on "the Street" enjoy far higher gross salaries, and even bigger incomes net of tax, than their opposite numbers in Britain. They tend to work far into the evening, take work home at weekends, have brief, non-alcoholic lunches and generally behave, responding to the stimulus of a financial carrot, as the capitalist text-books say they should. Many in the City, although denied this carrot, behave—remarkably—in the same way; others, perhaps more understandably, do not do so. Long vinuos (or spiritous) lunches, "swinging" of items onto expense accounts, days off to see the Derby or merely to play golf, long weekends, indispositions from a currently fashionable form of 'flu lasting much longer than is the wont of that virus . . . these things are not unknown.

It may be argued, of course, that the American approach to life, with all its disadvantages—such as perhaps more coronaries, higher blood pressure, more alcoholism, more violence, more pressure, in short an allegedly uncivilised life—is emphatically not preferable to the ostensibly more relaxed life of the British. That may be so; on the other hand it may not necessarily always be so. But either way it is a moot, subjective point, essentially a non-economic one, which is not germane to this chapter, or indeed to most of this book. If the problem is, and it is indeed, how to get a higher economic growth rate in Britain then the shape of the tax structure on earned incomes must inevitably be a major factor.

There was a serious deterioration in the taxation structure during the years 1964–70, quite apart from the 6d-in-the-pound increase in the standard rate of income tax: notably the new taxes on capital, the notorious "closed company" legislation, the introduction of the inequitable Selective Employment Tax, and successive increases in Corporation Tax and indirect taxes, such as purchase tax.

ESTIMATED YIELD OF EXISTING INDIRECT TAXES
FOR 1970–71

	£million
Purchase tax	1,260
Petrol/oil	1,380
Tobacco	1,160
Alcohol	905
Betting	120
Other duties	240
SET (net)	588
Total	5,453

The switch of emphasis of the taxation system from direct to indirect taxation involves the introduction of an added-value tax as a substitute for the highly discriminatory Selective Employment Tax and for purchase tax. In essence it is a tax on the value which each firm adds to the materials and services which it uses in the course of producing whatever it finally sells. In theory there are a number of possible forms of such a tax. In practice, if more than one rate is needed—and in this context any exemption constitutes a rate—it would probably be levied on the difference between a firm's purchases and its sales.

Collection would be on the basis of invoices. At the end of each period (be it one, two or three months), a company adds up its sales and the tax on them, at the appropriate rate, and likewise its purchases and the tax upon them. The tax on the purchases is deducted from the tax on the sales, and the difference is the tax due, for which a cheque is sent to the Customs and Excise, not to the Inland Revenue. Spot checks could help towards enforcement, but there is a certain amount of self-enforcement since a claim for rebate on purchases must correspond to a payment on someone else's sale.

Since the tax is rebated on all business purchases, including investments, it is a tax on final sales, that is on consumption. Its main advantage is that it involves, almost by definition in that it is levied on many goods at a relatively low rate, a widening of the tax base. It is also a powerful incentive to cost-cutting. And in its purest form, that is with no exceptions, it is non-discriminatory. To the extent that it raises a lot of money, make possible cuts in income tax and surtax, and reduces some of the archaic anomalies which were apparent even before the advent of SET, its introduction forms an invaluable part of a programme of tax reform and tax-cutting.

The added-value tax also has the advantage that, unlike SET, besides being an incentive to cost-cutting in business, it can be charged on imports and fully rebated on exports. The extent to which it is a significant export incentive has long been a matter of dispute. The Richardson Committee which considered such a tax's pros and cons when Reginald Maudling was Chancellor of the Exchequer decided that it did not provide such an incentive, or at least did not provide one which could not be more easily and cheaply provided in other ways such as the remission of purchase tax on exports. But anyone such as the author who, while working for Guest Keen and Nettlefolds, was concerned in preparing evidence for the Committee may question whether it asked the right questions, let alone found the right answers.

Suffice to say now that other countries *do* regard it as a significant incentive to exports, and that all six Common Market countries are harmonising their tax systems on the French model of the tax. British firms would therefore be at a comparative disadvantage compared with most of the rest of Western Europe (certain European Free Trade Area countries have it as well), if this country did not introduce such a tax. And if Britain joins the Common Market she must have the tax in any case.

Hence the absurdity to put it no higher of Labour "Europeans" such as Roy Jenkins and Harold Wilson in the 1970 election taunting the Tories with inclining towards the introduction of such a tax. The only pity is, indeed, that the Conservatives did not make a more specific pledge. Before he died Iain Macleod was strongly in favour, but certain of his colleagues were thought to have serious doubts about the merits of the tax. They appear to have included Reginald Maudling, who took much advice on the tax when at the Treasury, and is probably temperamentally inclined, as the point of decision about radical changes approaches, to see a hundred difficulties where only one existed before. Happily Anthony Barber has over-ruled the objections.

That is not to say, of course, that the added-value tax is perfect (what tax is?). From its lofty eminence in Downing Street, the Foreign and Commonwealth Office has always argued against export incentives—assuming for the moment that the added-value tax is such an animal—and has for long worked manfully, if without much visible effect, for their demise. The Treasury, the Bank of England, and the Customs and Excise, which will bear the brunt of the tax's introduction, have naturally been conscious of the considerable immediate administrative difficulties which would be caused thereby. The author remembers hearing a then Labour Minister saying at the time of the introduction of Labour's Corporation Tax to replace company Profits Tax: "You can only make such a big tax change once in a generation, and we've probably done the wrong one" (that is missing the opportunity to bring in the added-value tax).

So it has proved. Thus a superficially strong argument in recent years has been that the tax-gatherers have seldom been so busy since Matthew sat at the seat of custom; and that therefore all further tax changes should be postponed sine die. Yet can the welfare of Britain's over-worked and conscientious tax-gatherers, however worthy—who number, relative to population, three times as many as their American opposite numbers—really be weighed against reforming Britain's archaic tax system? It should be remembered, too, that in so far as the State has cleverly ensured that much of the cost of collecting SET and purchase tax should fall on industry and commerce, which are faced with endless form-filling, the true total cost of collecting those existing taxes is much more than it appears to be.

Labour has moved steadily against the added-value tax on the grounds that it is allegedly regressive, that is that it hits the poor harder than the rich. Clearly in so far as the money raised by the added-value tax is used to reduce direct taxation, it will help those in the upper income brackets who are still taxed here more heavily than in almost any other comparable country. For if it is applied to certain goods that now pay neither purchase tax nor SET (indirectly) it must put up the price of those goods.

Yet the price of certain other goods which now pay purchase tax could actually fall, for it has never been suggested that an added-value tax should be levied at anything approaching the average, let alone the upper, purchase tax rates. Such a tax apparently will not be levied on food (other exemptions, according to Iain Macleod in 1969, would include books, newspapers, journals, life assurance and farmers, and small traders would also be excluded in order to simplify administration). So there could be food price reductions to the extent that in many cases SET is now (indirectly) levied on food. It would at least help to offset the food price increases involved in phasing-out deficiency payments for farmers, as the Conservatives propose to do, and the additional food price increases which would be involved in joining the Common Market.

In 1969 the National Economic Development Office calculated that, if food and housing were exempt, a tax designed to raise £250 million *over and above* the yield of purchase tax and SET (money, that is, which could be used to take a further 6d off income tax) would involve a once-and-for-all increase in the cost of living of 1½–2 per cent. This would be less than a tenth of the rise in prices in the five years to 1964–69, and only about a quarter of the price rises caused in that period by increases in indirect taxes.

It is a mistake, however, to get bogged down in too much detailed calculation about the precise costs and revenue-raising powers of this tax or that. The advent of an added-value tax should be seen as part of a wider programme of tax rationalisation and reduction, going hand-in-hand with substantial cuts in Government expenditure. If the latter were achieved, as it could and should be, there ought to be no net adverse effect on the cost of living: rather the reverse.

The added-value tax certainly constitutes the most palpable means to hand—apart from doing such obvious things as phasing-out housing and agricultural subsidies—of making it possible to reduce the penal rates of direct taxation in Britain. And from that, as is pointed out elsewhere in this book, much could flow.

The concomitant of shifting the emphasis of taxation from direct to indirect taxes must be a drastic reduction in the *total* burden of taxation. This involves, in part, reducing the power and influence of the State in our national life (see Chapter Nine). A simplified tax structure and far fewer interfering para-State bodies would produce big savings in the office space and money pre-empted by non-productive civil servants; their numbers did after all increase by some 65,000 between 1964 and 1969. There would be considerable "invisible" savings, too, from a much reduced number of man hours wasted in industry answering often futile questions from Whitehall.

Yet the potential savings from cutting out "waste" in government should not be exaggerated (they are always argued for strongly by opposition parties) although they could be considerable. The logic of Chapter Five, after all, which argues that many bureaucrats work so hard that they cannot see the wood from the trees, is that in *some* categories, such as that of the top administrators, there should actually be more of them. The biggest savings on State expenditure will only come from difficult policy decisions, which will inevitably hurt some people. Some are obvious, such as phasing-out the present support system for agriculture and housing subsidies, costing some £250 million and £1,100 million a year respectively, and correspondingly compensating the poor.

Other possible savings are less obvious. They centre largely around greater "selectivity" in the social services. The welfare state—once Britain's pride and joy and the wonder of the world two decades ago—has become an anachronism in its present form. Thus when the National Health Service was introduced in 1948 a great weight of worry, the fear that at one fell blow through unexpected illness a family's savings could be wiped out, was lifted from many poor homes.

Now people are far better off than they were then and many, if not most, can afford to pay more for their own welfare. Parts of the State welfare services, and in particular of the NHS, moreover, are showing signs of grinding to a standstill from their sheer cost and inner contradictions. The evidence is, indeed, that fewer people want to pay more taxes for State welfare; and more would pay directly themselves for private welfare (there is widespread public dissatisfaction at the amount of "scrounging" off un-means-tested State hand-outs):

OPINION POLL ON WELFARE AND TAXATION

	% in favour of higher taxes for better State services		*% in favour of fees for private services, with lower taxes*	
	1963	*1970*	*1963*	*1970*
Education	51	44	47	55
Medical care	41	29	57	70
Pensions	43	31	56	68

Source: "Choice in Welfare, 1970", published by the Institute of Economic Affairs.

The fundamental problem of the indiscriminate, across-the-board welfare services as we have come to know them since the 1939–45 war, is, quite simply, that they cost too much. They therefore pre-empt too high a proportion of national resources and force taxation up to dangerous levels. Moreover, since so many people benefit from them it is impossible to concentrate their benefits where they are most needed. This was apparent during the years 1964–70 when the then Labour Government would clearly have liked to have done more for certain particularly deserving old age pensioners, for instance, but could not do so because it was irrevocably committed to the 1930's catch phrase of "no means test" and to the principle of undiscriminatory, universal, State benefits.

There is not space in this book to do more than outline the parameters of the problem posed by the sheer size and cost of the latter-day State welfare services; and to indicate the potential savings that could arise from a more rational structure of welfare in this country. It must be admitted, moreover, that there are difficult problems to be solved in the whole concept of "selectivity", of concentrating State benefits where they are most needed. In particular, there is the danger that if those benefits are concentrated too generously on certain of the "deserving poor" they will have little enough incentive to bestir themselves and earn an honest living, and especially so if direct taxation remains high. There are warning signs even now. On the one hand, many car workers and coal miners, for instance, tend to "go absent" and to work only a four-day week because to do more is "not worth the effort". And on the other, strikes tend to go on longer, and be more frequent than they otherwise would be, if there were less generous State welfare payments to the strikers' dependants.

A striker can live on his strike dependants' benefits and income tax rebates for weeks before he feels the pinch—and particularly so if, as they usually do, building societies and hire purchase companies take a lenient view of his "poverty".

In other countries, which order things differently, these British payments are regarded with wonder. It was encouraging that Tory Ministers after taking office in 1970, realised the problem and sought a solution.

Arthur Seldon, an expert on the social services, pointed out in a leader-page article in the *Daily Telegraph* on 31 July 1970 that: "Even with rising incomes, or perhaps *because* rising incomes have taught that choice and competition in everyday and household shopping can give rising standards, improving quality and personal service, people are reluctant to pay more in taxes for Government welfare. State services of all kinds—but especially education and medical care—are short of funds, yet we do little or nothing to tap the vast sums—now around £23,500 million—spent on consumption." He pointed out that, in round numbers, the gross national product in 1970 would be some £40,000 million, of which about a half would be spent by the Government. And of the £10,000 million which would be spent on the social services, about a half would go in benefits in cash (allowances, grants, pensions and so on), and the other half on services in kind (mostly education, medical care and housing).

Thus there are substantial resources to be tapped. Soon after taking office in the summer of 1970, Sir Keith Joseph, Minister for the Social Services, asked for time to think about new sources of revenue for the Health Service (an independent body had recommended large pay increases for doctors which the new Government only partially accepted). He might well do so. The Conservatives' ideas for earnings-related National Insurance contribution to be accompanied by earnings-related benefits, for pensions and the Health Service, will be regarded by the public as merely a form of taxation; and as unattractive taxation at that —even more so than in the case of Richard Crossman's unlamented earnings-related pensions scheme, which at least promised higher benefits for higher contributions.

The Conservatives will be tempted to take the easy way out and keep charging more for the social services; their civil service advisers will surely advise them to eschew radical ideas for raising more money. Sir Keith could take a leaf from Douglas Houghton's book and make charges for Health Service hospital boarding, and fees for visiting Health Service doctors. He would raise a lot of money thereby but he would be involved in cumbersome means tests, which are expensive to administer, and in a lot of exemptions, for such people as old-age pensioners. The same would be true if the Government charged for a proportion of State education, for which in principle there is much to be said.

Something quite new is required; and the eventual answer is a reverse income tax. When in Opposition the Conservatives are thought to have studied, behind closed doors, the possibility of introducing such a tax. But answer came there none, no doubt largely on the grounds of its alleged enormous administrative cost. Yet, as Sir Brandon Rhys-Williams has pointed out, the advent of the Post Office Giro has at last made it practicable for every citizen to keep an overall "account" with the State. All the welfare payments he received, in effect from the Exchequer, which are now handled by several Ministries, would be concentrated in this one account; so, too, would his tax liability. Whether he was in credit or debit with the State at the end of a particular year would depend on his particular circumstances— notably his income and family obligations or otherwise.

A negative income tax could, and should, be so pitched that the "submerged tenth" who have small or no incomes, could afford, through their credits with the State, to pay directly for at least a proportion of their own education and medical care. More important, they would acquire a new dignity as customers on an equal footing with those who can pay out of their own income. The possible disincentive effect on effort of such a reverse income tax would be limited by the fact that those who would most benefit directly therefrom would be such people as the old, the incapacitated, and widows with children. It would in effect replace and improve on existing welfare benefits.

For the other nine-tenths of the population who are less poor it would be necessary, too, to devise new incentives to regard welfare as a family purchase, and to spend more of it directly out of household budgeting. If other countries can provide refunds, as they do, of income tax on health insurance premiums and school fees, then why should not the British go and do likewise? People should be encouraged to spend more directly on their medical care by the State waiving the health insurance contribution for those who insure privately. And they should be allowed to contract out of the basic State pension at whatever age they like.

A difficulty of a negative income tax is that less well-off people largely pay their taxes indirectly on the goods they buy, and these cannot be allowed for in a system of tax refunds. But, as Arthur Seldon has suggested, possible solutions might be a refund equivalent to a proportion of that private expenditure, or a fixed sum per pensioner; or matching finance (it could be, a grant for each £2 of health insurance premium or school fees); or a certificate to pay for a certain amount of premium or fees.

The effect of all this would be to increase prices, charges or fees in the short term—for supply would be unlikely to increase at once as rapidly as demand. The Government would therefore need to move swiftly to encourage commercial investment in medical schools, hospitals, equipment and nursing homes. It should also consider tempting back, perhaps by a guarantee of a good income for say five years, some of the doctors who have emigrated to North America (see Chapter Sixteen) and elsewhere.

It is enormously important to solve as far as possible the disincentive problem involved in greater selectivity in the social services. Professor Prest, in his 1970 pamphlet, "Social Benefits and Tax Rates", has pointed out that because of varying means tests for rents, school meals, student grants, nurseries, rate rebate and so on, social benefits may be reduced by anything from 10 to 100 per cent (or even more) for an additional pound of income. At the same time the advantage of so-called reverse or negative income tax schemes would be their greater rationality—with income tax, social security and social benefits systems related to each other. Yet the dilemma, which may never be solved completely, would remain that if, under such a scheme, marginal tax rates were kept low all along the line, the poor would remain poor through the lack of the wherewithal to help them; and if marginal tax rates remained high the problem of incentives would also remain.

Nevertheless, the first step must be to reconsider from first principles radical solutions entirely different from the present cumbersome, costly, expensive-to-administer, means-tested grants. Such solutions should include, for instance, loans to students and housing reliefs attached to individuals rather than to houses. In a nut-shell, over £6,000 million goes to people who pay more in taxes than they receive in social benefits in the broadest sense. Thus there is scope here for tax cuts which would be massive compared with the small beer which is still wasted on "scroungers".

The Conservatives must also bend their minds to the over-due reform of company law. Labour's 1967 Companies Act was in general good as far as it went—which was not far enough. It compelled companies to give more information than hitherto in their reports and accounts about turnover, directors' emoluments, export sales, trade investments, information about subsidiary or parent companies, particulars of asset valuation, and so on.

The Conservative Government is only committed to appointing a working party "to consider any recommendations for change that are needed in the law relating to accountancy procedures" and to bringing in early legislation to amend the law where necessary. In opposition the Tories felt that the 1967 Act's disclosure requirements concerning private companies were unduly harsh, while not going quite far enough in forcing disclosure by public companies. Fuller disclosure of their trading results would spur management to greater things and enable the market to judge relative performances.

This is certainly along the right lines: in the more competitive economy which Britain badly needs (almost) everyone in industry needs to know more about (almost) everyone else. In the past too many companies have sat for too long on too many under-utilised assets, safe from the unblinking gaze of their shareholders, competitors and employees. Was it only four short years ago that most British firms, including some of the largest in the land, made a point of not disclosing their turnover? They thus made a nonsense of any calculations aspiring investment analysts might attempt to do on their vital—but partially hidden, bikini-like—statistics. What use are profits figures if they cannot be related to turnover and a company's performance be thereby assessed? Most British companies still lag far behind those quoted on Wall Street (even if they are far ahead of many Continental firms) in the statistics they provide. On the other side of the Atlantic companies tend to obligingly work out such relatively esoteric—to the average small investor—but important things as earnings per share. Significantly, in August 1970 the British Trade Union Congress called for a much greater disclosure of company information (but see Appendix 2: both major political parties have argued that employers should be made to tell their work people more).

Changes in company law should also make at least some meaningful genuflections to the concept of "worker participation". With certain honourable exceptions, such as Julian Amery, the Conservatives have taken relatively little interest in this topical matter. When in office, Labour, and in particular Barbara Castle at the Department of Employment and Productivity, made vague noises in the direction of "giving the workers a greater say in running their own affairs"; and a few worker directors were appointed in, for instance, the British Steel Corporation. But nothing much emerged from much deliberation, and the topic was hardly mentioned in the 1970 election.

Yet a *Daily Telegraph* Gallup Poll in the autumn of 1969 showed that, although the people interviewed were somewhat hazy about what they meant by it, there was strong support for more "participation"; and in particular for the idea that workers should be consulted more about their own jobs. And that really is the crux of the matter. Whatever the merits or otherwise of the more cosmic aspects of "co-determination" in Germany—and both sides of industry have mixed feelings about the effectiveness of having workers' representatives at boardroom level—there is no doubt that at the factory level their contact and co-operation is, by British standards, remarkably close.

In a large company, such as Daimler-Benz, Board directors regularly and personally inform their workers through the works council about the progress of the company. Subjects which are in many British firms regarded as vaguely indecent and "not for the workers", such as profit, turnover and export figures, are freely discussed. The works council is truly effective in Germany and complaints and grievances are aired at an early stage, usually

long before they become festering sores, embittering manage-
ment-labour relations and often leading to strikes.

Can it be doubted that a major cause of Britain's poor
industrial relations is the legacy of bitterness from the past?
And that part of that legacy is poor communications between both
sides of industry and the frequent secretiveness of management?
The author remembers working in a factory near Birmingham
and being amazed how little the workers there knew about their
(relatively small) company, or indeed the purpose of their own
jobs. Many actively resented this and said that none of the
"bosses" had even been near them and talked to them about
their working life and their aspirations. The managers just
thought many of them were "bolshy". Thus when a crisis came
both sides were slow to take action. When there was one such
crisis in the export department and the relevant invoices had to
be cleared urgently, the clerks concerned were not asked to work
overtime because it was felt that they would on no account do
so. Yet those clerks said in private that they would have certainly done so had they been asked to and had the reasons for
the urgency been explained!

Many such instances abound and constitute the cobwebs of
British industry. It would be difficult, of course, to change
quickly by legislation the legacy of decades. Thought must be
given, nevertheless, to encouraging the more practical aspects of
worker participation. Any changes in the company law, in the
general pursuit of a more competitive and less secretive industrial ethos, for instance, might stipulate minimum standards of
"information-giving" by managers to their employees: and
revamped and strengthened works councils could be the vehicle
for this.

On the wider front, the success of Germany's experiment in
"co-determination"—ironically, foisted on her in the hour of
defeat by the occupying powers, and in particular by Britain,
after the 1939–45 war—is having an increasing influence on the
Continent. The Dutch, in particular, are tempted to adapt their
company law in the direction of Germany's. The Common
Market Commission in Brussels, moreover, is most anxious to
achieve common standards of company law: now the differences
between countries can, *ceteris paribus*, persuade a large international company to avoid, for instance, Germany, if it dislikes
her advanced approach to industrial relations.

Thus if Britain joins the Common Market the German

example seems bound to have some influence here—and for the better. To enable workers' representatives to sit on the boards of companies would mean major changes in company law: in Germany they sit on the upper or "supervisory", that is policy-making, board, and appoint the Labour Director; but not on the lower, day-to-day, management board. In Britain there is, of course, only one board. But the German legislation applying to work councils, to the lower rungs of the industrial ladder, as it were, should be eminently transplantable to Britain.

So a more competitive Britain would take many forms—lower tariffs, less taxation, fewer State hand-outs, fewer interfering para-State bodies, changes in company law, less secrecy in industry, more worker participation. There seems no reason why the British should not respond, as others have done, to a more bracing climate (see Chapter Sixteen). Is it not worth trying "competition", in this wider sense, when almost everything else has been tried and failed?

CHAPTER NINE

Boards, Corporations, Commissions and Councils: *"let us have done with you"*

Competition must take the form, too, of winding up certain of the State and para-State bodies which multiplied during the Labour years of 1964–70 like princes of the Blood Royal in Hanoverian times. Stern Tory Ministers might well use Cromwell's famous words of dismissal to the Long Parliament:

> Depart I say, and let us have done with you. You have sat there too long for all the good you have been doing. In the name of God go.

For a trenchant—if unconsciously ironic—commentary on the hazards of Labour interventionism Ministers need look no further back than the summer of 1970. Lord Kearton, chairman of Courtaulds, a former part-time chairman of the Industrial Reorganisation Corporation, and thought to be a Labour supporter, said in Courtaulds's annual review that the Monopolies Commission report on the supply of cellulosic fibres was both "illogical and prejudiced"; and that the Prices and Incomes Board report which recommended that acetate prices should be reduced and Courtaulds itself "kept under review" was "an embarrassment to Whitehall".

"In our experience, the members of the teams doing the investigating, and the report writers, are as much subject to prejudices, whims, liverishness and general bile as any ordinary mortals. Some debunking of these bodies, as they have operated, is overdue". It is indeed, and it is as well that it has at last come so clearly from the horse's mouth. Never glad confident morning again for interventionism and planning.

Within a year or so of the 1964 Labour victory many in Fleet

Street, television, Whitehall, industry and even the City, who
felt that things could scarcely be made worse by a change of
Government, were disillusioned. While often not Socialists, they
had been prepared to reserve judgement at least, and to give
the Wilson Government's ideas on how to run the economy a
fair wind. The new Prime Minister's white-hot technological
revolution seemed more promising than his predecessor, Sir Alec
Douglas Home's, fumblings with his match sticks.

Such benign feelings towards Labour—a posthumous tribute
in part to Hugh Gaitskell's old battle against Labour's wild
men—did not, of course, last long. They collapsed with George
Brown's ill-fated, unlamented, National Plan in 1966 and certainly with devaluation in 1967.

There had, nevertheless, been good reasons for dissatisfaction with the dog days of the 1951–64 Conservative Governments. They had achieved a good deal in raising living
standards and expanding the social services. But there was a
growing realisation in the early 1960's that they had not
effectively tackled Britain's basic problems of, for instance, an
absurd tax structure, archaic industrial relations, an uncompetitive economy and continuing exclusion from the dynamic
market of the Six. During Harold Macmillan's later years his
Chancellor, Selwyn Lloyd, in effect recognised that there was
something rotten in the state of Denmark by taking the first
tentative steps towards indicative planning and an incomes
policy. Unfortunately, although his diagnosis may have been
right, his cure certainly was not. And, when adapted and
expanded by Labour in office the "cure", as with a mediaeval
doctor applying leeches to a stricken body, merely exacerbated
the disease and was in danger of killing the patient.

It is as well to recall the full paraphernalia of Labour
"planning" while there is yet time, before the memory fades
like some nightmare with the dawn. It could happen again and
it explains in part why certain members of the Conservative
Government, such as Sir Keith Joseph and Edward Heath himself, are so vehement that there must be root-and-branch changes
in economic policy if this country is ever to get out of its
perennial difficulties.

The PIB saga, in particular, was worth analysing in some
detail in Chapter Seven because it will surely stand for all
time as an awful reminder of how, in consensus Britain, so
many can for so long pursue a mirage. Millions of pounds went

on the salaries of, in the latter years, over 300 expensively-qualified people, and on maintaining expensive offices in Victoria Street. The staff would have been much better employed elsewhere contributing to an increase in the gross national' product. So would the myriads of people who had to answer their time-wasting questions, in both the private and public sector industries. And when the PIB in effect finally died the death of a thousand Tory cuts inflation of prices and incomes was almost unprecedentedly rapid. Moreover, in so far as the Board succeeded in keeping prices down more successfully than wages, it was actively harmful.

The other para-State bodies—which often in effect provide the means whereby Governments can off-load difficult and potentially unpopular decisions—have on the whole more tangible achievements to their credit. Whether those "achievements" will rank as a debit or a credit at the bar of history is, of course, another matter.

One of the least harmful, and arguably even effective, has been the National Economic Development Council, and its children, the "little Neddies" for different industries. It was, it is true, set up by a Conservative Chancellor, Selwyn Lloyd, during the high noon of Macmillanesque planning. The trade unions, who are represented at all levels in the Neddy network, took to them at once, as additional forums for airing their views. They therefore achieved more prominence, if not necessarily more actual power or influence, when a Labour Government which believed whole-heartedly in economic planning came to power.

"Big Neddy", on which sit the unions, the employers, and representatives of the NEDC office in Vickers Tower, is on the whole valued by those who take part in its discussions. Chaired by the Prime Minister or the Chancellor, it provides, with its able secretariat, a useful counter-weight to the Treasury for the generation and consideration of ideas, although it is clearly impossible to estimate precisely what has been its contribution in this respect. It has the merit of costing "only" a million pounds a year—chicken feed in the context of modern State expenditure. To that, however, should be added the cost of the considerable (although often exaggerated) time spent by busy executives on manning its many committees.

The danger to the Neddies is that they will be left high and dry in a world, or at least a Britain, which no longer believes in "planning": they were after all conceived in that context. It was perhaps to forestall such a fate that NEDC's Director-General in June 1970 sent the new Conservative Ministers, within a week or so of their arrival in office, a memorandum suggesting ideas for its future programme. He apparently asked that planning exercises should continue, in the form of regular exchanges of forward plans and forecasts between the public and private sectors of the economy. He is also thought to have mentioned some ideas for future NEDC discussions or inquiries, including: the issues, costs and choices involved in framing environment policies, to what extent economies of scale justify mergers, the terms of Common Market entry, the impact of trade liberalisation on productivity and growth, the impact of industry's cash flow problems on investment spending and the range of possible Government incentive schemes.

Predictably, such proposals met with an unenthusiastic response from Conservative Ministers. In the end "big NEDC's" future will turn largely on whether or not Conservative Ministers want to make anything of it. Although the TUC and the CBI undoubtedly value their regular confrontations with Ministers they do need to feel that they are achieving something constructive in return for the considerable time involved. And in the present "anti-planning" mood of the Tories that may not be possible.

The "Little Neddies" also face an uncertain future and already some have been wound up. It is almost inconceivable that they would survive if the National Economic Development Office, which services them, died. It has all along been willing, indeed anxious, to stand down those which appeared to have out-lived their usefulness (if any). Their performance and *raison d'être* has automatically come up for review every two years. But even among the weaker brethren—the "little Neddies" have included machine tools, chemicals, electronics, mechanical engineering, wool textiles, building, civil engineering, agriculture and, remarkably, the Post Office—one party or the other has usually found a compelling reason why they should not be disbanded. Like most institutions they have acquired a momentum of their own which only deliberate action will reverse.

In Opposition Sir Keith Joseph said that his party would stand down those "little Neddies" which "had served their purpose". Their most solid contribution—now largely achieved—has probably been to improve the supply of managerial information in their respective industries. Many British businessmen are remarkably secretive, often for historical reasons lost in the mists of time. The "Neddies" have persuaded some of them, no doubt, to "think big", to look at the problems of their industries in the round, to compare their own performances with those of their ostensible competitors, both at home and abroad.

This is important. The "blind-man's-buff" state of ignorance of the outside world in which firms in some industries worked until quite recently had to be seen to be believed. The author remembers doing a market research exercise some years ago in an attempt to establish a rough idea of the size of the nut and bolt market, and hence of his then employer's share of it. It was not easy. The trade associations in the fastener trade at that time were—although ostensibly they existed, as in other industries, in part to collect, collate, and exchange information between their members and with the outside world—in profound ignorance of the size of the trades which they represented. A major difficulty was that members deliberately withheld, or even occasionally falsified, information in order not to "give anything away" to competitors: this though returns to the associations were made on a strictly confidential basis! In such an odd situation a "Neddy" could hardly have avoided doing more good than harm.

Was it right to dismiss the Industrial Reorganisation Corporation, one of Labour's most controversial children? Its deficiencies were at first sight more obvious than its virtues. In the months before the June 1970 election, at a time when grants and loans were coming thick and fast from the IRC, the Conservatives were highly critical of the Corporation on the grounds that it usurped the normal functions of the market; and that anything useful which it did could be done as well, or better, by some other agency, such as the Industrial and Commercial Finance Corporation or the Finance Corporation for Industry.

The issues were: the extent to which the IRC had exceeded its brief in recent years, and whether that brief was desirable in the first place. The theory behind the IRC was that it could take over where merchant banks leave off; and that, in particular, a merger which was, at least in the short term, financially unattractive, might nevertheless be "in the national interest". The Corporation could offer the necessary financial "carrot" to persuade recalcitrant companies to move in the direction it wanted. But, as Lord Kearton pointed out, all men are fallible—even the servants of the State. The staff of the IRC had, therefore, to be guided by their own hunches, and by politicians only too eager to prop up moribund industries, as to what mergers were "desirable".

Thus the loans to Cammel Laird and to Rolls-Royce were intended to carry the two companies over a bad patch. The money came from the Government in the first place, and the motives, such as preserving threatened jobs in shipbuilding, if mixed, were on the whole transparent. The British Leyland loan was different. It seemed that the IRC, at least temporarily, had grown tired of "rationalising" industries, particularly the machine tool industry, through mergers and takeovers which were so slow to show results. British Leyland is one of the biggest buyers of machine tools in Britain, spending about £15 million a year on them, but importing about a third of its requirements. On balance exports in recent years have exceeded imports by only a small margin; whereas Germany exports two-thirds of its machine tool production Britain exports little more than a third.

The decline in orders for the home market in 1970 was therefore serious. The IRC was in danger of being forced to put good money after bad. It had helped Plessey to put together a group incorporating Airmec and the machine tool division of Ferranti: cost £3 million. It also gave a total of £4 million to Marwin and Herbert-Ingersoll. Yet Alfred Herbert had two disastrous years. The IRC then provided a revolving credit for British Leyland to buy machine tools at a time when it might otherwise have been reluctant to do so—in other words to buy at home some of that £5 million worth of machine tools a year which it would otherwise have imported. The money, at $8\frac{3}{4}$ per cent, was relatively cheap and only $\frac{1}{2}$ per cent above the IRC's own borrowing rate from the Government. But the IRC would advance money only if it approved of the companies with which British Leyland was placing the orders, that is if it thought that they deserved help.

This is the nub of the matter, and in an important sense the nub of the whole dilemma about British industrial policy. Such a gambit by the IRC was, of course, a distortion of free trade and an interference with competition. Yet it happens in other countries—not least in that bastion of capitalism, America, where companies getting Government contracts are frequently told what machine tools to use on the job. So can Britain afford not to do the same?

The problem of finding new markets for advanced new products (and some machine tools are ultra-advanced) for long exercised the Ministry of Technology and, before that, the National Research Development Corporation. The failure of British industry to buy new technology after it has been developed here is a major reason, combined with a low level of investment here over many years, why this country has lagged so far behind America in economic growth. With no space industry, little defence production and a truncated aircraft industry, the scope for boosting new technology is severely limited.

Conceivably the IRC could have provided a new avenue for Britain to do this: certainly it is vital for her whole economic future that new technology should flower. In effect, as well as encouraging certain British companies to become larger and hence, it was hoped, more competitive in world markets, the IRC was experimenting in lending money to companies to buy advanced equipment in which they would not otherwise take risks. This could, therefore, conceivably have played a part in helping British industry to break out of the whole "stop-go", high taxation, low investment, reluctance to take risks, syndrome—from which this country has suffered for so long.

Many root-and-branch Tories, both in Parliament and industry, saw the IRC as merely a device for bribing otherwise unwilling firms to merge. They therefore wished to kill it off. There is now the problem of winding up its existing commitments to, for instance, British Leyland, Rolls-Royce and Cammel Laird (over two-thirds of its original capital of £150 million is so committed). The IRC had obvious dangers, such as the increase in the power of the State which it represented (see Chapter Ten) and the risk that it would have become increasingly a vehicle for propping up declining industries and inefficient companies.

The logic of the IRC's last industrial moves could clearly be that, having encouraged the formation of particular groups in industry, it then had to lend out money continuously to other companies in order to channel orders to those groups. For the Corporation said specifically that it was prepared to extend the facilities granted to British Leyland to other big machine tool users. So why should not such large companies as

Babcock and Wilcox and General Electric line up for help, too? The IRC became involved in some of the largest regroupings this country has ever known. In one case, that of the General Electric Company—Associated Electrical Industries merger of 1967, it ostensibly wrought a near-miracle by achieving the result it intended without committing any money (although the participants knew, of course, that it had virtually unlimited State money at its beck and call if it were needed). Thus the IRC threw its considerable weight behind an opposed takeover but made no investment. In contrast, when British Motor Holdings and Leyland agreed on a merger, the IRC came up trumps with a loan of £25 million ostensibly for rapid rationalisation and development. In the resulting enormous company (since then there has been a fair amount of both, but the sagging British Leyland share price, reflecting in part persistent labour troubles, suggests that the results may take longer than originally anticipated to appear, despite the legendary daemonic energy of Lord Stokes.

Meanwhile, back in London's West End, the IRC had been surveying "in depth" the instrument industry. It thus felt qualified to take part in the sequence of events which led to Cambridge Instruments being purchased by George Kent, after the rejection of the bid by the Rank Organisation. There were, indeed, both bids and counter-bids and the IRC ended up with a £6.5 million stake in the resulting merger. In 1968 the IRC also played a further part in the GEC saga and supported its merger with English Electric. Flexible as ever, the Corporation even renegotiated its previous loan of £15 million to English Electric, made at the time of the latter's acquisition of Elliot-Automation.

On the other hand, it is undeniable that when the 1964–1970 Labour Government came to power there was much that was wrong about large areas of British industry. They were not delivering the goods in export markets as successfully as their international competitors. Often they were still not doing so when the Conservative Government wound up the IRC, despite the fillip provided by devaluation and much "restructuring". But by then there had been undeniably major improvements such as, for instance, the injection of Arnold Weinstock's expertise from the General Electric company into the vast, rambling, unprofitable Associated Electrical Industries empire—run not so long ago with what qualifications was never overwhelmingly clear, by Winston Churchill's friend, Lord Chandos.

Probably much of this improvement in the management of British industry would have happened in any case in a genuinely competitive economy. But Britain in 1964, as in 1970, was far from having such an economy. Hence changes which were widely regarded, and not only on the Left, as long overdue just had not happened. The State is already involved up to the hilt in British industry. It will take years to "unscramble" this commitment even if the political will to do so is there. So, regrettably, for the foreseeable future the job of the Ministry of Trade and Industry is to make that partnership work better—while reducing its scope where possible.

The IRC could have become a hybrid creature, mixing private and State capital to taste; it could have played a part in gearing up the State industries with mixed capital structures (see Chapter Eleven). The City might have underwritten such issues. The Corporation could have been re-fashioned as a vehicle for a more selective approach to industrial aid-giving whereby more selective industrial "carrots" in theory went where they were most needed.

The Corporation could certainly have been used as a channel for the more selective investment of State funds, so that major capital goods industries, such as machine tools, cars, and commercial vehicles, which have a central role in the economy, would have had access to working capital as a cushion against periodic credit squeezes, which can discourage capital investment plans. But great care would have been needed: the process of State aid can be insidious. It is by definition arbitrary and the problem of "where does one draw the line, whom does one favour, who is most deserving?" is in a fundamental sense insoluble.

Sir Joseph Lockwood, chairman of the IRC, argued that: "There are about 100 companies absolutely vital to this country. So why should they go short of money? The Government has been pushing about £800 million a year into industry and we have got to make sure it goes into the right channels." Yes—but should £800 million have gone into industry in the first place? And what were the right channels?

The IRC had also accumulated a useful dossier on the strengths and weaknesses of major British companies, and of the personalities who run them. It had become particularly interested in the balance between exports and imports in certain major sectors of the economy; and in what, if anything, it could do to tip the balance in a direction favourable to the balance of payments. Thus if imports of, it might be, jam seeds had for years risen more rapidly than their exports the implication was that British jam seed manufacturers were becoming steadily less competitive than their international competitors; and perchance something could be done about it.

The Corporation was also interested in "Europe", analysing Continental industry and exploring the possibilities of link-up arrangements between British and other European companies. Charles Villiers, Managing Director of the IRC, even suggested—not surprisingly perhaps—that there should eventually be a European IRC organisation as the ultimate counter to, and bastion against, American industrial domination.

But was the IRC ever the right vehicle to execute the many ideas it generated? Should not desirable and overdue change be left to "market forces"? Was it not dangerous that it had the power to intervene openly, to deal as a principal, in the Stock Exchange? Did it not by its very existence represent an undesirable increase in the power and influence of the State? If difficult decisions have to be made about State intervention in industry is it not right that they should be taken by Ministers themselves? Rather than being shuffled off on to some para-State body? On balance it was surely right to wind up the IRC.

In Conservative industrial policy the Government's approach to monopolies, or "anti-trust" as the Americans call it, is key. In this respect Government intervention probably will, and probably should, be actually strengthened. In Opposition the Conservatives rightly gave a good deal of thought to this, and they came up with some firm and attractive proposals. But the problem is in an important and final sense insoluble. For in many industries and activities modern technology has out-grown the nation State. There is not room for more than one, for instance, Rolls-Royce, GKN, ICI or Unilever in an economy of only 55 million or so people. But there would be in a Common Market of 250 million or more people. In many major sectors of the economy, such as cars, motor components, aero engines, advanced engineering, where economies of large-scale production apply, monopoly and restrictive practices policy only really has much meaning on a Continent-wide basis. And even then, such is the increase in the cost of modern technology that there may well be no more than one or two, for instance, large European aircraft manufacturers by 1980.

Even were it not for these wider, European, considerations, the Tories should lay down flexible criteria for their monopoly policy. Arbitrary edicts that a company's share of the market should not exceed a quarter, or a third, or a half of the total, often do more harm than good. In the vast American market (some ten times that of Britain in terms of income), where anti-trust regulations really do have some meaning, companies are in general debarred from attaining more than a third of the market for a particular product. But such a criterion is not meaningful even in America in certain industries of advanced technology. How many mighty Boeing-type companies, sustained by Government defence contracts and orders from a relatively few airlines, can even America sustain? And for how long?

The Conservatives are right to streamline and strengthen the Monopolies Commission with a full-time Board, and to establish a Registrar of Monopolies, parallel with the Registrar of Restrictive Trade Practices. This would take over from the Commission the task of looking for appropriate situations for the Commission to investigate.

Ever since Edward Heath was at the Board of Trade in 1963–64, in the dog days of the Conservatives' "thirteen years", the Tories have been keen to create a Registrar of Monopolies who, like the Registrar of Restrictive Trading Agreements, would have wide powers of independent action within a brief laid down by statute. But, in the monopoly and merger field, he would be subject to Ministerial veto. At the same time, the offices of the two Registrars would probably be merged.

Another long-standing Conservative proposal is that the investigatory and judicial functions of the Monopolies Commission should be separated. The assumption behind this is that the issues involved should, as far as possible, be decided by the rule of law rather than by the rule of men; and that the outcome, again as far as possible, should be predictable and certain rather than uncertain and arbitrary.

The objective would be to create a sensible division of function by removing from Ministerial discretion the day-to-day pursuit of obstacles to competitive pressures; and to provide a means whereby the preliminary appraisal of situations of market power and of proposed mergers can be conducted swiftly and expertly. Hence this approach would need to be relatively simple and capable of being clearly understood. In practice it would tend to concentrate on so-called restrictive practices, such as companies setting the same price for the same product (a persistent habit in Britain—see Edward Heath's Herculean labours to abolish resale price maintenance in 1964), market-sharing, discriminatory buying, and discount or "loss-leader" selling policies used by large companies to retain their dominant market position. The Conservative approach would mean, moreover, that any challenge to, and dispute about, proposed mergers would come at the time they are proposed rather than possibly at some subsequent stage, as was suggested for Labour's abortive Commission for Industry and Manpower Bill.

Conservative monopoly policy is not necessarily different in essence from that of Labour. The principle remains that a full-scale investigation should be called only in the small minority of cases where damage to "the public interest" may be involved. But the changes made by the Conservatives will clearly make it possible to adopt a more aggressive approach to the control of monopoly power. And in the context of mergers and takeovers—which admittedly is not the major part of the Commission's work—it will mean that a closer check can be kept on the intentions of the companies concerned; and possibly, too, as an "after sales service", on whether or not they have kept their promises to the Commission.

This is all very well as far as it goes, and should certainly be an improvement on the somewhat ad hoc and unpredictable monopolies "policy" Britain has suffered in recent years. For the endless attempts by the State to control monopolies and mergers has undoubtedly become a major irritant to industry, even though relatively few companies are directly involved. In particular, Barbara Castle tried to broaden the scope of the Commission's work by asking it to examine the implications "for the national interest" not only of alleged monopoly situations, but of size itself. In other words the briefing for the proposed ponderous CIM, to be chaired by (who else?) Aubrey Jones, implied that, *ceteris paribus,* size was a crime unless proved otherwise.

The thesis was well illustrated in the "conglomerate" investigation in 1969 of the Allied Breweries-Unilever merger plan; in Rank's bid for De La Rue; and in the abortive attempt in early 1970 to follow these up with a look at the Burmah bid for Laporte Industries. In all these cases the basis for reference was merely the size of the companies concerned rather than their technical monopoly situation or otherwise in the markets for their products. This despite the fact that through the IRC, for instance, Labour had actively encouraged "size through mergers".

The Monopolies Commission reported that the problem of size as such had not yet developed so far as to cause real concern. It also rightly pointed out that international competition, rather than the domestic market only, is often the proper criterion for judging the impact of size. And it suggested the disclosure of more and better information by companies involved in mergers.

This is the crux of the matter. If British companies could be persuaded by outside pressure—which can only come from the Government creating the right conditions—really to compete, to be much less secretive, to tell their shareholders and employees what they are doing and what they are attempting to achieve, then "policing" Commissions, Boards, Corporations and Councils would be largely unnecessary. Many firms do the right things already, and more than hold their own in export markets with the best companies in the world; but many do not do so.

Sir Keith Joseph put the matter well in the spring of 1970, when Conservative spokesman on industrial affairs. He said "It is above all a combination of measures—increased disclosure so that shareholders and analysts are aware of management performance, coupled if we can with lower taxation on investment income so that shareholders have an interest in better management, coupled ideally with the removal of bias against distribution so that shareholders have an even more intensified interest in performance ... coupled with sharper Government buying on a narrow firm front, coupled with the gradual rolling back of the public sector, coupled at the extreme with tariff cuts. The interaction of all these is likely, it seems to me, to put more lively top management in a larger sector of the economy."

Certainly better management is essential if the Conservatives are ever to "get Britain moving."

CHAPTER TEN

The Power of the State has Increased . . .

Can it be doubted, in any consideration of what we should do to find economic salvation, that "the power of the state has increased, is increasing, and ought to be diminished"? The conventional wisdom is that this trend is inevitable, that it is happening in almost all countries, and that in Britain Left-wing Governments push forward the frontiers of the State, and right-wing Administrations are then brought in to consolidate the good work and provide a much-needed period of "stability". As Burke said, "we adjust, we reconcile, we balance".

Such is the genius of the British people. Or is it? Clearly the frontiers of the State have indeed been pushed steadily forward for decades, if not from the beginning, and the trend accelerated between 1964 and 1970. But that did not necessarily make it a Good Thing. Nor does it mean that it cannot be reversed. It would require a great effort by the Conservatives, and by those who believe in human liberty, to reverse the steadily expanding influence of the public sector of the economy—but it could be done.

The reasons why it should be done are simple. They are libertarian and economic. And the first, although less often mentioned, is the more important. The failures of certain nationalised industries are obvious, their ill effects relatively quantifiable (of which more anon). Much less easy to assess, and therefore more insidious, are the creeping tentacles of the State, which now stretch out into almost every aspect of national life. Not fortuitously but deliberately—for Socialists revelled in it— the pace of the creeping gathered momentum under the last Labour Government.

Taxation in monetary terms doubled in six short years; and

increased from 33.1 per cent to 44.1 per cent of the gross national product. Another large basic industry—steel—was nationalised. The number of civil servants increased by 62,000. State and para-State bodies, such as the Prices and Incomes Board, the Industrial Re-organisation Corporation, the Ministry of Technology, the Ministry of Overseas Development and the ill-fated Department of Economic Affairs, multiplied like amoeba (see Chapter Eight).

More sinister, because the immediate results were more immediately pleasing to the average citizen, there was a large increase in State hand-outs of (almost) all kinds. Harold Wilson was proud of this and seldom let slip an opportunity to boast of the expansion of welfare expenditure under his Government—by over two-thirds between 1964 and 1970. The assumption was, of course, that such social "progress" is by definition desirable. Traditionally indeed, it has been almost as difficult to be intellectually against the welfare state as it has been to be against the Deity, or the Commonwealth or an incomes policy. In the British Pantheon all have had a respected, if not equal, place.

Yet honoured heroes can prove to be false gods. The British have had a particular fondness for the welfare state because in a real sense they pioneered it. There were, it is true, communes of "togetherness" from the early Christians to Paris in 1871; and Bismarck's social insurance, whatever his contrary motives, gave a boost to socialist ideas of welfare throughout Europe. But it was really the philosophy of the People's Budget, and in particular the introduction of old age pensions at five shillings a week, by the Asquith Government which laid the foundations of the welfare state as we know it today. And this concept of State paternalism, and especially the 1948 National Health Service, which—though singularly dog-eared now—was in its time much admired abroad (see Chapters One and Eight). Indeed, that phrase beloved of politicians, "the admiration of the world" was seldom far from Labour lips.

However, times change, and British welfare services have in many respects fallen well behind those prevailing on the Continent, even though the public sector has accounted for a steadily increasing share of the economy. This reflects, of course, largely the much more rapid economic growth rate in other European countries. There is also the fact that a much higher proportion of the cost of the social services there falls directly on the employer (amounting in effect to a non-discriminatory payroll tax which encourages the introduction of capital-intensive, labour-saving equipment) rather than on the taxpayer. Thus the cost of employing labour in most Common Market countries is a good deal higher than in Britain, although average wages are about the same—if rising in real terms much more rapidly. In contrast, in Britain welfare payments are in effect paid out of steep, discriminatory taxes on incomes.

The libertarian arguments, moreover, apply equally strongly against the extension of the power and influence of the State into economic "planning" of even ostensibly privately owned industries. We become pensioners of the State if we are ever more dependent on its hand-outs for our daily bread. An increasing number of us have also become its dependants and employees as a result of the steady expansion of the public sector of the economy. And Labour has promised to take the process even further in the future. Logically—assuming an alternation of Left- and Right-wing Governments, and that the latter never seek actively to reverse the trend—there is no reason why the entire economy should not one day be owned by the State. The examples of Russia and Czechoslovakia, for instance, do not suggest that this is desirable to say the least, either on libertarian or economic grounds.

When the State controls everything, including ostensibly men's minds, it is impossible for it to relax its grip, to make even the smallest concessions towards a freer society, without threatening the whole basis of the regime. This is the long-term dilemma facing the leaders of such countries as Russia and South Africa. By their own lights they are quite right to keep their people on as short a rein as possible. Human freedom is indivisible. A taste of freedom, however limited, feeds on itself. No doubt Stalin would never have had the difficulties his successors are having with the Russian intellectuals. Under his harsher regime they would have remained completely docile, or found themselves in a Siberian slave labour camp, or under two feet of quick-lime.

The Communists have discovered, too—the hard way—that there are insuperable difficulties in running an efficient, wholly socialised, economy. Tito of Yugoslavia realised this two decades ago and has been trying ever since, with indifferent success, to restore the profit motive and some measure of incentive without reverting to unfettered capitalism. The Russians and Czechs realised it more recently but it will do them little good. For an incentive-orientated, profit-motivated, "market forces" form of Communism is a contradiction in terms.

The inherent difficulty, the basic contradiction of complete Socialism (Marx's common ownership of the means of production, distribution and exchange) and to a lesser extent of the mixed economy prevailing in Britain, is that there exists no mechanism whereby economic resources can be efficiently allocated. The planners are there, of course, in Moscow and in Peking seeking that elusive and undefinable concept, the "national interest", but they have no defined criteria on which to work. Everything they decide must be arbitrarily based on their own value judgements, on subjective assessments of situations which can be as easily reversed by their successors. When things go wrong, as in the case of Kruschev's "virgin lands" scheme for making the desert bloom or the post-war African groundnuts scheme, they go very wrong indeed. And, needless to say, although happily now only metaphorically in Russia today, heads roll as a result.

Under complete Socialism there is no way of deciding how to allocate resources between competing claims on their use. A batch of ingot steel, for instance, may be urgently needed by the motor, construction and engineering industries all at the same time. How then does the planner choose between them except on some abstract, and inevitably highly subjective, criteria of the national good? Soviet planners do not know the true cost of making things because that cost depends on the use of components and labour whose prices are themselves artificially determined. And when the Russian manufacturer comes to sell his product he receives—despite recent modifications of the pure milk of Marxism—a price for it which in effect, directly or indirectly, is determined by the ubiquitous and all-seeing State. Errors can be serious. There was, for instance, the Russian steel works which sent its steel ingots in the early 1960's all the way to South Wales for re-rolling. Clearly some planner had miscalculated the re-rolling capacity required in Russia, or he had no idea of his costs—or both.

In contrast, in a free market economy prices, and therefore ultimately costs, are determined by a complex mechanism which can be compared to ripples on a pool. Every action of the producer and consumer has an infinite number of repercussions (however small and almost imperceptible to the naked eye), which through the price mechanism determine how a country's resources should be best distributed.

Lord Coleraine put the matter well in his book *For Conservatives Only* when he said:

> The true antithesis is not between individual freedom and the needs of society, but between an order which is spontaneous and self-regulating and one which is imposed.
>
> The sheer impossibility of detailed economic planning is now generally recognised, at any rate by Conservatives, but there remains what is called "indicative" planning. If government cannot organise supply and demand, and if it cannot supervise the minutiae of production and distribution, then it must have the duty of identifying economic trends and of persuading industry to conform to them.
>
> But there is no reason whatever to suppose that government is able to identify economic trends as accurately or as speedily as industry itself. A spontaneous order in the economic field does not depend on the supposed infallibility of a few individuals at the centre, supported and nourished by a mass of information coming in from the periphery with varying degrees of unpunctuality and inaccuracy. It is created and sustained by the self-regulating activities of an almost infinite number of individuals, each of whom is in communication with only a very small number of others. Each of these is linked to others again.
>
> Thus, the needs and ideas of a single person can be communicated through an endless chain to those utterly remote from him; and everyone in the chain is free to respond to information reaching him, in any way he pleases—or not to respond at all. It is this process, infinitely complex in its operation but infallible in its effects, which causes packets of tea, for instance, to appear in the grocer's shop in convenient sizes, with blends and flavours suited to the varying tastes of the housewife, and matched to the length of her purse, an operation carried out so smoothly that its complexity is not even suspected.
>
> This kind of intercommunication covers the whole field of economic activity. The same process which creates economic trends, by changing the pattern of supply and demand in oil, or copper, or machine-tools, or tankers, identifies these trends as they appear, more accurately and more swiftly than any centralised planning agency could conceivably do.
>
> . . . Why, one asks, is it to be supposed that any group of people, no matter how intelligent or high-minded, is fitted to form the general character of a community of which it is so small a part?

This is the classic view of the open society, of the free market economy. Competition is more likely than the alternatives to it to encourage economic efficiency, and hence economic growth and a rapid improvement in the standard of living. The infinite number of independent judgements on which its working depends means that it is less likely to produce the frequent monumental errors of central control—such as Britain's postwar fuel policy which assumed for far too long that a shortage of coal would for the foreseeable future continue to be a law as immutable as the laws of the Medes and Persians; and that the demand for electricity would grow much more rapidly than it did in the event. Competition is also more sensitive to changing markets and improving techniques. And better able to give people full scope, and adequate reward, for their abilities.

In this context the diversity which is the essence of competition is the other side of the coin to human freedom. In every aspect, it gives the citizen a wide choice: as a consumer buying goods and services, as an investor placing his savings, as an employee earning his living. It provides a plethora of sources of liberty and of economic power, encourages the individual ownership of capital and hence personal independence (who can afford to resign on a salary of £2,000 a year, with hire purchase debts of £500 and mortgage repayments of £10 a week?); and as such is a bastion against increasingly authoritarian politics.

The point about choice of jobs, although seldom made, is particularly important. Nationalisation of the fourteen large steel companies in 1967, the most recent and one of the most massive examples of a State takeover for instance, has enormously reduced job mobility in that industry. The author knew a number of young men in the GKN Steel Company before its nationalisation who, if they fell out with their firm—it might be for the best of reasons—had at least thirteen other potential employers to talk to. They now have none unless they go on a conversion course and move to another industry, which becomes progressively more difficult as they grow older. Or unless (a slim chance) they transfer to one of the smaller steel companies so far left unscathed by the State, such as the re-rollers, which may well require different skills. Theoretically no doubt they could move from one part of the vast, sprawling, British Steel Corporation to another; but it is stretching credulity too far to believe that, if a man puts up a serious "black", there are no central records to be used in evidence against him if and when he seeks a new job.

It may well be that the State taking a part share in ostensibly private companies rather than outright nationalisation is the more insidious and therefore the more dangerous in the long run. It is less obvious and its results are less easy to assess. Hence the success, from his and his party's point of view, of Harold Wilson's form of socialisation compared with the old-style "Clause Four" version of Aneurin Bevan. How could Hugh Gaitskell ever have opposed Wilsonism in the courageous way he attacked Bevanism? How can one grapple with a jelly-fish?

Not only are the full consequences not yet generally realised; the actual extent of the increase of State influence on industry between 1964 and 1970 is not generally realised even now. This took many forms, which are worth recapitulating briefly. There was the burden of additional costs: the increase in company taxation via the new 1965 Corporation Tax and other new imposts; the 1966 Selective Employment Tax; five increases in petrol tax and two in fuel oil duty; two substantial increases in vehicle licences; four increases in employers' National Insurance and Health contributions; and the new 1965 Redundancy Fund contributions. Whatever the merits or otherwise (mainly otherwise) of these new burdens on industry, and some were arguably an incentive to reducing labour costs, they represented a big advance in State influence. Their total cost was after all over £2,000 million a year, at least nine-tenths of which fell on the private sector of the economy. In addition there was the cost of persistently and inordinately high interest rates, the "forced loan" element in SET and the import deposit scheme, the effects on cost of the involuntary 1967 devaluation, and substantially higher charges by the nationalised industries and the Post Office.

The counterpart of all this was large increases in State subsidies, to nearly £1,000 million a year, of the type which Labour Governments tend to approve as if by reflex action. About half this was accounted for by the investment cash grants which replaced the investment allowances (the major difference being, of course, that companies only qualified for the allowances, unlike the grants, if they actually earned a profit) and which the Conservative Government has since disavowed. There was also introduced in 1967 the Regional Employment Premium designed to encourage employment in the Development Areas and as such was ostensibly self-financing. Thus money, needed for capital investment, the seed corn of future growth, was taken

9—WES * *

from industry by the State's right hand and given back, on its own terms, with the left. So does the State make beggars of us all!

In addition, there were the absurdities of the futile attempts to control wages, prices and dividends—which almost certainly wasted even more man hours, and created more frustration, in industry than they did in Whitehall.

The administrative burden of all this on industry and on the professions, such as accountancy, though difficult to assess, has been enormous. The cost will never appear in any Government White or Green Paper, it will never fall as a direct charge on the taxpayer, it will never have to be sanctioned by the ever-watchful Treasury. But it exists and the effort involved would be much better diverted to such wealth-creating pursuits as expanding exports.

There have been investment grant forms to fill in. There was a constant flow of official papers of various colours to digest: about tax changes and their amendments and about prices and incomes policy. SET payments have to be kept track of so that the appropriate refunds may be claimed. And there have been endless forms and questionnaires from Ministries (on the lines of: "are the prospects for your exports better, the same, or worse than they were six months ago?") and their multiplying para-State offshoots, such as the Prices and Incomes Board.

Government interference has borne particularly harshly on small businesses, and notably those which are family-owned. The close company and disclosure provisions of the Corporation Tax put smaller companies at substantial disadvantages compared with their larger rivals. And these companies tend to predominate in certain industries such as building, hotels, shops, and road haulage, which have been especially badly hit by discriminatory taxation like the SET and by endless, almost unprecedentedly severe, credit squeezes. Small family businesses are often regarded as a thing of the past in an era of vast corporations. Yet they often, even in an economy as vast and advanced as America's, provide much of the dynamic for new ideas, for new products, for risk-taking.

Meanwhile, the large companies have tended to get bigger— and not only by mergers. With their large credit lines to the banks they can usually ride out credit squeezes, which in part reflect the remarkably high level of Government expenditure, relatively well (notwithstanding the Rolls-Royce débâcle). This applies also, but even more so, to the nationalised industries. Until 1967, and only then as a result of Conservative pressure they were not even scrutinised under the prices and incomes so-called policy.

Again, apart from the outright re-nationalisation of steel, there were the more subtle extensions of State ownership under Labour. Existing nationalised industries were given, and indeed were encouraged, to expand into new fields or even to buy into existing private companies. Examples included chemicals, brick-making and buses. In this context the "tidying up" takeover by the Transport Holding Company of British Electric Traction's privately-owned buses in 1968 was indefensible. BET was the largest bus company not owned by the State. The then THC also took over more than twenty private haulage companies between 1964 and British Road Services was incorporated into the new National Freight Corporation, successor to the THC, in 1969. By restrictions on the work which private road haulage firms are allowed to do, the NFC could, in certain circumstances, undercut them. Its very existence represents, compared with 1964, a substantial shift in the pattern of ownership of road haulage towards the State.

There were also after 1964 wide-ranging enabling Acts, giving either the Government or its para-State offshoots far-reaching powers to create new companies or to take shares in existing ones: the Science and Technology Act of 1965, the Industrial Re-organisation Corporation Act of 1967, the Industrial Expansion Act of 1965 and the Shipbuilding Industry Acts of 1967 and 1969.

Of these much the most significant, at least in the short term, was the setting up of the Industrial Reorganisation Corporation, whose operations are discussed in Chapter Nine. An independent statutory body, the IRC was given wide powers, including the provision of loans, to further the reorganisation or development of any industry or part of it. In the heyday of the cult of "rationalisation" George Brown expansively outlined the job of the new IRC: "To search for opportunities to promote rationalisation schemes which can yield substantial benefits to the national economy, especially in terms of increased exports and more rapid technological advance."

In other words, in that glad confident morning of planning, "restructuring" and rationalisation (January 1966) it seemed that the sky was the limit for the IRC. A little can be made to go a long way when the State controls the levers of power, and a lot goes even further. The IRC was given £150 million of Exchequer funds and truly has it laboured in four years to give the taxpayer "more bang for his buck". The game was one that any number could play indefinitely: ingenious and flexible indeed were the permutations deployed by the IRC.

Of the other "hamper" socialising legislation of the Labour Government, the 1965 Science and Technology Act was mainly concerned with re-casting the administrative framework in this field. But in 1964 Labour had promised to "go beyond research and development (in Government establishments) and establish new industries either by public enterprise or in partnership with private industry". Thus in the 1965 Act the Ministry of Technology was given wide general powers to spend money in "furthering the practical application of the results of research"; and the Atomic Energy Authority was enabled to undertake research and development outside the atomic energy field.

The archetypal Socialist measure, however, which could mean all things to all men, and particularly to those in economic difficulties, was the 1968 Industrial Expansion Act: "You name it, we will do it." Doing it, for Ministers, included the power to provide assistance for industrial investment schemes, to create, expand or sustain production capacity (whatever that means), and to support "technological advance". Finance up to a limit of £100 million—which could be increased to £150 million with the approval of the Commons—was provided for expenditure on industrial investment schemes. It could also be used for schemes of general industrial reorganisation, not restricted to individual projects. And a board for the industry concerned could even be set up!

Highlights of developments under the Act included supporting, to the tune of £13.5 million, the merger of the computer and scientific computers business of International Computers and Tabulators and English Electric Computers, with the participation of Plessey and the Ministry of Technology. Any number can also play at the computers game, at dispensing, and absorbing State money and there seems to be no good reason why, in the fullness of days, Uncle Tom Cobbley and all should not join in. Who goes home?

There were, too, the 1968 aluminium smelter schemes which were even more ambitious: loans of up to a total of £63 million to the British Aluminium Company and to Anglesey

Aluminium Metal for the aluminium projects at Invergordon and Anglesey. The loans were to be deployed towards the capital cost of the new electricity generating capacity involved. In comparison, loans of up to £24 million to Cunard towards the construction of the *Queen Elizabeth II* seem unimpressive. But the same cannot be said, alas, about the raising of the limit of advances to the National Research Development, which seeks to secure the development and exploitation of inventions in the public interest, to £50 million. Nor of the development, with France, of the enormously expensive Concorde supersonic airliner which was, however, originally a Conservative concept.

Under the 1967 and 1969 Acts the Government could guarantee loans at favourable interest rates up to a limit of £400 million to British residents building ships in "approved yards" in this country. British ship-owners were undoubtedly encouraged to buy British thereby. But was this necessarily in the long-term interests of Britain?

Moreover, large borrowing powers for the new nationalised industries were created. Under the 1968 Transport Act, the new National Freight Corporation was given immediate borrowing powers of £200 million, which could be extended by Ministerial order to £300 million. It was also provided with grants of £60 million to cover any losses (Labour Governments have learnt the hard way not to have over-sanguine views about their nationalised protégés' prospects) in the first five years. The possible implications for the deliberately already hard-pressed free enterprise haulier were obvious.

In the same Act the National Bus Company was given immediate borrowing powers of £50 million. There were also to be subsidies for rural buses and ferry services. There was an arbitrary reduction in the equally arbitrary fuel oil tax (designed largely to help the ailing coal industry) for bus operators. In the 1968 Act the Scottish Transport Group was given immediate borrowing powers of £50 million. These new borrowing powers in the 1968 Act amounted to nearly £500 million. They included the "commencing debt capitals" which offered substantial scope for further borrowing, and were available for further purchasing of privately-owned road haulage, bus and coach concerns had there been no change of Government.

Again in the same Act British Railway's capital debt was reduced from £1,562 million to £300 million; in the previous decade the Government had provided BR with nearly £2,000 million of capital investment, largely for successive and in part ill-starred modernisation schemes. The capital of the Waterways Board was at the same time reduced from £19.25 million to £3.75 million. All these debt reductions were in effect a recognition, or at least a reluctant acceptance, by the Government that the industries concerned were unlikely ever to remunerate the capital with which they had been so generously provided by the State in the past. This might well not be so under different management, of course, but that is another story.

Perhaps the greatest step forward in the upward march of Socialist man was the 1968 Transport Act, aptly described as seven in one (Acts) and one in seven. It reorganised the railways, nationalised the bus companies, set up passenger transport authorities, created a new national freight authority, dealt with inland waterways and road haulage licensing, and—most significantly for this cautionary tale—extended substantially the powers of the nationalised transport undertakings concerned. Thus British Railways, British Waterways, the new National Freight Corporation, the new National Bus Company and Scottish Transport Group were given general powers to manufacture anything they believed that they could make profitably and to retail anything they purchased in the course of their business— that is in effect *carte blanche* to do virtually whatever they liked. Moreover, the PTAs were told that they could do anything from running taxi services and coach tours to petrol stations and motor accessory shops.

The power of the State did indeed increase greatly in six short years under the rule of a party which no longer officially— at least for the purpose of fighting elections—believes in anything so crude as nationalisation. The time has come, is long overdue, to reverse that trend.

CHAPTER ELEVEN

Exchequer Dependants

The performance of the nationalised industries has for too long been a political shuttlecock to be bandied around as the small coin of political exchange. For a quarter of a century, since the Attlee Government was returned to power with a commitment to take over the basic industries, both main political parties have taken up doctrinaire positions on the issue. The Labour Party, at first enthusiastic about the prospect of "the workers" at last owning the industries which employed them, and hopeful of a more rational organisation of the means of production, distribution and exchange, has clung to a shibboleth, to a romantic concept, long after its early hopes were seen to be unjustified.

Labour's greatest mistake—apart, that is, from the original error in believing, on the basis of a partial understanding of Marx and Engels, that State ownership was the panacea for almost all evils—was to set up vast, unwieldy amorphous State corporations. Accountable only to themselves on a day-to-day management basis, they have behaved as a law unto themselves for long periods. The day of reckoning has come eventually, of course, and then the State dinosaurs have been brought sharply to heel by a Treasury weary of putting good money after bad. But usually in the meantime a great deal has gone wrong, more often than not because of sheer bad management and a maldistribution of national resources, resulting from an uncommercial pricing policy.

Let it be said that the fault has often been that of Ministers who have been reluctant to let State industries raise their prices to realistic levels: ostensibly to set an "example" to the private sector in the perpetual war on inflation, in fact often to buy the housewife's vote by attempting to usher in a period of bogus relative price stability. Although much worse has happened since, Chancellor Harold Macmillan's "price plateau" of fifteen years ago, which offered the nationalised industries as sacrificial cows on the altar of one of the earlier versions of a so-called incomes policy, was a classic example of its kind. By restraining prices in key sectors of the economy it artificially stimulated demand for the products concerned (to reduce to absurdity, there is an unlimited demand for a product priced at zero) and unduly depressed the profitability of the industries concerned.

This was the era, dating back to the original nationalisation statutes of the first post-war Labour Government of 1945–51, when—almost unbelievably—State industries were enjoined to do no more than "break even, taking one year with another". In other words, few things could have been further from the minds of the nationalised industries' founding fathers than that they should earn a proper return on the capital they employed.

In their thirteen years in power the Conservatives did little to change the organisation of the nationalised industries—much less did they apparently even consider their phased denationalisation. Temperamentally opposed to their existence, virtually devoid of ideas on how to improve them, disinclined largely through inertia and lack of forethought to returning them to the private sector, they were concerned mainly to let sleepings dogs lie. If occasionally one woke up and barked and caused embarrassment, then so much the better. The resulting political row could be blamed on the Socialists, who created the situation in the first place, and then afterwards everyone concerned could go back to square one and things would drift on as before. The Conservatives' almost complete failure until late on in their long period of office to do anything constructive about the depressed condition of the State industries is one of the greatest reproaches against their post-war Governments. It certainly reflects badly on their leaders, some of whom were far from unmindful of, and untutored in, economic matters.

Moreover, when the initiative for reform came, by and large it was not from the politicians at all. The full story of how Treasury officials, to their great credit, pushed hard against entrenched opposition, over quite a long period, for a proper financial discipline for the nationalised industries, has yet to be told. When it is, it will surely rank as a classic example of how in history institutions seldom, if ever, reform themselves without severe outside pressure.

This pressure the Treasury provided. After months, if not years of labour, its Public Enterprises Division produced the revolutionary White Paper, "The Financial and Economic Obligations of the Nationalised Industries" in July 1961. Out of the window went the concept that State industries were social services, largely provided indiscriminately for the welfare of the citizen. Instead was introduced the principle that they must earn—continuously, and not merely "taking one year with another"—a return on their assets sufficient to justify their existence. In retrospect it seems an obviously desirable economic aim, but at the time it was a vast improvement on what had gone before. The White Paper appeared not long after that great leap into the unknown, the modernisation of British Railways under the leadership of General Robertson, son of the First World War Field-Marshall. Such was the predominance of "the military" on the railways at that time that one newspaper commented that nothing like it had been seen since Cromwell's rule of the Major-Generals. Vast sums of money were invested at that time—the late 1950's—without any proper sums being done about anticipated returns on capital invested and so on. Worse, when Lord Beeching took over the railways in 1961 he found that their management had little idea of rates of return on *existing* equipment, let alone what might be expected from new investments. Many a branch line remained opened for years losing proportionately large sums of money because no one knew how much it lost. The activities of General Robertson are only mentioned as an example (there were, and to a lesser extent still are, many others) of the amateurism which then dominated the management of much of Britain's business, and indeed of its life generally.

It is true that Ministers asked for the 1960–61 examination of the nationalised industries to be made in the first place. But they had no particularly constructive ideas about what it might achieve. They were mainly concerned with the organisational forms the State industries should take and in chains of command. They were much less interested in the criteria on which decisions should be taken. Indeed, in the Conservative Party regional decentralisation had for long been fashionable: there was even talk, absurdly, of competition between British Railways' regions (the number of competing lines on which this had any meaning could be counted on the fingers of two hands (if that). Thus the public sector industries were constantly reorganised and the last state was usually worse than the first. But the 1961 reforms have endured; their few omissions were largely corrected by a further White Paper, "Nationalised Industries: A Review of Economic and Financial Objectives", prepared by the same section of the Treasury, in 1967.

Since then the public sector industries have by and large been run—within the limitations of their institutional framework, and accepting that genuine competition is not usually "in the nature of the animal", nor indeed possible in the quasi-monopolistic positions which most of them enjoy—on commercial principles. Morale, which had been low before 1961, largely because the industries concerned had no clear idea what they were supposed to be doing, improved substantially. Profitability, rather than keeping down prices artificially, became the aim. And some industries, such as electricity, did indeed earn respectable profits in relation to the assets they employed. The importance of getting the targets "right" and ensuring an adequate overall return from the public sector industries was under-lined indirectly by the 1967 White Paper: "With the nationalisation of steel, their net assets are now valued at nearly £12,000 million and they invest annually around £1,700 million, over half of which is at present financed by the Exchequer. Their annual investment is equivalent to the whole of that for private manufacturing industry; they contribute about 11 per cent of the gross domestic product and they employ around 8 per cent of the total labour force."

Where applicable, each industry was set a financial target and was expected to achieve it in good times and in bad. The targets, defined in terms of profitability on the assets employed by the various State industries, varied considerably. This was to take account of their different trading prospects (capital-intensive electricity, for instance, is inherently more profitable than, say, the declining but in some respects competing, coal industry).

The financial targets also took account of the State industries' differing "social" obligations, often inherited from the dim and distant past. A case in point was the Post Office, on to which since the inauguration of Rowland Hill's penny post in 1840 has been grafted the telephone system. From the beginning it was an accepted principle that postal charges should be at a flat rate throughout the country, whether a letter went a mile or from Land's End to the Western Isles.

This cross-subsidisation was allowed for in the setting of the Post Office's financial target. So, too, was the fact that the capital-intensive telecommunications side, with far fewer social obligations and a much higher general profitability than the mails, must in the nature of things contribute much more to the combined target. Similarly, although its contribution to the Exchequer was negotiated annually with the Treasury, the Transport Holding Company's obligation to run, for instance, unremunerative buses in remote rural areas was allowed for.

British Railways had more "social" obligations than any other State industry. Its financial target was therefore—perforce—merely to break even as soon as possible. This has, alas, never been achieved in the subsequent decade except in so far as under Labour the loss-making but "socially desirable" railway lines have been hived off and given specific subsidies for a stated number of years. What happens after that is very much an open question; predictably, the rate-payers in the areas these lines are supposed to benefit are showing distinct signs of not wanting to underwrite the losses involved. Logically, therefore, they should be either run more efficiently, or closed. The introduction of un-manned halts instead of manned stations and the collection of fares on trains can be an effective, if obvious, way of boosting branch line profitability. For some reason, possibly the tacit opposition of the railway unions, this has not always been tried where it might have paid off handsomely.

A case in point was the old Cambridge-Sandy-Bletchley-Oxford line, one of the relatively few East-West rail links in this country, and running close to the proposed new "growth point" town of Milton Keynes, and possibly, although it is to be hoped not, to the proposed third London Airport. It might have been thought desirable to make a special effort to keep this line open, if only for its substantial freight traffic which went far towards covering its overheads. Moreover, substantial sums were spent, under the Robertson programme, on modernising the line a relatively short time before closure of all but the Bedford-Bletchley section. Yet no attempt was apparently made to boost takings by offering a better service, or to reduce costs in the sort of ways already mentioned, against a probable future increase in traffic. Indeed, the line seemed to be deliberately allowed to run down. This is merely mentioned as an example (there are others, no doubt, among the branch lines now under threat of closure) of what could be done if the railways showed more initiative, were more prepared to brave union opposition, and were less inclined to take unsatisfactory situations as "given" and immutable. The Treasury, the Ministry of Transport (now part of the Ministry of Environment), not surprisingly, have long been dissatisfied with the railways' management. The latter have, nevertheless, shown remarkable initiative in other directions—such as the speeding up of the "Inter City" train services. In some cases passenger revenue has increased by two-thirds or more after electrification. There has been, too, the pioneering of the "freight-liners" for the movement of containerised goods.

Some idea of the effectiveness of the new approach to the financing of State sector industries may be gained from a few figures. Thus the profitability of the Post Office rose from a return on assets of only 4.4 per cent in 1955–56 to 8 per cent in 1958–59 and has fluctuated around that level since then. The corresponding figure for the Electricity Councils and Boards in England and Wales rose from 4.6 per cent in 1955–56 to 6.9 per cent in 1963–64. And for the Gas Council and Area Gas Boards from 3.6 per cent in 1955–56 to 5.9 per cent in 1964–65. There were, however, certain lame ducks, such as the British Waterways Board which remained laggards, with continuing deficits, despite all the ingenuity of the Treasury, the Ministry of Transport, and indeed the Board itself, in thinking up new ideas, like for instance filling in little-used canals, to boost profitability. For all nationalised industries, including the Post Office, average profitability, however, rose from 2.9 per cent in 1955–56 to only 4.3 per cent in 1964–65—by any standards an unexciting return. The enormous sums written off the capital debt of the nationalised industries since they were taken into public ownership is no great advertisement for them and, with other aspects of their performance and general position in the economy, raises important questions about their present status. The total write-off has amounted to over £2,600 million, and in the process more than £420 million a year in interest and other payments has been foregone. Notable write-offs have included £487 million for the then British Transport Commission in 1962, £415 million for the National Coal Board in 1965, £110 million for British Overseas Airways Corporation in 1966, £1,262 million for British Railways Board in 1968 and £270 million for the London Transport Board in 1969.

Where will the process end? Logically there is *no* end to the process. A single-minded State determined to put bad money after good could indefinitely waste vast sums of the taxpayer's money. Some State industries, indeed, such as the National Coal Board and British Railways already resemble the proverbial bottomless pit. Surely the time has come—is long overdue—for the Conservatives in office to consider much more seriously than they appear to have done so far denationalisation for certain industries. As was pointed out in Chapter Ten there seems no good reason why the public-private ownership pendulum should stay fixed for all time where it happens to have come to rest now, or alternatively in the long run should move only Leftwards. Steel was denationalised a long time ago, in the early 1950's, it is true, but since then Enoch Powell and Ernest Marples have stood out as exceptions among the Conservatives in urging some measure of denationalisation.

The Conservative party's official attitude on this subject is all right as far as it goes, but it does not go far enough. Thus its 1970 pamphlet "Make Life Better" said:

> "We will put a stop to further nationalisation. We will reverse the Labour Government's process of using the taxpayer's money to buy its way into private firms. We will repeal the Industrial Expansion Act. . . . We are determined to restore a competitive framework for steel. We are pledged to repeal the nationalisation provisions of the Socialist Transport Bill. We are also examining wider schemes for selling shares in other State concerns to the public. . . . The industries that remain nationalised will be made as efficient as possible. We will set them clearer targets. Then we shall let the managements get on with the job, and stop messing them around with damaging political pressures and detailed interference by government departments."

Yet why stop there? What is the philosophical or practical objection to re-examining from first principles the whole vast edifice of State ownership? Or, put another way, what is the case for allowing the public sector to continue to pre-empt such a high proportion of the economy's overall resources? Are the British Steel Corporation, the British Railways Board, the National Freight Corporation and all (as now constituted) to be regarded as immutable for all time?

There have, it is true, already been signs of a greater flexibility in the capital structure of the State industries and in the long run from that much could flow. Thus the reduction of British Overseas Airways Corporation's debt to the Government by £110 million (largely representing past accumulated deficits) left it with an outstanding capital of £66 million. This was divided into £31 million of loan capital, on which interest will be paid, and £35 million of new "Exchequer Dividend Capital", on which payments will vary according to profitability. In other words, in a good year BOAC will pay a lot to its pay-master, the Treasury, but in a lean year will pay little or nothing. The scheme, which in cautious Whitehall is regarded as strictly experimental, is to last five years in the first instance.

There seems to be no good reason why British European Airways should not also participate in the same experiment, however. Indeed, the case for so doing is if anything stronger. For BEA's short-haul operations are intrinsically less profitable than those of BOAC, so that the interest charges on its substantial debts have in recent years rather more than outweighed its unexciting operating surplus. On cue, the Labour Government reacted by reducing BEA's capital liabilities by some £25 million with effect from 1968. It also made provision, should it be needed and subject to the approval of the Commons, for the conversion of a further tranche of borrowings of up to £12.5 million into a special account to support BEA's revenue accounts in the three years 1972–75. But why should not BEA be allowed to enjoy the same flexibility as BOAC with its new EDC?

If the hope was to limit the new type of capital for State industries to BOAC for the foreseeable future, it was singularly unsuccessful. Almost at once the new British Steel Corporation made a pre-emptive bid for a similar capital structure to that which BOAC enjoys. Its Chairman, Lord Melchett— surprisingly, a merchant banker by training—is rumoured to have pressed a reluctant Government and Treasury long and hard before getting his way. But the upshot was that under the 1969 Iron and Steel Act (which increased BSC's borrowing powers to a maximum of £650 million) £700 million of the £834 million commencing debt was converted into Public Dividend Capital paying a variable return. Curiously—for why not go the whole hog and make all the capital PDC?—for some reason the remaining £134 million pays interest at $6\frac{1}{2}$ per cent. Even more curiously, since the whole idea of PDC was to give greater flexibility in a State corporation's payments to the Exchequer in any one year, the return by way of dividend and tax payments is not to be less than would have been received if the commencing debt had all been fixed interest! This seems in fact to be a classic case of a "now-you-see-it-now-you-don't", ostensibly radical, reform.

Yet the BOAC and BSC *démarches* are important, even so: more for what they could imply for the future than for what they now are in themselves. Once the principle of a mixed capital structure for the nationalised industries is accepted—however tentatively—there is no good reason why it should not be rapidly extended. The British Government has after all for long owned 51 per cent of British Petroleum's equity. The introduction of private capital into State industries is the next logical step to Public Dividend Capital. If the Treasury is prepared to accept a variable return in BOAC and BSC, with all the attendant risks and potential rewards, then why should not the great British public be let in on the deal? The argument that there is something special about the nationalised industries which requires an unusual capital structure (that is, all fixed-interest debt) falls to the ground when that structure more nearly corresponds to that of a private company, and when the whole concept has in any case been made to look ridiculous as a result of successive, arbitrary write-offs of their capital.

It is improbable, in a country where change tends to take place gradually, that whole State industries would ever be de-nationalised at one fell blow. The difficulty which the 1951–55 Churchill Government had in disposing of the steel industry's assets has in any case persuaded many people that an operation on such a scale in a relatively short time is impracticable, if not impossible (although the threat of renationalisation by the Labour Party was a major fortuitous deterrent to would-be purchasers of steel shares for most of the 1950's). It is argued, too, that the London capital market, although by far the largest in Europe, would be incapable of absorbing quickly the capital of a whole State industry. This though the sums involved for any one such industry would be small compared with the present total size of the vast gilt-edged market; and although the reduction in the size of that market, which would be involved in the conversion of "x" million of nationalised stock into equity, would make available at least part of that money for investment in the new equity. On the other hand, the institutions—the large pension funds, insurance companies, investment trusts and so on—which are nowadays the biggest market influence would almost certainly want to convert some of their money which had been invested in the fixed-interest debt of the industry being denationalised into similar (fixed interest) stocks elsewhere in order to maintain the balance of their portfolios.

Clearly there would be much to be said for phasing the denationalisation of State industries over a period. One obvious advantage would be that it would give the Labour Party time to get used to the idea. It is sometimes argued that denationalisation should not, indeed cannot, be even attempted in this country because the Labour Party and trade unions would automatically oppose any such proposals ferociously. And that in so doing they would make it at least as difficult to return State industries to the private sector as the steel denationalisation of the 1950's proved to be.

There is a classic undynamic British circularity in this argument. If radical change is never attempted because of the difficulties it would involve, how then is Britain ever to see happier days? It might just as well be argued that the Conservatives should not attempt to reform the archaic British taxation structure, or bring the trade unions within the ambit of the common law like everyone else, for fear of the fuss which would be created. If the Labour Party needs educating in the facts of economic life, then that is its problem. Probably one day it will happen, and the non-doctrinaire radical party which Hugh Gaitskell sought will emerge kicking and screaming into the twentieth (or twenty-first) century. This is much more likely to happen soon if it is shown beyond a shadow of doubt that a really competitive capitalist society delivers the goods in the shape of faster growth and a higher standard of living. How wrong Adenauer and Erhard would have been to have heeded the protests of the then German Opposition Social Democrats against their highly successful policy of unfettered free enterprise in the 1950's. In the end it was the Social Democrats who changed their ground, in line with public opinion, and dropped their nationalisation proposals.

A steady, sustained, phased, manifestly successful process of denationalisation over a period could be invaluable in so educating the British Labour Party. It should also, with the other measures which could make the British economy one of the most dynamic in the world one day, by its obvious success win for the party which implemented it a long period of office—like the German Christian Democrats. And clearly an ambitious programme of denationalisation, combined with other such radical measures of reform, would require more than one Parliament to carry out.

At the first chance, therefore, the Conservatives should use the opportunity provided by Labour's introduction of mixed capital structures into two nationalised industries to build something new. For a start they could introduce Public Dividend Capital, or its equivalent, into more of the State industries, and announce that they intended to do so for all of them in due course barring quite unforeseen snags. Meanwhile they could start selling off in tranches some of the existing PDC. British Overseas Airways Corporation would be as good a beginning as any. Other State airlines, such as Belgium's Sabena, allow the public to buy their equity, so why not BOAC and BEA—or, preferably, a combined airline?

Steel, which already has PDC, would also be another good early candidate for sales to the public. The PDC, or whatever it was renamed, would have to be converted, perhaps also in tranches, into proper equity with voting rights for shareholders and so on. Steel was after all nationalised in the dying months of the Attlee Government, which by then had a tiny majority, against the doubts of many prominent Socialists and by what is thought to have been a small majority in the Cabinet. Since then it has become the aimless shuttlecock of British politics. Unless some new solution is tried, or Labour changes its spots, or preferably both, the issue of steel, its nationalisation and de-nationalisation, threatens to roll endlessly down the years perpetuating a pointless, bitter *jehad* between the parties.

For this reason alone the Conservatives have been understandably reluctant to promise outright denationalisation of the steel industry once more. They have also, of course, been conscious of the alleged difficulties of selling off its assets; and of "unscrambling" an industry in which the old private companies are no more, and which is now organised "vertically" into product groups. That is indeed a problem which was almost certainly created in part deliberately by Labour for its successors. But it is no less a problem for that. Over a long period what is now the British Steel Corporation could doubtless be broken down into several competing companies, based it might well be, on certain areas, such as South Wales and North-East England. Doubtless, too, this should be done. That is, unless the "economies of scale" argument—so potent in the most technologically-advanced industries, such as the manufacture of supersonic aeroplanes or computers—comes to mean that there is only room for one steel company, or more relevant one steel factory in Britain. This seems most improbable.

The phased conversion of BSC's Public Dividend Capital into proper equity and its subsequent sale to the public, might well, therefore, help to reconcile Labour to denationalisation of steel. The State could continue, if it wished, to retain BSC's prior charge fixed-interest capital indefinitely. It could even do the same with part of the PDC. Thus Labour would be left with the thought that it could, if it really still wished to do so later, "rephase" a proportion of BSC's capital back into public ownership. Or do it all at once. But at least there would not then be the irrevocable ideological all-or-nothing gulf which now separates the parties on the tired old issue of who should own the steel industry.

Another obvious candidate for such treatment is the telecommunications side of the Post Office. No doubt there are good reasons why the mail should remain in public ownership. It is so owned in virtually every country in the world. It is difficult to see a private company ever regarding it as a profitable proposition, for instance, to take letters to Mull or to the Scillies. Nor does competition have much meaning in this context where a national, all-embracing, network of distribution of letters and parcels is essential. The postal strike of early 1971 nevertheless showed that not even the daily mail is essential; and that the Post Office's services can be duplicated by entrepreneurs.

The same arguments do not apply to the telephones. And the sensible bisecting of the Post Office under Labour into two semi-autonomous parts, mails and telecommunications, each with its own financial target, again gives the Conservatives something valuable on which to build. The great disparity between the relative profitability of the two sides of the Post Office will soon be obvious to all—though it has, of course, always been apparent from a study of the annual report and accounts.

No investor in his right mind would want to buy into the mails side of the Post Office, earning as it usually does only $2\frac{1}{2}$ per cent on its assets—unless he had good reason to believe a substantial improvement was on the way. But he should leap at the opportunity to buy into the highly profitable telephone system, already earning some 8 per cent on its assets and doubtless capable of even greater things under new, more "commercial", management. No doubt the development of a more reliable STD service (which should surely not be too difficult) and a greater availability of telephones for immediate installation, to name but two random if obvious thoughts, would do wonders for turnover, and in the long run for profits.

There seems to be no ideological objection, in principle, not even on the Left, to the denationalising of telephones. After all, Hull has had its own separate telephone system from the beginning. And as Hull goes today, why should not Britain go tomorrow? No doubt if any political party had had any rooted objection to the Hull set-up, it would have excised this harmless—but significant—anachronism long ago. But the fact is that local calls are cheaper in that great city than they are elsewhere, and this gives every appearance of reflecting a greater efficiency than prevails at the Post Office dinosaur.

Admittedly, the Hull telephone service is municipally-owned. But in an important sense that does not matter. The principle of separate ownership has been conceded by allowing it to co-exist with the State telephone network. As a result it is impossible to maintain in logic that one single, all-seeing, monolith is necessary to control Britain's telephonic communications. Indeed, in America many cities and areas have their own privately-owned telephone companies, which are linked, of course, on the national grid. The service has deteriorated of late in certain areas—notably New York—owing largely to a lack of automatic exchange equipment and consequent traffic congestion. But there can be little doubt that even now the American telephones service is one of the finest, if not the best, in the world, and certainly one of the cheapest in relation to the distances involved. For years it was possible, for instance, to telephone anywhere even at 3,000 miles distance for only a dollar after 9 p.m. And there have been proportionate flat, but rather more expensive, rates for the earlier hours of the evening.

A privately-owned telephone system in Britain would not necessarily ever be as cheap or efficient as America's now is, of course. The accumulated high level of capital investment in that system over a long period, and the sheer wealth and size of the market, make it difficult if not impossible for any other country to catch up with it. With greater drive and commercial sense, however, there should be considerable scope for expanding the British telephone market. The dead hand of Treasury control of the Post Office's capital investment programme, despite the high returns on its telecommunications side, has contributed to a perennial shortage of equipment in certain areas, and therefore to a severe restraint on the rate of overall growth of the service. Steep increases in charges in recent years have also contributed to a slackening of demand. As a result Britain has only twenty-five telephones for every 100 people, a proportion far lower than in, for instance, Sweden or America.

The inherent illogicality of State ownership of so many industries was never more vividly illustrated than in the case of telephones. In spite of such relatively big increases in charges, the Post Office was only about 40 per cent self-financing for its capital investment programme (most of which went on the telephone side) in 1968–69. No doubt this will continue to be roughly true in the next five years, during which it is planned to spend some £2,000 million on investment. No doubt, too, were it not for the constraints of State ownership, whereby about £1,200 million of that total will have to be found by the taxpayer, the £2,000 million should be much greater. Almost certainly whatever money the already relatively profitable telephone system needed to fulfil its true potential for growth would be forthcoming on the open capital market. And to the extent that that was so the demands on the over-burdened, depressed Government gilt-edged market would be eliminated.

Other candidates for denationalisation must surely include the road haulage and bus interests of the former Transport Holding Company, a large proportion of which have only recently been absorbed by the State sector. There is no good reason whatsoever, except ideology, why they should not operate in a genuinely competitive environment. The *raison d'être* of the rag-bag NFC as a whole is indeed difficult to discern and it must surely be an early candidate for the abbatoir under any Right-wing radical Government. Its formation effectively decapitated British Railways by removing from it the profitable freight liner service.

The railways have shown vision in fostering the concept of containerisation of goods for transportation, and particularly for export, well ahead of other countries; they little deserved to have this, potentially one of the greatest areas of expansion, removed at such an early stage. Yet, ironically, the freight liner train service and British Road Services, removed from the former

Transport Holding Company, are expected to make losses of an average £10 million annually for their first five years. Ominously, the NFC has borrowing powers of £200 million, which the Minister can extend by order to £300 million, and these could clearly be used under a Left-wing Government to buy up further private sector road haulage firms. And, in order, meanwhile, to tip the balance further against these concerns a system of quantity licensing of their larger lorries, restricting their journeys above 100 miles, was threatened. As a result manufacturers' unfettered freedom to decide whether their goods go by road or rail would be restricted, and industrial costs significantly increased.

This nonsense could be ended by a straight act of denationalisation which sold off the NFC's road haulage and bus interests to the private sector. The freight liner train service could then be returned to British Railways, pending consideration of its longer-term future. Although there is no intrinsic reason why it should be owned and run by the State, there is logic in its being integrated with the railways and in its boosting their flagging finances.

This raises the question of how far denationalisation should be taken. Enoch Powell has correctly pointed out that everything, even an unsuccessful nationalised industry, has its price; and that therefore there should be no problem in logic in disposing of even the coal industry, the railways and the waterways. If London Transport, never a high-flier financially, can be "unloaded"—albeit to a Conservative-controlled local authority rather than to a privately-owned concern—then why not the flotsam and jetsam of the State sector? The case is beguiling and no doubt the least profitable nationalised industries could all be disposed of, perhaps as job lots, that is in parts, in a knock-down auction at a fraction of their asset value. To say that this would represent a waste of all the vast sums of taxpayers' money which has been sunk in those industries over so many years is to beg the question. The money has *already* been lost (witness the successive write-offs of State industries' debt) and will not be seen again by the taxpayer whether or not he continues to "own" so many industries. The only question is how best he should cut his losses and move towards a more satisfactory situation in the future.

There is another point, however. "Market forces" as we know them would undoubtedly hasten the decline of already contracting industries such as coal and the railways. That is in principle a good thing—in the long run good even for the work people concerned who are thereby redeployed more profitably, and good for the nation. Yet it would not necessarily be good for Britain if in the 1980's she had virtually no railways except the fast, profitable, inter-city services. New Yorkers, for instance, have come to bitterly rue the day that their ostensibly unprofitable commuter services were allowed to wither on the bough of pure market forces. The "social cost" of traffic congestion at rush-hour in that great city, though largely unquantifiable by economics at its *present* stage of development, is clearly enormous, in terms of lost working (and relaxing) hours and the impeding of commercial traffic.

Almost certainly in time much more sophisticated techniques will be evolved than we know today for assessing in economic terms such inconveniences and cost to everyday life as pollution, noise, congestion and so on. Invaluable work has already been done in the economics section of the former Ministry of Transport, for instance, on the possibilities of road pricing—whereby vehicles will be charged according to how much road space they use and for how long in the centre of cities.

This is relevant to the railways, as well as to London Transport, in that probably few people would really like to see a relatively railway-less Britain; nor in their heart of hearts do they probably imagine that such a state would be good economics. One of the conveniences (which has an economic value) of living in Britain, as opposed to America, is that one can make many journeys in the comparative comfort of a train—relaxing for the traveller for pleasure but also invaluable for the businessman who has papers to read, topics to discuss, thoughts to brood on. In the Great Republic, on the other hand, almost every journey has to be made by air or car and neither are anything like as conducive to doing business en route. Moreover, without the Southern Region of British Railways, which has the largest and densest commuter service in the world, life in the metropolis would be almost unbearable, and would certainly be seized up for a large part of the day.

Yet there is surely a good prospect that in time it will be possible to assess the "social benefit" of such a commuter service much more accurately than it is today. The granting of specific subsidies to certain loss-making lines is a small start.

This social benefit could then be included in the economics of running the services concerned and appropriate conclusions drawn about who should pay—user, local authority, Treasury or some source as yet unthought of. But the point is that all this could be much more easily worked out if the industry concerned, such as the railways, was still in State ownership, at least in the initial stages.

There is virtually no prospect anyway, of the less successful State industries being sold off. There is a rather better prospect, of the moderately successful industries, such as gas, being denationalised one day, at least in part. Such industries are therefore ideal candidates for a mixed capital structure where part is owned by the State and part by private investors.

The Treasury might also be persuaded to remove its indiscriminate and relatively recent guarantee on the debt stock of such industries which continued to be held by the State. That guarantee, which in effect lumps together the stock of all the State industries on the same interest-rate basis, greatly increases the problems of managing the vast gilt-edged market, and therefore of controlling the money supply. It would be much better to let, say, the gas industry pay more for its new money for capital investment than the more profitable electricity industry, if that is what the market believes it should be paying, and is only prepared to lend on those terms. There would then be a better distribution of national resources between the various State industries, and between them and the private sector, than can ever be achieved by the sophisticated but somewhat artificial techniques of State investment appraisal now prevailing. In other words, if investment by one industry, and particularly investment on a marginal project, were considered more risky and potentially less profitable than investment by another, it would pay more for its money. This effect would be achieved, of course, by the introduction of privately-held equity into State industries. But it could also be achieved, perhaps as an interim step, by inviting the public to subscribe to the prior charge debt stock of State industries without the Treasury guarantee of capital and interest. It would cost some of the industries concerned a good deal more money a year in interest charges. But it would be worth it in so far as it eliminated some of the worst excesses of over-investment in unviable propositions.

The paragraph in the 1967 White Paper quoted earlier in this chapter emphasises the importance of the State industries to the economy. If only a proportion of the assets they deploy were transferred back to the private sector over a period the economic and "libertarian" advantages (no less important for being unquantifiable: see Chapter Ten) would surely be great. They are certainly worth working for.

To the surprise of many, the Conservatives in office soon showed that they had been in earnest when in opposition they looked favourably on the possibilities of denationalisation. What was more genuinely surprising was that, as well as talking of injecting private capital into whole industries hitherto wholly owned by the State, the Conservative Government dallied with "hiving-off" parts of those industries to the private sector. At the new Ministry of Trade and Industry John Davies' radical lieutenants, Sir John Eden and Nicholas Ridley, in particular were rumoured to be beavering away energetically at possible ways of reducing the State's stranglehold on the "means of production and distribution".

In January 1971 it was announced that Thomas Cook—a by-word around the world for travel since intrepid Victorian maiden ladies first used its services to penetrate the Nile as far as the Third Cataract, was to be sold—along with certain other transport interests of the Transport Holding Company was to be sold. Potential buyers had been sniffing around the company for years, and Ministers were justified in asking for a high price. Its profit record, it is true, was chequered, despite the highly profitable travellers' cheques side. But the scope for further growth, in a dynamic market with vast potential, was correspondingly the greater. In Whitehall there had long been a feeling that the company was insufficiently thrusting: it had been slow for instance to exploit, in conjunction with the State airlines with which it inevitably worked closely, the buoyant package holiday market. Cooks had in any case only been nationalised almost fortuitously by the war-time Churchill Government to safeguard "the national interest". Nevertheless, in the interests of instant opposition, Labour opposed strenuously the proposal to sell the company.

At almost the same time, and with a degree of poetic justice, the announcement of much improved profits by the State public houses was rewarded almost at once with another to the effect that they were to be sold. At the end of the thirteen Tory years the Home Government in 1964 was steeling itself to denationalise the Scottish and Carlisle pubs in the following Parliament. But this belated resolve was overtaken by Labour's election victory that year. These pubs had also been taken over by the State as a war-time measure—by the Lloyd George Coalition in order to discourage the munitions workers from drunkenness. Since then they had come under the benign eye of the Treasury which sought, commendably and continuously, to garner reasonable profits from the State Management Districts. From the side-lines other Departments intermittently pursued other and more obscure objectives, such as urging that the State pubs should "set an example" to other less highly-principled publicans, by keeping their prices down in the interests of "incomes policy" or some such nonsense. Fortunately their success was temporary and limited, if not actually invisible to the naked eye.

These were obvious targets for early denationalisation. Much more difficult was the concept of selling only the profitable parts of industries. The chairmen of State industries could reasonably claim—and did so—that losing their favourite sons, often reared with loving care and at some risk, was to increase greatly, if not to make impossible, their proper task of earning a reasonable overall return on their assets. Certainly the industries concerned would be less attractive to prospective private investors to the extent that their profitability was diminished (there was an analagous argument against the so-called Public Dividend Capital for State industries: to the extent that Ministers urged other objectives on them, such as price stability which eroded profits, they were correspondingly less attractive to potential holders of that PDC).

The rag-bag hamper of State holdings which were candidates for hiving-off was indeed diverse. The eighteen large parent State undertakings in fact included altogether nearly 800 individual companies. Thus British Rail had thirty-four hotels, fourteen railway workshops and 187 refreshment rooms, besides hover-craft, harbours, ships, and (often underdeveloped) real estate. And the Coal Board owned farms and houses, made bricks, sold chemicals, and drilled for natural gas and oil. In addition it owned an air distribution equipment manufacturer, five building supplies companies, seven fuel distributors, and six chemical companies (wholly or in part). The Electricity Boards had 1,300 showrooms, selling electrical appliances.

Moreover, as has been pointed out, the 1964–70 Labour Government actively encouraged the spread of these peripheral State interests. The Gas Council Bill, which (with the Electricity Bill) was overtaken by the 1970 election, would have allowed the Gas Council to refine and market oil. And the Central Electricity

Generating Board would have been able to make electrical plant and fittings, and even—"you name it, we will do it"—to do anything it believed was "requisite, advantageous, or convenient".

It was remarkably difficult to manage efficiently such varied activities, since the discipline of control through the market was non-existent. They had, moreover, often been deliberately favoured. Thus the electricity showrooms, in contrast to their private competitors, were at first exempt from Selective Employment Tax. When the law was changed to make them pay SET their profits took a severe toss. Moreover, the protection long enjoyed by the Coal Board in the shape of the fuel oil tax and the ban until 1970 on imports of foreign coal was a standing affront to the idea of a more competitive Britain.

An obvious candidate for the knife was the British Steel Corporation. Great was the battle about its future behind the Whitehall scenes. Its mixed capital structure, for which Lord Melchett had struggled so hard; its interests in special steels, chemicals and construction engineering; its recent reorganisation into product as opposed to area groups (which many believed to have been a deliberate anti-nationalisation gambit); and its low profitability; all these were reproaches to impatient Tory Ministers. Many were the options—some discussed in this book— which were canvassed. The peripheral activities could be sold to private enterprise. Or the whole vast Corporation, much the largest steel company in Europe, could be given an injection of private capital—possibly on the lines of the so-called "British Petroleum formula", whereby private investors would take part of the capital. The Corporation's existing PDC might suffice with relatively little alteration, for this. Another possibility would be dividing BSC into two competing units, whether wholly or partially owned by private enterprise.

At least as important as the form and proportion private capital should take in the present State industries is the degree of independence they should enjoy from Whitehall interference. The historical reasons for their present equivocal position have already been touched on. It is a moot point whether there was less Ministerial interference in the running of the nationalised industries before or after the change of Government in June 1970. Certainly Heath's Ministers were much more involved behind the scenes than they would admit in public. Inevitably so: their early experience showed how impossible it is for he who pays the nationalised piper not to call the tune, if he wishes to see the colour of his money (which is yet another reason, if one were needed, for reducing the economic commitment of the State).

In the first months of the Heath Government Ministers were, *inter alia*, trying hard to control the Post Office, and in the process painfully dismissing its Labour-appointed chairman; arguing with Lord Robens about the terms on which he might or might not stay on as chairman of the Coal Board; asking Lord Melchett what good reason the Steel Corporation had for keeping its more lucrative side-lines; reading the riot act to the chairmen of all State industries about the rate of their own wage inflation; and wondering how many of their heads would have to roll before the leadership of what remained of public sector industries agreed with the aspirations of the Conservative Government.

There were a number of possible organisational structures for the revamped industries which are now owned wholly by the State. A non-political financial structure or investment board, or "conglomerate" holding company, might be interposed between the Whitehall civil servants and the boards of those industries owned, or partially owned, by the State. This would reduce interference by the Executive or by Parliament (or by both) in the day-to-day running of those industries to a minimum. Alternatively if hybrid corporations, in which State participation was relatively low, eventually evolved—and particularly if they were not near-monopolies—there would be no valid reason why they should not be allowed to do anything which a commercial company might do. Certainly there would be no justification for detailed surveillance by Parliament or by officials. The State, with the other shareholders, would merely expect a viable balance-sheet and respectable profits at the end of the company's financial year.

Clearly difficulties abound, as in the case of any radical change. Such formulae are inevitably compromises, as long as *any* State interest persists, between the need for the taxpayer to ensure a proper return on his money and the equally important need for the companies concerned to be allowed to get on with the job in relative freedom from outside interference. As long as the State has any stake in industry, there is a danger that it will have to put good money after bad.

The Conservative policy of disengagement by the State from

involvement in industry, preached so enthusiastically by the Prime Minister to the party conference in the autumn of 1970, soon ran into some predictable snags. What could have been more embarrassing for a new *laissez faire* Government than the financial difficulties of Rolls-Royce, a company whose name had been for long almost synonymous with British know-how and engineering brilliance? Ministers felt that such a priceless national asset could not be allowed to wither on the bough, or perhaps even worse pass into foreign hands, and accordingly launched a massive rescue operation in late 1970.

Apart from some justified teasing by the Labour Opposition and rumblings from Enoch Powell, there was little coherent criticism of their decision to support Rolls-Royce to the tune of a £600 million rescue operation. Few pointed out that it was not self-evident, to say the least, that if Rolls-Royce was not helped by the Government it would disappear from the face of the earth, or at best be sold off as a job lot at knock-down prices. Every firm has a price at which it is attractive to a potential buyer: Rolls-Royce might well have been taken over by an international company prepared to give it the necessary financial transfusion. And had it been an American concern, then so much the better in the sense that American investment in this country is on the whole so much more efficient than the British norm, and so correspondingly beneficial to its employees.

Yet, it is true that Conservative Ministers had repeatedly said that advanced, sophisticated, high-technology industries, such as aerospace and computer manufacturing, might in the last resort qualify for special assistance. Rolls-Royce was after all one of the three leading aero-engine manufacturers in the world. Its high-value exports earned a lot of foreign exchange. Derby was one of Britain's few centres of high-technology manufacture. To let Rolls-Royce fail in its great adventure of selling advanced engines to the American giant Lockheed, on which it had embarked with such acclaim and national pride, would have been unforgivable; future generations would rue the day, and so on. Such at least was the argument.

This was the situation of, these were the arguments about, Rolls-Royce until the crash in February 1971. The largest bankruptcy to have taken place in Britain since the 1939–45 war was a shattering blow to British morale and pride. It was true that aerospace companies in most countries were in some sort of difficulty for one reason or another—usually the sheer cost of research and development in such advanced technology. Lockheed itself, which was hit so badly by Rolls-Royce reneging on its contract to sell the revolutionary RB-211 engine at a fixed price, had for some time been far from viable. Lockheed was correspondingly less able to pay Rolls-Royce more generously for its engines, short of massive aid from the American Government, which seemed improbable despite the Prime Minister's use of the hot line to President Nixon.

Nevertheless, a company as large as Rolls-Royce, employing tens of thousands of people and renowned for its technical expertise, inevitably occupied a special place in British hearts. Its bankruptcy, moreover, raised the haunting question: if Britain could not make, and as important sell, such sophisticated products as aero engines, in which it had a technical lead, at what precisely could it excel whereby to earn its daily bread?

This was admittedly a special case (which cases are not special in some way?) The company's accounting had clearly been hopelessly wrong and optimistic; its board, even after the injection of Lord Cole, former chairman of Unilever, had been heavily weighted in favour of technical men; development costs for the £150 million contract had doubled since 1968 to some £135 million in a period of almost unprecedentedly rapid inflation; too many projects had been on the stocks simultaneously, and the company was probably making too many products in any case.

Yet a crash is a crash and could not be explained away. Its repercussions were serious. Many smaller firms which supplied Rolls-Royce were put in jeopardy. Thousands were thrown out of work. Britain's reputation for advanced technology and commercial rectitude had taken a severe knock. The British Government had side-stepped any obligation on its part to supply the ailing Lockheed company, at a heavy loss, with the engines which it so badly needed.

In the emergency Commons debate on the Rolls-Royce débâcle on 8 February, which coincided with the Government's legislation to temporarily "nationalise" the company, Opposition MPs pointed sadly—as well they might—to all the ill effects of the Rolls-Royce bankruptcy. Yet it was indeed difficult to see what else the Government could have done. The State had already committed nearly £900 million of taxpayers' money and, as Anthony Barber said in the debate, the loss on the production alone of the RB-211 engine would have been £600 million or more. And when the receiver for Rolls-Royce was appointed there were substantial open-ended commitments concerning potential claims for delay in delivery, on top of the huge losses on development and manufacturing.

Labour presented Ministers' decision to take into public ownership the main assets of Rolls-Royce for a while as the opposite of their professed faith of non-intervention in industry. They were wrong. Temporary State ownership would be used merely to sort out the rag-bag of disparate interests which had been Rolls-Royce. Some activities had to be retained for defence reasons or to fulfil Britain's obligations to her European allies. Others, such as the prestigious car plant, in which David Brown among others apparently showed an interest, could be sold as going concerns. Yet others were no longer profitable. To the extent that the Rolls-Royce umbrella had hitherto embraced prestige, defence and commercial considerations, the Government's decision was an overdue move away from State intervention (albeit indirect) in industry.

Much more straightforward, much easier for harassed Ministers rightly intent on rolling back the feather-bedding of decades, was the decision in late 1970 not to help the ailing Mersey Docks and Harbours Board. Clearly a second Rolls-Royce operation would have been disastrous for the credibility of the Government's policy of disengagement. A loan to the Board might have opened a Pandora's box of similar concerns seeking similar State aid; labour relations on Merseyside, Britain's second largest port, had for long been notably bad; and as a port Liverpool had been losing ground to more go-ahead ports such as Felixstowe, Southampton, and Tilbury.

It was, nevertheless, a brave decision—one almost inconceivable under the 1964–70 Labour Government. There was a fearful row in the City, that traditional bastion of the Conservative Party, over the terms proposed for the Board's bondholders, who were in effect billed to take the loss incurred by past mistakes and inefficiency. Rationalisation of the Board's activities and the injection of financial expertise seemed certain to exacerbate labour relations before it improved them. Increases in the Board's charges totalling about 45 per cent would not endear it to its customers. And selling off assets to raise the necessary cash is not always easy, and was certainly painful to an old-established company.

But then no one had ever argued that disengagement itself

was likely to be easy and painless. The new style of government involved for Britain by definition a new type of self-reliance and risk-taking which had been alien to the British scene for decades. As with the balance-sheet of entry into Europe, the pain involved was almost immediate and there for all to see; the advantages to the individual and the nation would take longer to appear but would be none the less great for that.

CHAPTER TWELVE

Industrial Relations—The Locust-eaten Years

As sad a tale as any in Britain since 1945 has been the mis-handling, or failure to handle, her chaotic industrial relations. And for this the Conservatives must take much of the blame. They have after all been in power for slightly over a half of the last quarter century. Yet there is little evidence that, until they went into Opposition in 1964, they took anything like seriously enough the threat to, indeed the steady erosion of, Britain's economic strength caused: by wild-cat strikes, which often throw out of work far more people than those involved in the immediate disputes; her unbelievably complex trade union structure, which leads to endless demarcation disputes about who-does-what-from-which-union and to "leap-frogging" wage claims; and restrictive practices, which by definition reduce productivity and discourage the installation of new, more productive machinery.

It was apparent by the early 1960's, and arguably well before, that Britain had a relatively low economic growth, and that her industrial relations were exceptionally bad by international standards—and that there was at least some connection between these things. Yet virtually nothing was done to change this state of affairs during the long Churchill-Eden-Macmillan-Home years.

Surely it is reasonable to ask: if the Conservatives' proposals for reforming Britain's industrial relations, enshrined in "Fair Deal at Work", their pamphlet published in opposition, are now (rightly) regarded as so fundamental to the Tories' approach to "getting Britain moving", why were they barely hinted at before they lost power in 1964? British industrial relations have not deteriorated *so* markedly in the last six years.

The fact is, of course, that the essence of the Conservatives' approach to Government during their thirteen years was usually to avoid a head-on approach to problems. The implicit thesis in their style of Government for much of that time was to hope, in a very British way, that the less they thought about basic problems, such as industrial relations, the more likely they were to go away and solve themselves. To that extent the bills, the post-dated cheques, for the thirteen Tory years are still rolling in, after a six-year Labour interregnum, under another Conservative Government. How different a place this country might be by now if the running sores of a highly disincentive-making tax system, chaotic industrial relations, a cosy, highly protected, uncompetitive economy, exclusion from Europe, had been tackled at the right time—ten, fifteen, or preferably twenty years ago.

If this is thought to be a rather harsh judgement, delivered with the benefit of hindsight, perhaps one example will suffice to prove the point (and there are many, including the author, who were highly critical of those Conservative Governments at that time for precisely the reasons given in this book). The abolition of resale price maintenance was by 1964, when the Conservatives made it the ark of their latter-day economic covenant, long overdue. The benefits which would spring from it, such as a reduction of shop prices on a wide range of consumers goods, from gramophone records to cars, had long been obvious. The disadvantages were less easy to detect, except that such a move was bitterly opposed by small shop-keepers and their representatives in the Conservative Parliamentary Party, who assumed (wrongly, as it turned out) that the demise of RPM would *necessarily* be bad for the shop on the corner which still offered "service".

A proposal to abolish RPM appears to have gone to the Macmillan Cabinet more than once but to have been rejected as "politically inopportune". In other words, the game of making Britain more efficient was not worth the candle of incurring unpopularity, even temporarily, with a section of the electorate which usually voted Conservative.

In the event, of course, such fears proved largely groundless. Traditional Tory voters have "nowhere else to go" when forced to chose between the two main parties at an election. Prime Minister Sir Alec Douglas-Home and Edward Heath, then at the Board of Trade with a brand-new, high-powered Ministerial title, showed rare courage in pushing the abolition of RPM in early 1964 through the Conservative Parliamentary caucus by one vote in the face of the rage of the squires from the shires and other special interests. Yet by the October 1964 election all was forgiven and forgotten—well, almost—and more "competition", epitomised by the abolition of RPM, was the new, or rather revivified Tory slogan. And in 1965 Heath was elected Conservative leader.

This cautionary tale in political courage has clear lessons for the more important issue of Britain's industrial relations. It seems improbable, to say the least, that if, for instance, Harold Macmillan had made an issue of industrial relations in the 1959 election he would have been returned to power with a majority any whit the smaller than the 100 seats he enjoyed at the beginning of the 1959–64 Government. Indeed, it is not impossible that his majority would actually have been larger: there has been evidence for years that there is widespread support for Government action to reduce Britain's strike-proneness—not least by trade unionists, and particularly by their wives.

Who can doubt that Macmillan, with one of the largest majorities any Prime Minister has enjoyed in peace time, could not have enacted some at least of the proposals similar to those Robert Carr has espoused? It may be said that all this is water under the bridge; that "jobbing backwards" is no more profitable in politics than on the Stock Exchange. Yet the British economic failures of the last quarter century, which were often apparent at the time, cannot be emphasised too often if this country is to see happier days in the future. The abiding British tendency to try and put off the solution to problems for as long as possible, thereby exacerbating those problems—epitomised to some extent by the Macmillan, and more so by the Wilson years—must somehow now be recognised. And as far as possible, although a nation, like an individual, can only work within the limits of its virtues and faults, that tendency must be mitigated.

In official Tory folk-myth little more could have been done (in other words, virtually nothing) than was done in the thirteen years of Conservative Government, about industrial relations. The 1970 Conservative Campaign Guide, in what will surely rank for all time as a classic statement of the quietest British approach to politics, says: "The Conservative view during the 1950's was that the best way to deal with industrial relations was to let unions and management put their own house in order. At this time this policy had the overwhelming support of the British public".

An unusually large number of major points are begged here. What is the evidence, to invert the argument, that the electorate, in so far as they thought then about such matters, were "overwhelmingly" opposed to changes in industrial relations (such evidence as there is is surely to the contrary)? What evidence is there that the sustained attitude of "live and let live" of successive Conservative Governments in this field had any beneficial effect whatsoever, and was not, indeed, an abdication of what might be thought to be the obligations of any responsible democratic Government? And if by some mischance public opinion was as apathetic as is now claimed, do not the Ministers who presided over such remarkable apathy also bear some responsibility for it?

The argument is unhealthily reminiscent of Stanley Baldwin's pathetic plea in mitigation of his Government's sleepy (but by no means totally unaware) attitude to German rearmament, that had he gone to the country in 1935 on a programme of more arms he would not have had a chance of re-election. It is also reminiscent of the post-ante plea in mitigation of the Churchill-Eden-Macmillan Governments' failure to explore soon enough the chances of joining the Common Market, and the subsequent half-hearted 1961–63 approach to Europe, that public opinion was not prepared for such a radical move.

It indeed was not. And nor, for that matter, is it now. Public opinion, perhaps surprisingly, in view of the short-sighted nonsense it is often fed "from on high", to some extent follows what its leaders reveal as the truth. In the case of "Europe," apart from Reginald Maudling's 1958 doomed wild-goose chase around the European capitals attempting to build a free trade area scaffolding around a Market he appeared not to understand, the British people a decade ago had little enough reason to be aware of what was happening twenty miles from their south coast. This though the unification of Europe happened to be one of the greatest historical events of all time. Conservative and Labour leaders had seldom mentioned it. They preferred to utter platitudes about a Commonwealth which already had little meaning in hard political or economic terms. And in so far as the Macmillan Government did mention the Common Market in the 1959 election it was only to taunt the Liberals with wishing to join! And subsequently when in 1961 the decision was made to negotiate to see if there could be a negotiation with the Six, where was the "Midlothian campaign" to tell the people what was involved, and why the longer-term opportunities pointed overwhelmingly in favour of British entry? Where, for that matter, was that campaign in 1970 as public sentiment moved steadily against "Europe"?

The Conservatives' attitude to public opinion (or what in the days of less comprehensive public opinion polls than now operate was thought to be public opinion) and industrial relations in the 1950's and early 1960's is worth illustrating by these two examples from the sphere of foreign policy. For the principles are the same: that political leaders should not merely take public opinion as "given", that it is their duty to lead, and to inform, as well as to take note of, the consensus view at any particular point in time.

Where is the historical evidence, moreover, from, for instance, the example of the monasteries on the eve of the Henrician Reformation to that of the trade unions on the eve, it is to be hoped, of the Tory reformation, that institutions ever voluntarily reform themselves? Why should they when the power and privileges their leaders enjoy whether they be wealthy Mediaeval abbots or power-hungry trade union leaders, are so much to their liking?

In the case of Britain's industrial relations it was surely clear well before the Conservatives left office that, far from reforming themselves, the power of the trade unions, like that of the State itself, had increased, was increasing, and ought to be diminished. Indeed, George Woodcock, former General Secretary of the Trade Union Council, in a new version of a do-it-yourself kit, had graphically demonstrated, single-handed, the futility of the 1950's Conservative thesis on industrial relations. He took office, after all, in 1960 quite determined to bang all available trade union heads together and to create, on the German model, a rational, simple, trade union structure in this country. In 1962 the TUC even passed a resolution asking the Congress to report "on the possibility of reorganising the structure of both the TUC and the British trade union movement with a view to making it better fitted to meet modern industrial conditions". He soon discovered, however, that the cajoling powers of his job were minimal and the persuasive powers ineffective, and in time retired—perforce—disillusioned from the field. There has, of course, been some amalgamation of trade unions (such as the Amalgamated Engineering Union) since the glad confident morning of Woodcock's high hopes of trade union reform, but there are still hundreds of trade unions affiliated to the TUC, compared with only sixteen for the whole of West Germany.

Britain's industrial relations, have deteriorated further in the 1960's. Figures for the number of strikes, and the number of working days lost directly from them, should be treated with caution. There are times and conditions when a relatively large number of strikes can even be a good thing if it indicates an increased determination by management to put its house in order, or to stand out against outrageous wage demands, or both. Moreover, an almost unique feature of the British scene is the relatively large number of people thrown out of work by strikes with which they are not directly concerned—witness the repeated, disastrous wild-cat strikes in the car components firms which are apt to dislocate much of the motor industry at the drop of a cloth cap.

Even so, the British strike figures of the last two decades have *some* significance. Thus during the 1950's the average number of strikes, excluding coal-mining, was 590 a year. In the 1960's the corresponding figures was 1,590, over two and a half times as many, and nine-tenths of them were unofficial, that is not backed by trade unions—another particular feature of the British industrial relations scene. Moreover, the situation had deteriorated markedly in 1969, with roughly three times as many days lost by strikes as the annual average for the years 1963–67, and the figures for 1970 were a post-war record. There were 3,888 stoppages, involving nearly 1.8 million workers in 1970, compared with respective figures of 3,116 and 1.7 million in 1969. Working days lost rose from 6.9 million to 11.0 million in 1970. This deterioration may be not unconnected with the Labour Government's climb-down over its proposed anti-strike legislation in the White Paper "In Place of Strife". The unions were thereby given the green light for almost anything which took their fancy, including enormous wage claims.

By the time it left office in 1964 the Conservative Government was at least aware that there was an industrial relations problem; the Liberal and Labour parties in their 1964 election manifesto ignored the Tory pledge to set up a wide-ranging enquiry on the trade unions if they were returned to power.

Harold Wilson said quite specifically: "I see no need for a Royal Commission ... which will take Minutes and waste years." He duly set up the Donovan Commission in 1965, and it reported in 1968, advising in effect no radical trade union legislation which might upset anyone unduly.

Meanwhile, as a result of the labours of a specialist study group, the Conservatives had within a year of losing the 1964 election, produced a radical programme of reform, which was duly incorporated in their 1966 election programme and spelt out in detail in the 1968 "Fair Deal at Work". This wisely made no promises that the new Tory proposals would automatically usher in an Augustan age of peace in British factories: "it would be nonsense to claim that a new framework of law will inspire a new atmosphere of responsible co-operation overnight". But the hope was that over a period the comprehensive industrial relations Act foreshadowed in "Fair Deal at Work" (the first Act of its kind in British history) would make a radical difference to the whole atmosphere of industrial relations in this country.

What the Conservative proposals involve, and what they might mean for the future, can best be judged by what the other parties fail to mention. The Liberals apparently have no known views on this knotty problem, except for their proposals on industrial partnership. The Labour Party transitorily had views on what to do about the unions, but after the Government's climb-down on its proposed legislation in 1969, in effect had none.

The 1964–70 Labour Government first produced the Trade Disputes Act 1965, which was designed to give legal protection to union officials, or anyone else, against civil proceedings for intimidation. It is not uncommon for workers to be intimidated for not belonging to unions and for unions to ask for their dismissal if they stand out against the majority of their work-mates. The Conservatives are rightly pledged to repeal the 1965 Act.

The Donovan Royal Commission's diagnosis of the ills of Britain's industrial relations was much more impressive than its suggestions for action, such as they were. It was perhaps predictable that the Commission, under the Chairmanship of Lord Donovan and staffed with the usual Establishment worthies (no doubt culled from the Treasury's "Great and the Good" list) would produce a weak and divided report. The report of a Royal Commission can be predicted fairly accurately on the basis of its composition and in this case the Donovan Commission included among its members none other than a sadly chastened George

Woodcock, still General Secretary of the TUC before going on to be (guess what?) first chairman of the Industrial Relations Commission at a salary of £11,500 per annum.

The Donovan Report was adamant—and rightly so—on the need to overhaul Britain's archaic industrial relations but, as for the means it proposed to achieve this desirable end, it brought forth mice. Notably:

(i) it suggested that companies should be compelled to register their collective agreements with the Department of Employment and Productivity; or, if they had none, to state why;

(ii) and that an Industrial Relations Commission should be established to watch over these agreements and their observance. It would have no powers and would have even had to wait for a reference from the DEP before it could investigate such agreements.

There was much also besides, of course, but such basically were the results of three years (admittedly part-time) labour of able-bodied men.

The history of Labour's attempt to deal with Britain's worsening industrial relations is too recent and too painful to need recapitulating in detail. Seldom has there been such a total fiasco, such a remarkable lack of foresight, even in British post-war history. It may be argued, of course, that Labour, traditionally dependent on the trade unions for moral and financial succour, was wrong even to attempt union reform. No doubt Douglas Houghton, chairman of the Labour Party, was right in warning the then Prime Minister in May 1969 that: "No good that any contentious Bill of this kind can do to industrial relations or to the economy will redeem the harm we can do to our Government by disintegration or defeat of the Labour Party." He then referred to the "marginal damage of unconstitutional strikes".

No doubt he was right that *at that point in time* there was no hope of pushing even his party's inadequate reform proposals through a Parliamentary Labour Party roughly a third of whose members were trade unionists themselves, and often in part dependent on a union for their daily bread. But if this was so it reflects (like the other examples, such as Macmillan's volte face on the Common Market) in large measure the unremarkable fact that changes in Government policy as radical as this need some careful preparation, some education, some explanation of the reasons why they are necessary. Such a process may take months or even years but it is worth it. Ironically, in this case there was (and is) as has been pointed out, widespread public support for proper industrial relations legislation, and especially so among the wives of unionists—but not, alas, among Labour MPs.

It had been assumed that the Labour Government would go no further (if that) than the milk-and-water proposals of the Donovan Report. If that had proved to be the case Labour MPs could have lived happily with their consciences and with their sponsoring unions. Yet seven months after that report, in January 1969, the Government produced a White Paper, "In Place of Strife", which included not only some of the Donovan proposals but also others, some apparently culled from the Tories "Fair Deal at Work" and others, often ambiguous, thrown in for good measure from no obvious source.

There was immediate, predictable, dismay in Labour and trade union quarters but ominously for them, Roy Jenkins as Chancellor in his April Budget Statement announced immediate legislation of "some of the more important provisions" of the White Paper—many thought as a *quid pro quo* to the bailiffs at the International Monetary Fund for the simultaneous dropping of the compulsory powers to freeze wage increases. The Chancellor referred to the economic harm caused by "unnecessary and damaging disputes", and the next day Barbara Castle unveiled her proposals (see Appendix 2):

1. The right of the individual employee to belong to a trade union would "become part of every contract of employment";
2. If an employer refused to recognise a trade union, the union could complain to the Commission on Industrial Relations, which might then hold a ballot. If the CIR recommended action the Minister could then make a Recognition Order and if this were disobeyed it would be up to the union to take the employer to the Industrial Court.
3. When more than one union was involved in a recognition dispute, the TUC would at first negotiate and the CIR would then investigate. If subsequently the Minister made a Recognition Order it would be enforced by summoning the offending party before a new "Industrial Board" (apparently identical with the existing Industrial Court), which could impose a financial penalty.
4. In the case of unconstitutional strikes the Minister could impose by Order a 28-day pause on both sides: thus the

employer would return to the *status quo* and the strikers would go back to work. Any party which disobeyed such an order could be brought before the Industrial Board and made to pay a fine.

5. Unemployment benefit would be made available to workers laid off by strike action in several cases where they did not hitherto receive it.

On the face of it these were hardly revolutionary proposals and indeed similar legislation is but the small coin of industrial relations in most advanced, civilised societies. But in Britain all hell was let loose at the mere mention of "sanctions" against the unions, which for decades had been effectively exempt from the normal provisions of the otherwise hallowed Common Law.

When the White Paper had been debated on 3 March 1969 fifty-five Labour MPs had voted against the Government and about forty appeared to have abstained. And three weeks later the National Executive Committee of the Labour Party voted to inform Barbara Castle by a majority of three to one, which included Home Secretary James Callaghan, that they could not agree to support legislation on all the suggestions in the White Paper. When in February Callaghan, as Treasurer of the party, had met the unions they had made it clear that Ministers would have to drop their strike legislation if they wanted more cash for the Labour Party.

The Trade Union Congress had, of course, been opposed to the Government's proposals from the start. A week after Mrs Castle announced her proposals the General Council called a special Congress of the TUC, the first for nearly four decades. The approach was not, however, entirely negative. The Congress had before it a Report explaining the reasons for the TUC's opposition to the Government's proposals and suggesting what the unions themselves might do to deal with certain industrial problems. "Programme for Action" was duly adopted, but with the proviso from important unions that their support was conditional on the Government dropping its Bill. The Prime Minister, meanwhile, was still stoutly maintaining that his Governments' Bill was an issue of confidence and that in the case of defeat of it he would call an election. The Bill was apparently essential equally to Britain's economic recovery, to the balance of payments, to full employment and to the survival of the Govern-

ment. The relative merit of these various objectives was left to
his listeners to decide.

Wilson's fierce stand was reiterated the day after the
publication of "Programme for Action": "I believe that the life
of the country is at stake on all these issues" and Mrs Castle's
Department promptly announced that the Government had
"considerable reservations about the effectiveness of the General
Council's proposals for dealing with unconstitutional strikes".
But subsequent meetings with the TUC led nowhere and, after
the ultimatum from the Labour Party's Liaison Committee of 16
June that there was no hope of carrying the strike-curb Bill (even
though the Conservatives had undertaken not to oppose it),
Wilson and Barbara Castle met the TUC General Council at
Downing Street for the last time. They had decided in effect to
climb down under intense pressure and announced that in view
of the "solemn and binding undertaking" by the General Council the notorious Bill would be withdrawn. If the TUC ratified
the amendments made to the rules at Croydon "we should not
proceed with penal powers for the life of this Government".

The TUC undertaking applied only to Rule 11 which, with
Rule 12, gives the General Council the right to intervene in
disputes. At Croydon it was made clear that both official (that is
union-sanctioned) and unofficial strikes were covered by the
Rule; that a recalcitrant member union might be suspended from
the TUC if it did not observe the new procedure; and that the
General Council *would*, rather than might, intervene in every
serious unconstitutional strike.

On paper the TUC's Croydon commitment was undoubtedly an advance. In practice Britain's industrial relations have
deteriorated steadily ever since. Immediately after the Government's climb-down the Port Talbot steel men came out on a
six-week unofficial strike—followed in quick succession by the
dockers, the dustmen, the coal miners, and the underground
train guards. Meanwhile, almost every morning anew the key
motor industry was (and still is) disrupted by lightning unofficial
strikes which tend to throw out of work far more people than are
immediately concerned in the dispute.

Victor Feather, General Secretary of the TUC, was commendably active in his attempts to settle strikes of all kinds.
Sometimes he succeeded, as in the tangled case concerning Fleet
Street wage differentials in May 1969. More often the intervention of the TUC was ineffective, if not actually counter-

productive, as in the Pilkington glass works dispute of the same month.

It was in this situation that the Conservatives took office in 1970 unequivocally pledged to the reform of Britain's archaic industrial relations. It was obvious to all but the most obtuse, or those most interested in the preservation of the *status quo*, that things could not be allowed to continue as they were. The Conservatives at least have a carefully thought-out policy. There seems to be a good chance that it will work in practice. Robert Carr, then Shadow Minister of Employment and Productivity, in July 1969 put his finger on the fundamental weakness of the Croydon formula:

"The TUC's commitment is to be welcomed. It is an important gain. However, it cannot be enough on its own and the TUC's powers are nothing like equal to those minimum powers which the Government said were so urgently needed..."

Mrs Castle tried subsequently to tidy up the loose ends left by the collapse of her "In Place of Strife" approach. But her (revised) Industrial Relations Bill, published on 30 April 1970 and overtaken by the June election, was a mouse of a Bill. It would have changed nothing fundamentally and in some ways tipped the balance further in favour of the unions. In deference to the susceptibilities of the unions, legal sanctions of any sort were omitted. The battle lines were drawn for Robert Carr's attempt, at the Ministry of Employment and Productivity to get through Parliament his party's industrial relations proposals in the face of bitter opposition.

No one can possibly say in advance, of course, whether such a programme of reform, as Carr is the first to admit, would do the trick of making Britain's industrial relations as rational and orderly as those in other civilised countries at a similar stage of development. If it did not, the law would obviously have to be amended. But at least it is a programme and goes a good deal further, and contains more carefully thought-out ideas, than did Labour's "In Place of Strife". In particular, it puts more emphasis on legal processes and, as might be expected, less on the arbitrary intervention of the Government to ensure a proper conduct of industrial relations.

The objections to, and the difficulties of, in particular, making industrial contracts legally-binding are by now well known. Labour leaders have gone out of their way to taunt the

Tories with the possible draw-backs of this concept, even though only in 1969 they were proposing precisely that (albeit to be administered in a somewhat different way)! It was said, although the Tories put the onus of good behaviour on the unions, rather than on their members, that thousands of otherwise law-abiding trade unionists would have to go to gaol if the Conservatives' proposals were implemented. Would the prison building programme support such an influx? Alternatively, or in addition, the difficulties of deducting fines at source from workers' wages were said to be almost insuperable. This in a country which proudly boasts of having invented pay-as-you-earn!

There are times, indeed, when it seems that God speaks only to his latter-day Englishmen; that the writ of economic laws and codes of civilised conduct which apply elsewhere for some obscure reason does not apply in the offshore island. Thus in most countries the law makes a clear distinction between "lawful" and "unlawful" strikes and lock-outs. And those who incite or participate in unlawful strikes are held liable for their actions. In contrast, in Britain the law defines a "trade dispute" to cover an enormously wide range of circumstances, and then protects those involved from liability for loss or hardship caused to anyone else as a result of the dispute.

Similarly in most other industrial countries freely-negotiated contracts are binding on both sides (and why not when other contracts are?). Not surprisingly, "wildcat" strikes in breach of agreements are uncommon, and in some countries virtually non-existent, elsewhere. Yet in Britain they account for all but a twentieth of all strikes and their unpredictability, and often sheer wilfulness, cause serious disruption to highly-capitalised, mass production industry. Again, a "cooling off" period to delay or stop a strike or lock-out is quite common in other countries, and notably America. This, too, can have its snags, but surely almost anything is better than the present situation where major exporting industries can be disrupted overnight by unofficial unexpected, strikes? The harm these do to Britain in terms of broken delivery promises and lost (often for ever) goodwill is incalculable—but undoubtedly enormous.

There are, too, the great problems of union recognition and demarcation disputes. Britain, in this as in so many other ways, is still in a sense paying the price of being first in the field with its trade unions in the last century. Too many unions, not enough discipline, a lot of "poaching" of members between unions in

some industries, "leap-frogging" wage claims to maintain existing differentials—this is a formula for chaos. A classic example
was the dispute in the steel industry (appropriately if no doubt
fortuitously) just after the Labour Government's surrender on its
Industrial Relations Bill in the summer of 1969. It revolved
around whether or not the industry's white collar workers should
join the appropriate white collar or industrial union, and which
union for that purpose should be recognised by the management.
The dispute dragged on seemingly interminably, cost the British
Steel Corporation much money which it could ill afford to lose,
was settled inconclusively, and will no doubt erupt another day
in one form or another. The absence of recognised, democratic
procedures, for which not even the ubiquitous Victor Feather
was an adequate substitute, was never more apparent than at
that time. The Conservatives' proposals should go far to meet
this deficiency.

Yet the problem goes deeper than that. It really is, as has
been said, the structure of unionism itself which is badly at fault.
The absence of powerful centralised industrial unions is a profound structural weakness in the British economy. There have
been some mergers since then but not nearly enough. The model
for Britain should be I.G. Metall of Germany, or the United
Autoworkers of America—unions large, rich and well advised
enough to offer both workers and management a better deal. It
also happens, of course, that in their pursuit of plant bargaining,
of "picking off" individual factories one by one in their quest for
higher wages and better conditions, the American unions often
positively encourage higher productivity and profits: a far cry
indeed from Britain.

Surely Britain should model itself on Germany and America
in this respect. Here the multiplicity of unions in such industries
as steel and newspapers makes rational wage negotiations almost
impossible. The rectification of every ancient abuse, of every
unjustified, time-hallowed, wage differential only creates new
problems. The "injured" unions immediately spring to the
defence of their allegedly wronged members, and then after an
interminable dispute between, it may well be, the craft and
manual unions concerned, as often as not everyone eventually
goes back to square one. The whole process is irresistably
reminiscent of the card from the game of "Monopoly" which
curtly orders: "Go back to Go, do not collect £200" (your
wage differential).

It is, of course, easier to say that Britain has too many unions than to do anything practical about it, as George Woodcock learnt the hard way. The Conservatives' proposals on union recognition, or a development of them, might speed up the process of amalgamation. Could not the Government encourage on site elections at big plants to choose one of the many unions and then encourage employers to deal with the winner, which would then represent the whole factory? Such ideas need more careful thought before legislation or administrative action could be contemplated (enhanced powers for the TUC would obviously help in this respect: what price a new Croydon Declaration?).

Clearly, however, as in so many other spheres of Britain's industrial relations, things cannot be allowed to go on as they are. The nineteenth-century craft structure, and the loose federal on which it is based, is almost as inappropriate for rapid growth, retraining, technological development, automation, the need for wider differentials to encourage greater enterprise, and so on, as it is possible to be.

In the summer of 1970 the new Minister for Employment and Productivity, Robert Carr—soon acclaimed by the Press one of Heath's early successes—swiftly showed his mastery of the different aspects of Britain's industrial relations tangle. As important, he showed every sign of bracing himself for his personal Armageddon with the trade unions in the Fall when he duly introduced his controversial industrial relations proposals.

There were at first predictable but wholly inaccurate rumours—no doubt inspired, at least in part, by the unions themselves—that Conservative Ministers were preparing to climb down on the proposals enshrined on their party's tablets, "Fair Deal at Work". It seemed improbable. Heath had said repeatedly both before, during and after the June 1970 election that he was prepared to consult with, and listen to, the union leaders but that the essence of his party's industrial relations proposals was not negotiable. Carr followed this dictum to the letter, in so far as he could: the unions sulked in their tents, and sabre-rattled from afar.

Even so there were some relatively minor changes in the new Government's approach. Like the other para-State bodies, the Commission on Industrial Relations was in limbo immediately after the Conservatives' surprise election victory. But in early August Carr told the CIR to carry on as usual. Indeed, it seemed that the Commission, hitherto a voluntary body with no obvious effective purpose in life, was to be given "teeth". It would have powers to intervene in companies and industries which had records of labour troubles and unofficial strikes. The CIR's main task would still be investigation and conciliation. Like the Race Relations Board, it would investigate complaints and attempt to arrange a voluntary agreement between the disputants. But if that failed it would be able to on those concerned. There would be penalties for those who ignored the procedure imposed by the CIR.

Such a brief would be wide-ranging and substantial for an institution which was not even mentioned when "Fair Deal at Work" was published in 1968—for the good reason that it did not then exist. The Confederation of British Industry was unenthusiastic about such proposals. In their representations to Carr it had asked specifically for a strong Registrar of Trade Unions with the power to punish unions whose members kept striking unofficially. The Minister did indeed intend to establish a new Registrar, but did not envisage that he should supervise collective bargaining. He would act primarily as a kind of ombudsman dealing with complaints by individual trade unionists against their union. He would seek to ensure that union rules and elections were as democratic as possible—which in many cases had for long been far from the case.

Yet in a sense all this was by the way. Conservative Ministers were as determined as ever to stick to essentials and to bring Britain's chaotic industrial relations within the rule of common law. Their legislation, for which they had a clear electoral mandate, might, if the union chiefs were so minded, precipitate the worst industrial strife in Britain since the General Strike of 1926 (union militants, at the express disapproval of the TUC, early organised a series of one-day strikes against the Industrial Relations Bill). But the Conservative leaders knew that that was a risk they must take if Britain was ever to emerge from the tragic situation where, for instance, the motor industry was prostrate and idle at the drop of a spanner in some components factory.

Such a state of affairs, almost unique among civilised industrialised countries, was a clear formula for economic decline and atrophy. By seeking to exorcise it Tory leaders made amends for the locust-eaten years when they could have, but did not, tackle Britain's achilles heel.

In the event there were relatively few changes, and none of them of fundamental importance, from the "Fair Deal at Work" proposals evolved in opposition, in the Heath Government's Consultative Document and subsequent Industrial Relations Bill, published in December 1970. Robert Carr and his lieutenants had done their home-work thoroughly in opposition, and the officials at the Department of Employment and Productivity (now "of Employment" only) were clearly unable to fault their broad approach.

The most notable innovations in the Bill were: the new Registrar of Trade Unions would be empowered to make a complaint to the court if on investigation he believed that a workers' organisation seriously contravened statutory guiding principles, or persistently breached its registered rules; the right to make a binding order was reserved to the National Industrial Relations Court, rather than to Industrial Tribunals. In addition, bringing pressure on a person, to prevent or hinder him from exercising any right or performing any duty, and dominating or seeking to dominate a registered trade union, were no longer defined as unfair industrial action.

The first offence—experience abroad had been studied—proved incapable of a tight enough legal definition. The second could have been interpreted to cover almost anything; and in any case a union dominated by an employer would cease to qualify for registration. Ministers had successfully resisted two recommendations by the Confederation of British Industry: that the special power given to the Court to impose a procedure agreement when those concerned did not agree should extend to industry-wide agreements, as well as to those for individual "bargaining units"; that the Registrar should be able to initiate proceedings for breach of a legally-binding contract.

By accepting these proposed changes the Government would have tipped the balance of the Bill against organised labour. And individual employers would have thereby been able to avoid managing their own work-people on a clearly-defined basis. In effect they would have been able to hang on to the collective coat-tails of their employers' federation or of the Registrar.

There were obvious potential weaknesses in Robert Carr's

Bill. One was imprecise—perhaps inevitably so—definitions, such as the provisions on disclosure of information (see Appendix 2) "in accordance with good industrial relations practice". Only time and the evolution of a case law based on precedent and on a code of good practice would eliminate these ambiguities; Carr clearly recognised this.

The Bill also attacked in a strange way that notorious institution, the closed shop. It proposed that: no one should be obliged to belong to a union; but where the majority of workers wanted a particular union to negotiate on their behalf the minority, whether it belonged to that union or not, would have to accept it as a negotiating body; and those who did not wish to belong to a union might still be obliged to pay their dues; or, if that was contrary to their consciences, to commute the payment by a contribution of equivalent value to charity. These complicated proposals are designed to meet the point that workers should not be able to enjoy the advantages of trade union membership without at the same time accepting its obligations. They also predicate the much more doubtful and very British assumption that all workers must at almost any price maintain proletarian solidarity.

Yet these were but minor warts on the face of Cromwell. And Carr himself conceded that to the extent that his industrial relations proposals did not work in practice they would need to be amended in the light of experience. They were in effect, like so much else in the Heath Government's programme, an act of faith—that the British would react sensibly and positively, as they had so often reacted before, to a challenge, in this case to a civilised framework of behaviour for civilised men.

The passage of the Carr Bill was storm-tossed. Carr himself narrowly escaped assassination at home, although those concerned may have merely used his Bill as a *casus bellum*. The Government, probably wrongly but understandably, "guillotined" discussion of the Bill in the face of wrecking tactics by certain labour MPs. Barbara Castle spent many moons explaining, to almost no one's conviction, how Robert Carr's approach to reform was totally different to that which she had proposed in that (it seemed already) far distant summer. The TUC foolishly opposed the Bill root-and-branch. It more sensibly condemned the one-day "spontaneous" strikes against the Bill in the winter of 1970–71, strikes which disappointed the militants who organised them in that the response was much less than they had hoped for. Labour in Parliament eventually came round to more constructive criticism of the Bill's individual clauses, but its militant back-benchers caused uproar in the Commons. Labour was inhibited by the embarrassing legacy of the past, by the sheer hypocrisy of opposing tooth-and-nail something which in effect it had so recently espoused, and by the knowledge that public opinion, including trade unionists, was overwhelmingly behind the Government on the issue. And it was also inhibited by the fact that Barbara Castle herself was chosen by the Leader to oppose the Bill, backed largely by Labour MPs of trade union background. Under severe pressure from his union allies, Harold Wilson promised the improbable and unpopular, that a future Labour Government would repeal the Bill *in toto*. He would almost certainly come to regret this rash pledge. Meanwhile, the industrial relations saga had all the makings of a tragi-comedy for Labour—in roughly equal proportions.

CHAPTER THIRTEEN

A Certain Idea of Europe

There is also the historic issue of Europe. Although ostensibly not a decisive issue in that the leaderships of all three political parties have since 1967 been in favour of Britain entering the Common Market on "reasonable" terms, "Europe" has haunted the British political scene like the ghost of Banquo for nearly a decade.

It will probably continue to do so until the negotiations for the enlargement of the Market, which opened in Brussels in the summer of 1970, are brought to a successful conclusion—or otherwise. The French have so far kept to their word given to their five Market partners at The Hague in December 1969 that they would negotiate with Britain, Denmark, Norway, and Eire in good faith once the European Economic Community (in this context largely the Common Agricultural Policy) had been "completed" to their satisfaction and great advantage.

The Pompidou Government has not only kept faith; the signs are that it positively wants Britain to join the Market, if only because of its fear of Germany's growing economic might. The Germans realise what France's motives are, of course, and even welcome them. Herr Brandt has no reason to modify his long-standing wish to see the offshore island take, if belatedly, its rightful place in Europe. The German Government believes that a triumvirate of the three large European powers, Germany, France and Britain, would be more healthy for Europe, and evoke fewer suspicions among the smaller nations of the Community, than a condominium of Germany and France, until recently the historic enemies of a millennium.

Moreover, Italy, Holland, Belgium and Luxemburg (and, the polls suggest, the majority of Frenchmen) together with

Germany, want Britain in the Market for a variety of reasons. The sheer trade arguments of an enlarged Community are obvious. The division of the ancient States of Western Europe between Britain's scratch team of the European Free Trade Area and the European Economic Community is becoming an increasing embarrassment to all concerned, despite falling tariffs between them. It considerably weakens Europe's voice in world affairs. And Britain is wanted for her political stability, her experience, her justified reputation as a civilised society, and for her substantial economic and technological assets.

The wind from France, and from the Continent generally, is therefore more favourable for British entry than for many a day. For some time hopes have been rising all over Europe that despite all the disappointments of the past—Churchill's failure to justify the hopes he raised about a united Europe when in Opposition, Britain's failure to become a founder member of the pioneering European Coal and Steel Community, the death of the European Defence Community, two French vetoes on British Market entry—this great thing, the enlargement of the Community and the building of a new Europe, may yet be done.

It is not often that a nation has a third chance to rectify the mistakes of the past. Yet, almost miraculously, within a short time of the unexpected departure of General de Gaulle as President of France, the signs are that his successor looks benignly on the prospect of Britain joining the new Europe. Gone is all the talk of, in effect it being easier for a rich man to enter the kingdom of heaven, or for a camel to pass through the eye of a needle, than for Britain to enter the hallowed temples of the European Pantheon.

What then is the answer the British should give to the Six if as seems probable a deal for her entry is negotiated in 1971? What are the alternatives to her accession to the Treaty of Rome? Is the alternative to not entering Europe quite simply going it alone?

The British people will be forced, within the next year or two at the most, to answer these questions whose solution has been postponed for so long for a number of reasons; not least their own temperamental inclination to avoid difficult decisions and the granite, unyielding, disapproval of the General who for three decades dominated France, whether in or out of office. If the answer is "no", from this or the Continental side of the Channel, to British entry—which is quite possible: the chances of success can hardly be rated higher than 60–40 on—then the festering perennial post-war problem of "what to do about Britain" will in a sense be solved, albeit negatively, in this generation.

It has been said that Edward Heath, that "European" of long-standing, in private takes a relatively phlegmatic view of the success or otherwise of any particular approach to join the Market, on the grounds that in the long-run Britain's future must inevitably lie in Europe. No doubt that is right. But, as Lord Keynes said, in the long run we are all dead. It seems improbable that if there were to be yet another failure in negotiations for the enlargement of the Common Market, "Europe" would remain an issue in British politics in this generation. The Six would be disinclined to hold up any longer their plans for political union (including, it may well be, defence integration). And British public opinion would be disinclined, even more so than now, to face the possibility of further humiliations for a once great, and still considerable, power.

The re-opened negotiations in Brussels will therefore be critical for this country's economic and political future, and it could be also for its defence, for as far into the future as most people can hope to peer. They could be critical, too, for the age-old dream of Europe, "a certain idea of Europe" (to paraphrase President de Gaulle's famous phrase about France). That idea in a sense goes back two millennia, to Gibbon's "happiest state of man', the golden age of the Antonine Roman Emperors, when as he said, a man could walk from one side of the then civilised world to the other in peace.

That idea of Europe, which has never been fully understood on this side of the Channel, the British people may soon have to come to terms with at last. The completed customs union we now see twenty miles from our south coast is only the outward and visible sign of that idea—and the first step to building something greater and more enduring.

The idea embraces the legacy of two thousand years: Marcus Aurelius, Charlemagne, his sons who divided Europe, Byzantium based on Constantinople, which did the same, the majesty of the Roman Church and its offshoots, the latter-day despots such as Napoleon who have tried to dominate the Continent, and the founding fathers of the Common Market, de Gasperi, Adenauer, Schuman, who sought at Messina to lay for ever the blood feud of a thousand years between Frank and Teuton.

It is a civilisation, as well as a political concept, this idea. It is a civilisation which has provided, as it has fanned out across the seas to the new countries of the European diaspora, many of the good things, as well as some of the bad, of the world. It includes Beethoven, Michelangelo, Dante, the vineyards of the Dordogne, the castles on the Rhine, the splendour of the Alps, the Baroque churches of southern Germany, the Renaissance splendour of Florence, the sombre beauty of Edinburgh and the pastoral peacefulness of the Netherlands.

This is what Europe is about—not merely the dry figuring, the careful weighing of pros and cons in Command 4289, the Labour Government's White Paper "Britain and the European Communities", published in February 1970. These are the ideals enshrined or implied in the 1957 Treaty of Rome, with which the British must make their peace if they enter the Community. The chances are that they would so come to terms with "Europe", for they are an unusually adaptable race. And who can doubt that some adaptation, some change, is needed now?

It is not too fanciful to see the British, indeed, becoming great upholders of the Community's institutions after entry into the Market. Their traditional reluctance to learn Continental (though not Imperial) languages would no doubt perforce be changed in time. Their brilliant civil servants would play at least their part in running the complex Common Market Commission in Brussels. Their innate democratic instincts would persuade them that the Commission should be brought under the equivalent of Parliamentary control. Within a decade a British Minister in an embryonic European Government could be taking the floor in the Strasbourg Parliament to plead for direct elections of MPs to that Market's Parliament.

Why should Britain, if she can obtain reasonable terms, after a decade of frustration and successive disappointments, at last enter the Common Market? The question may on the face of it seem curious after so many years of public discussion, of endless weighing of the pros and cons, of many learned academic articles purporting to show that the economic arguments on either side were "evenly balanced". And in particular because the leaderships of all three political parties, with varying degrees of enthusiasm, are in favour of Britain undertaking this great adventure. Yet the British people have never been told frankly what issues are involved, and as a result most of them are both ill-informed and suspicious about what would be involved in Market membership. Hence it is necessary to look afresh at the issues involved.

It might be thought that the question was whether the longer-term by definition unknowable advantages of Britain entering an industrial tariff-free market outweigh the well-known disadvantages of the application of the Six's Common Agricultural Policy. It might also be thought that one might disagree about the emphasis to be put on one side or the other, but not about the issues involved.

Yet in the aftermath of the departure of President de Gaulle and the resulting much improved prospects for British entry to the Market, it has become apparent that that is not so even in the case of otherwise well-informed and well educated people. There is widespread uncertainty, fourteen years after the signature of the Treaty of Rome setting up the Common Market, and despite much discussion about, and publicity for and against, the formation of various other customs unions and free trade areas around the world, what it is Britain is being asked to do. Fears of higher food prices and a dearer cost of living generally, seem to be the main result of the "educational" efforts of the British Governments, Conservative and Labour, which have tried to negotiate their way into the Market in the last decade.

It is difficult to say whether this ignorance on such a major issue denotes more a failure of democracy itself or a failure of the political leaders who have happened to be in power in recent years. Nor is this the place to speculate at such a philosophical level. It is a good reason, however, for recapitulating, at the risk of boring certain readers, the issues involved in entry to Europe. No book on the mistakes (and successes) of past British economic policy and the alternatives open to this country in the future could possibly neglect a thorough discussion of the problems posed for Britain by the mere *existence* of the Common Market. Although the author believes that, if reasonable terms are available, as seems probable, then Britain should at last take her rightful place in Europe.

If we do not join, this country will be faced with a very difficult situation, discussed more fully in Chapters Fifteen and Sixteen. Much of that difficulty will be caused by the emergence of an economic, and in the future no doubt increasingly political, colossus twenty miles from Britain's south coast. If Western

Europe were still divided and fragmented into ancient nation states dating back to the Renaissance and Reformation and even earlier, then the problem would be much less acute—although there would be other problems in its stead. There would still be the difficulties caused by the relative inefficiency of the British economy and by the deep-seated xenophobia, conservatism and resistance to change of many British people. But British foreign policy could continue in its traditional way: maintaining a diplomatic balance in Europe and only intervening actively, if necessary militarily, when that balance collapsed. (It is certainly to the credit of the British Foreign Office that it has grasped, albeit belatedly, the implications for British diplomacy of the existence of the Market.)

Moreover, Britain's economic problems would be less acute if there were no Market. The Market has made the Six more dynamic, diverted trade from the outside world (including Britain) and in so doing made the offshore island's *relative* economic stagnation greater. Repeated attempts by Britain over almost a decade to join the Market have in addition, contributed to the further, but inevitable in the long run, weakening of her traditional trade links with the Commonwealth countries. This process, which is almost certainly irrevocable and irreversible, would have happened anyway. But a visitor, for instance, to Australia or New Zealand, Britain's allies in two world wars, is left in no doubt as to how unfavourably many people in those countries view her European aspirations. Which is not to say, of course, that in the long run the fact that those countries were encouraged, indeed forced, at last to consider themselves Asian nations was not a good thing: it probably was. Whatever the ethnic, historical and sentimental ties between Britain and Australia, it is inevitable, as Australia becomes more highly industrialised and a greater exporter of minerals, that she should find trading partners closer to home. And the withdrawal from East of Suez will make it even more difficult for Britain, from the other side of the world, to make joint defence arrangements with Australia.

So the issue is Europe for Britain or no Europe. There is no doubt that temperamentally as a nation we do not like matters to be put in such stark terms. As the point of decision approaches on whether or not Britain should irrevocably, for all time, link its destiny with the countries of the Continent, British "doubts" may increase further. It is, admittedly, as big a decision as any country has ever had to make in peacetime. How many of one's acquaintances, ostensibly long-standing "Europeans", lean over confidentially these days and mutter "Something you ought to know, I'm having doubts about Europe . . . unacceptable cost of the common agricultural policy . . . but in principle of course, we should still join" : not outright opposition, just doubt.

Yet nothing basic has changed recently except the proximity of the point of decision. It has been apparent for at least several years that there would be a significant short-term cost, in the shape of the CAP, for Britain to bear if she joined the Market: in a sense that is the price of dithering about Europe for so long. Devaluation has undoubtedly increased that cost, but the case for entry, and particularly the defence argument, has become stronger, too.

But the British, and perhaps particularly the educated British, reared in a classical tradition which makes a virtue of seeing all sides of a case (sometimes to the extent of complete paralysis of action), like to avoid committal if possible.

A major factor in the present situation *vis-à-vis* Europe is that Britain is herself trying to make up for lost time, as well as being asked to pay a price for her original dilatoriness. She stayed out of the Coal and Steel Community; virtually killed the European Defence Community by refusing to give France the guarantees she sought against a possible revanchiste Germany; failed in a futile attempt to superimpose a having-it-both-ways free trade area on the newly-formed Common Market; and, perhaps worst of all psychologically, bitterly disappointed her friends on the Continent by raising high hopes in the immediate post-war years when Churchill was in Opposition that a European lead would come from London, only to dash them when the great man returned to power.

After the founding ECSC, which sought to fuse the basic coal and steel industries of the historic enemies, France and Germany, came Euratom for the pooling of the Six's atomic energy resources and the phased programme (now completed) for establishing a customs union, and eventually a full economic union, under the Treaty of Rome. The founding fathers, such as Adenauer, Monnet, de Gasperi, Schumann, assumed that economic unity would one day lead to a loose political integration. The evolution of a customs union, with no tariffs between member States, was thought to have a dynamic of its own, which it was difficult if not impossible to reverse.

The experience of the earlier years after 1958, when the Common Market started, suggested that they were right. Before then the Six's economic growth rate had already been high, that is without the stimulus of a new, vast, market. But before 1958 those countries, which were largely devastated in the 1939–45 war, were merely making up for lost time and repairing the ravages of, for instance, an almost completely flattened Ruhr.

It was difficult to sustain this argument for much more than, say, fifteen years after the end of the Second World War. Yet between 1958 and 1968 industrial production in the European Economic Community increased by 80 per cent; and in Britain by 38 per cent. And in that same decade the gross national product of the Six expanded at an annual average rate of 5.1 per cent; of Britain at 3.2 per cent. Trade among the Six, mainly in manufactured goods, behind the barrier to the outside world of an external tariff moving towards uniformity, expanded at a rate far higher than the world average—by well over three times as rapidly in the 1958–1968 decade. Experience shows that even a relatively low tariff round a customs union, as the Six's was, can have a quite disproportionate effect in diverting trade towards those within "the laager". Yet the Six's exports to the outside world more than doubled in the 1958–68 decade, while Britain's increased by 55 per cent: so much for the Market being an allegedly inward-looking community.

Living standards approached, and in some cases such as Germany, starting virtually from scratch in 1945, overtook those of Britain. Capital investment, the harbinger of future growth, stimulated in part by the advent of new and wider opportunities in the Market, ran at levels far higher than in Britain. Tariff reductions between the Market's member States took place on time and were even accelerated. Remote and depressed areas of the Market, such as Sicily, received the largesse—a total of £120 million in 1968—of the European Investment Bank, as Scotland, Wales, Ulster and parts of the north of England may do one day. Hundreds of thousands of unemployed Italians travelled north and fanned out across a booming Europe in a successful search for work. The German economy, in particular (like the Swiss in the European Free Trade Area), benefited greatly from this addition to its labour supply.

Meanwhile, back in Brussels, polyglot, multi-lingual, multi-national bureaucrats beavered away, mainly in French, to keep the European show on the road. Putting up proposals to the

Market's Council of Ministers they had, and have, considerable freedom to evolve new plans for European integration. Until President de Gaulle insisted on the resignation of the German Chancellor Adenauer's friend, Professor Hallstein, first President of the Common Market Commission, for his too "European" visions of Europe, it seemed that the Eurocrats had almost cast-iron security of tenure. They could only be dismissed en bloc, by a two-thirds majority of the European Parliament—a most unlikely contingency.

Eventually the Eurocrat's beavering produced the notorious CAP, which—in some guise or other—has all along been regarded as essential to the establishment of a true and total customs union with complete freedom of movement of men, money, and materials within its boundaries. For the same reason a common monetary policy, and even a common monetary unit, a common transport policy, a common tax system, all have been regarded as essential if often long-term goals, on which relatively little progress has so far been made. But until the advent of the contentious and so far unsuccessful agricultural policy, and until the first veto on British entry to the Market, it seemed that the sky was the limit for "Europe".

Increasingly the ancient States of Western Europe made the pilgrimage to Brussels. Those outside the laager soon came to do penance, like some minor satraps before a Roman Emperor. Professor Hallstein received them, like a Head of State, in quasi-regal splendour (to which General de Gaulle particularly objected), as if at a latter-day Durbar. Greece, for instance, negotiated associate status which involved favourable access for her exports to the Market and a very long period of adjustment before her own economy would be exposed to the full blast of competition from the highly-developed economies of the Six.

But, after, and largely because of, the first unilateral French veto on British entry the Market lost much of its momentum; member States were much less inclined to trade their national interests against the greater good of the whole Community; the common policies already mentioned, plus notably a common commercial policy towards the outside world, seemed to be increasingly still-born; members quarrelled almost continuously about the need to enlarge it, and, to their eternal credit, the Dutch kept the name of Britain always before the Council of Ministers.

Yet the achievements of the Market remain impressive—far greater than many thought possible in little more than a decade—and there has been significant progress towards economic integration even in recent years. Much more is promised and probable since the successful Heads of State summit meeting at The Hague in December 1969.

There is now effectively free movement of labour within the Community. Thus the former Sicilian peasant working in the Ruhr is increasingly employed on equal terms with his German contemporary. Even so the Six are a long way from achieving the medium-term goal of complete mobility between countries in the professions owing to the difficulty of harmonising educational qualifications. And the free movement of people will require some harmonisation of social benefits so that people will not lose by moving between Market countries.

Euratom has never gained the original momentum of the other two Communities, the Market itself and the European Coal and Steel Community. Indeed, under President de Gaulle the French, reluctant to divulge to others their atomic secrets, deliberately emasculated the embryonic Community of its purpose: the co-ordination of peaceful atomic research within the Six.

The fusion in 1967 of the three Commissions of the Six's three Communities has done little to improve the prospects for Euratom and the ECSC. One suffers from inanimation, the other from the steady decline of coal production in Belgium and Germany in particular—as in Britain. Yet the experience of ECSC in co-ordinating production on a Europe-wide basis could in time be invaluable as the basis for integrating the Community's basic industry and energy policies.

A common anti-trust policy is critical to the future development of the Market. In so far as modern mass-production industry and technology has outgrown the nation-State, there is room for only one ICI, Guest Keen and Nettlefolds or British Leyland to operate within the British market: but there could be scope for several within a market of ten or more nations (see Chapter Eight).

The Commission in Brussels is in principle in favour of mergers, if only to withstand the American economic assault on Europe. But it is also concerned that firms such as Fiat should not continue to enjoy such dominant positions in their own regions of the Market. In the longer run they may be an

insoluble dilemma here for the Commission and the High Court
in Luxemburg which administer and police the Market's laws
on restrictive practices. There is also the problem of the elim-
ination of non-tariff barriers to trade. Although internal tariff
barriers to trade have gone, such intangibles as differing road
safety regulations, technical standards, quarantine rules and
excise duties, are still important obstacles to the free movement
of goods.

In the past, until the 1969 Hague meeting at which the
French agreed in principle to the enlargement of the Market,
there was little prospect of further rapid development of integration between the Six unless the candidate States were
allowed to join. That is no longer so. If Britain fails to join
now, it may be because of the high cost of the CAP, or the
hostility of British public opinion, or both. But whatever the
reason, the Six will go ahead without her in developing the
Market into some form of political union. Such a course would
be a *pis aller* for many on the Continent, and especially for the
Netherlands, as it would be for Britain, but it would be clear in
such a situation, both on the Continent and here, that British
entry was not a practical possibility in this generation and
perhaps never. As Edward Heath rightly said in Paris in May
1970, neither side would want to try yet again in the foreseeable
future.

Enlargement of the Market is critical for the Six as well as
for Britain. This makes it all the more important that the
arguments in favour of British entry, now that another opportunity to join has come unexpectedly, are clearly understood at
last in this country. It is to be hoped that, if and when an
acceptable deal is on offer from the Six, Ministers will go out
into the country as they have never done before and deploy the
case for joining with all the strength they can muster. Geoffrey
Rippon, Britain's negotiator in Brussels, has already showed a
commendable impatience to do just that. There is little doubt
that much of the present British hostility to going into Europe,
apart from a natural fear of the unknown and an equally
understandable fear about the higher cost of living in the
Market, reflects understandable resentment at repeated humiliations for Britain in her belated attempts to join the Market.

For that reason Harold Wilson deserves credit for having
steadfastly maintained as Prime Minister his application to join
the Market when it would have been so easy, and so electorally

popular, to have "forgotten" about it; and Heath, as leader of
the Opposition, for as steadfastly supporting him in this in the
years since the second Gaullist veto of 1967. But if it became
clear that the Six were offering Britain reasonable terms, especially on the agricultural issue; that food prices would not rise as
much and as rapidly as many now fear; and that no more vetoes
and humiliations were in prospect; and if Ministers clearly
explained the case for Market entry in the country; then the
swing back of opinion could be as dramatic as was the falling
away in public support for entry in 1969–70. The opinion polls
show that even now, when the Market is ostensibly unpopular,
most people (and especially young people) regard eventual
Market entry as inevitable. And the signs are that *in principle*
they approve of this prospect. Nor is this surprising in that young
people, who have so many more opportunities to eat foreign
food, to consume foreign wine, to wear foreign clothes and to
travel are more outward-looking in their view of the world than
are their parents.

What then is the case for British entry that should be
deployed if and when the point of decision is reached? Many
pundits have long argued that the economic arguments for and
against British entry into the Common Market are evenly
balanced (this comfortable conclusion may chime well with the
British penchant for fence-sitting, but is hardly helpful to actual
decision-making), and the final decision is therefore solely a
political one. Times change. So do myths. At the time of the first
application to join the Market nearly a decade ago we were told
that the economic case for joining was powerful but that politics
hardly entered into the matter (the Six were perforce told
something rather different).

If the arguments for and against were indeed exactly evenly
balanced it would certainly be a statistical fluke scarcely known
to higher mathematics, a one in ten million chance, perhaps. It
would be more accurate to say that the short-term cost of Britain
entering the Common Market is more easily calculated—
although nothing like as definitely as the opponents of British
entry would have us believe—than the longer-term benefits.
Entry would be an act of faith: that over a period the enormous
considerable reserves of talent, intelligence, education, and
innate common sense in Britain will respond to the challege of
the changed environment which membership of the Common
Market would bring. In this wider sense the British approach to

Europe is indeed a political decision on a par with declaring war or making peace, or leaving India in 1947. If Britain joins in the journey to a new kind of Europe it will be a supreme adventure with no certainty about which port she will eventually reach but many challenges and opportunities along the way.

There will also be many uncertainties, however, if Britain does not join the Market. What is certain is that if Britain failed for a third, and probably last, time to join Europe, she would find herself in an extremely exposed position, which is analysed in more detail in Chapters Fifteen and Sixteen. Apart from Japan, which is a special case, if only because of her remarkable specialisation in certain lucrative export industries, Britain would be the only major industrialised country without access to a large home market.

So it is essential to compare the probable position of Britain in, say, 1980 as a member of the Common Market with her likely situation as a non-member *in the same year*. And yet it is common, notably in calculations about the short-term cost of the Six's notorious Common Agricultural Policy, to compare Britain's economic state in the earlier years of membership with her position *now*. The whole exercise of computing the cost of "Europe" is essentially dynamic. The cost of food would certainly increase substantially. But it will do so in any case, although to a lesser extent, if only because of the insupportable cost of deficiency payments to British farmers, and the fact that the Conservatives are set on changing over from deficiency payments to import tariffs which cost the taxpayer less and the consumer more.

The Conservative plans to phase out deficiency payments, and thereby save the Exchequer some £250 million a year, are likely to raise the cost of food by 5 to 6 per cent, and hence the overall cost of living by about $1\frac{1}{2}$ per cent. This would be spread over the transitional period of three years and hence would average about $\frac{1}{2}$ per cent a year. This compares with an average annual increase of nearly $4\frac{1}{2}$ per cent since 1964.

At the end of 1969 the Confederation of British Industry published an appraisal of the effects on British industry on Market entry (the report was broadly in favour of entry). The CBI gave the *maximum* likely increase in food prices at 18 per cent, equivalent to a rise of 4 per cent in the cost of living. The European Economic Community Commission in Brussels has put the figure rather lower, at 12–15 per cent for the increase in the price of food, or 3–3½ per cent on the cost of living. I contrast, the British Government in its White Paper, "Britain and the European Communities—An Economic Assessment", estimated that the increase in food prices might be 18–26 per cent, that is an extra 4–5 per cent on the cost of living (of which 1½ per cent will take place in any case under the Government's proposals for agriculture).

These estimates all assume that in an enlarged Community prices will remain at existing levels. This seems unlikely in view of the pressure on West Germany from her Market partners (including notably and perhaps surprisingly in British eyes, the French) for a reduction of prices. But the increase in food prices involved in British entry into Europe would be bound to be substantial. It underlines the need for this country to have a transitional period of the five years which Rippon has negotiated, in order that the British farmer and the British housewife may have a reasonable time in which to adjust to the implications of the CAP.

The White Paper said that the change in the food import bill could range from a reduction of £85 million a year, in that higher prices could stimulate even higher productivity and output in British agriculture, to an increase of £225 million a year, depending on how British producers and consumers reacted to changed price levels and what those levels were. In addition there would be the cost of contributing to the Market's Agricultural Fund, which might range from between £150 million a year and, most improbably, £670 million a year. The White Paper did not put much faith in its own estimate—rightly so—and indeed it is doubtful whether the exercise had any validity at all.

Certainly it alarmed the doubters on the Common Market issue, not to mention the housewives, unduly with its vague estimates. Yet the Prime Minister rashly promised to produce the White Paper under pressure from the anti-Marketeers at the 1969 Labour Party conference in the vain hope of taking the wind out of their sails! Predictably, they paid little attention (why should they?) to the White Paper's bald statement that: "in the crucial area of our financial contribution to the Fund, there is just not a sufficient basis ... for making reliable assessments either about its cost or our share of it".

However, a working paper submitted to Brussels by the new Conservative Government put the probable balance of payments cost of the CAP to Britain as somewhat lower than had Labour's White Paper.

The CBI was both more specific and more realistic in pointing out that the cost of the CAP to Britain would not be a constant factor—and indeed would fluctuate considerably over a fairly long period. This it implied a range of £150 million to £450 million a year for the cost of this country's contribution to the Fund at its peak in 1977. This would fall away to £100 million to £200 million a year in the 1980's. All these calculations assume that the CAP would be applied as it stands, and they emphasise the need to negotiate a limit (a not impossible task, given good will) to Britain's contribution. This is already implicit in the Six's rules, but Rippon has rightly asked the Six to put it in writing in order to reasure British public opinion.

Dr Tim Josling, a London School of Economics expert on the CAP, in an article in the *Daily Telegraph* in November 1969, pointed out that: "The real loss to the country is threefold: one, the loss due to employing more resources in agriculture than would otherwise be warranted; two, the loss due to the distortion in relative prices of food and other products; and, three, the loss due to net transfer payments to other countries, in the form of receipts from the variable levies and higher prices for Continental food supplies. In addition, there could be serious income losses if the balance-of-payments cost forced the country into a policy of deflation."

He put the two first "efficiency" losses in the order of £35 million and the third, or "transfer", loss at another £200 million a year. Writing before the publication of the Government's White Paper, he thought that the increase in the cost of living for the average family would be about 16s. a week; but against that there should be set the possibility of reducing income tax by about 9d. off the standard rate—or the equivalent distributed in other ways. Josling was somewhat depressed, but by no means overwhelmed, by such calculations. He concluded that the foreign exchange cost arising from the CAP would necessitate, other things being equal (which they seldom are in economics), a 2 per cent depreciation of sterling if Britain was not to place on the Community the burden of a weak currency. His preference in such a situation was a more flexible exchange rate for the pound. He thought that the net cost to the consumer of the CAP would be less than 1 per cent of the gross national product, or the equivalent of about four months' growth in income (on the basis of the White

Paper's upper estimates these figures would be somewhat higher). He concluded: "However much we might dislike the excesses of the CAP, we can certainly afford to join the Common Market if we wish."

What then are the industrial advantages that override these drawbacks of the CAP? And of some marginal damage to Britain's declining trade with her traditional Commonwealth trading partners (the Six have agreed in principle that New Zealand should be treated as a special case)? And of the "impact" effect of tariff changes on the industrial side (such as higher imports of industrial goods) which the White Paper put at £125 million—£250 million? The White Paper spoke truly, if obviously, when it said that: "The main consequences of membership for British industry are . . . that the 'home market' will be several times larger than our existing home market, including EFTA, and the new home market will be a more rapidly growing one than the present home market." Moreover, Market entry would encourage the rationalisation of production of British industry, greater specialisation, and a higher rate of capital investment, leading to a much-needed higher economic growth rate. The White Paper in effect agreed with the CBI report in concluding that these largely unquantifiable benefits of membership should exceed in the long run the more immediate (and largely agricultural) cost of joining.

The "industrial case" for British entry to the Market turns largely on the fact that trade in manufactured goods between highly industrialised countries—particularly so within the Community, but elsewhere too—has risen far more rapidly than world trade as a whole. And there is no sign whatever of this changing in the foreseeable future. Yet trade between those rich countries and the much poorer producers of food, commodities and raw materials is relatively static: witness the steadily declining share of Britain's trade accounted for by the Commonwealth.

Thus it is not surprising that, for instance, Lord Stokes of British Leyland (although even he was shaken by the Government White Paper's CAP figuring), and indeed most of the motor and motor components industries, are anxious to get into the Market as soon as possible. This despite the fact that soon after entry they would experience much greater competition from foreign imports, buoyant even now, in their home market. Which is a large part, of course, of the economic case for British entry: that it would give British industry an overdue shake-up. In the long run, if British firms cannot survive in the Market, where will they prosper? Significantly, with few exceptions the larger members of the CBI are strongly in favour of Market entry, and most of the smaller firms are in varying degrees in favour also. Their attitude is in sharp contrast to many carefully doubting, "evenly balanced" academic economists. The industrialists know how important are the dynamic opportunities thrown up by a market of 250 million people or more; how essential are long production runs in modern, advanced, manufacturing; and how harmful to our exports, how discriminatory, is even a barrier as low as the Market's external tariff as long as Britain is outside it.

The problem is urgent. The motor industry, which is vital to Britain's economic survival, is now in serious straits as a result of successive freezes and squeezes on the home market, superimposed on endless lightning unofficial strikes. A low volume of production, in an industry which must quite fully utilise its capacity to make any profits at all, is forcing car manufacturers to put up their prices rapidly in order to recoup their vast capital investment costs. British Leyland made a derisory profit in 1970. Car exports are likely over a period to suffer relative to their international competitors unless they can find new, compensating, opportunities.

It is sometimes argued that the relative success of the Kennedy Round tariff cuts makes our entry into the Market less urgent. Clearly to the extent that the Market's external tariff is now being reduced over a number of years it is becoming less of a barrier to the outside world. (The Market's common external tariff, uniform to the outside world, is on average only 8 per cent, a good deal less than Britain's average tariff.) Yet the psychological effect of one vast unified market with no tariff barriers whatsoever between the members of the Six is enormous. And the diversionary effects of even quite a modest unified external tariff—diversionary, that is, of trade from the outside world to those within the laager—can be considerable.

The purely trade argument, moreover, ignores the sheer scale of modern technology, which has outgrown the nation State as we have known it. The development costs of the Concorde airliner, which have already run into hundreds of millions of pounds for both France and Britain and escalate almost monthly, are proving to be on any rational economic grounds too much for even both countries combined. The production of modern aircraft, nuclear power, computers and the other advanced products on which Britain's economic future must turn needs an enormous, continent-wide, market and the investment resources of several nations to be viable.

For this reason Harold Wilson's 1967 technological Community for Europe—to be grafted on to the existing Brussels Communities, with the (combined) Commission to administer them?—was one of his best ideas, ill thought-out though it was in detail. The relative strength of Britain's advanced technology compared with the Six's, and the sheer size and efficiency of her large companies are powerful, if only implicit, cards to play in Brussels. Moreover, the scale of modern advanced technology has a major bearing on another burning, highly topical issue, which so much distressed, in particular, President de Gaulle: investment from third countries, outside the Market, and in particular America. It can be argued, of course, that American investment in Europe, and certainly in this country, has done little but good. By and large the American companies in Britain are unusually well-managed, profitable, and forward-looking (their average return on assets is about double the average for British companies).

Yet there must be a danger that, in the longer run, if vast American companies came to own much, if not conceivably most, of European industry, their subsidiaries here would indulge in a form of "economic helotry". European firms might well in effect become hewers of wood and drawers of water, producing the relatively unsophisticated products which did not interest the parent American companies. This is much less likely to happen if Western Europe becomes one vast unified market— soon. And also the danger that American companies would increasingly by-pass this country if she stayed outside the Market would be correspondingly reduced. It is relevant that at the beginning of the 1960's, American investment in Britain was more than that in all the Market countries combined. The balance since then has tipped very much in the Six's favour: the figure for the Market even in 1967 was about $84.05 million, and for Britain around $61.01 million. Moreover, large British companies such as Imperial Chemical Industries which have sought to by-pass the common external tariff of the Six by heavy investment on the Continent are not now, through no fault of their own, doing much to increase employment opportunities in Britain.

The recent dramatic improvement in Britain's "invisible"

trade balance—earnings from shipping, insurance, banking, broking and so on—must also be taken as a good omen for Britain's long-term chances in Europe. If she can do so well with her invisibles when still outside the Market (and the remarkable growth from scratch of the City's Euro-dollar market in a few short years must be rated a striking tribute to Britain's financial "know-how") then how much better still might she do as a member? The capital markets of the Continent, although improving, are on the whole puny compared with the City. Is it too fanciful to see London as one day the financial "capital" of an integrated Europe? Probably not.

There are several factors to be weighed in the Market balance. Against the increase in the cost of food if Britain joined would be a significant reduction in the prices of manufactured goods from the Continent. Thus, for example, Italian refrigerators, German cars, Belgian cake-mixers, and even French wine (although its high cost in Britain is largely accounted for by a high Excise duty rather than a tariff) should all be significantly cheaper if Britain went into Europe. This could amount to perhaps 2 per cent off the cost of living over the transitional period of several years.

To the cost of the CAP there must be added probably some (unpredictable) net outflow of capital as Britain perforce liberalised her investment policies *vis-à-vis* her new Market partners. It is probable, too, that imports might expand more rapidly than exports in the earlier years of British membership: again much would turn on the details of the transitional arrangements. Britain would also lose, of course, most of the residual tariff preferences with Commonwealth countries.

But, whatever the precise detailed calculations about the pros and cons of British entry to the Market—which by definition are bound to be inconclusive, and can only be proved or disproved by experience—the industrial, and therefore overall economic, case for British entry is simple. It is that over, say, thirty years the industrial benefits of entry should greatly exceed the more immediate disadvantages of the common agricultural policy, which in any case will almost certainly be modified by the Six themselves, and also tempered to Britain's interests if she joins them (after she joined Britain would have as much say as any country in amending the CAP). To argue otherwise is, in a sense, to take an unjustifiably gloomy view of this country's potential. For if Britain cannot hold her own in one of the world's largest and most dynamic areas of economic growth, comprising countries at a similar stage of development and extending to within twenty miles of her shores, then where precisely can she prosper?

Now at last all the Six want Britain in the Market as long as she genuinely adheres to the "European" ideas enshrined in the Treaty of Rome, and as long as France receives her "pound of flesh" on agriculture. Such a situation may not last for long. This chance for Britain may not come again. The opportunities offered by going into Europe would be immense and should be firmly grasped if, the terms available to Britain are reasonable.

CHAPTER FOURTEEN

Not so much an Economic Community . . .

More important than all the economic arguments about whether
or not Britain should join in building a new Europe must be the
defence and political issues. All the signs are that the Americans,
who have defended Western Europe for a quarter of a century,
and who learnt so well the lessons of the 1930's that equivo-
cation and cowardice lead to war, are in a mood for withdrawal
from her far-flung post-war commitments. They are tired of continuous abuse and ingratitude; some are even bitter. They feel
strongly that Western Europe should take on a much higher
proportion of the cost of defending itself. They are not so
impressed by the lesson of Czechoslovakia that Russian Communism is unregenerate as to conclude that they should go on
bearing an unduly high proportion of the cost of NATO defence.
This is so even though it has, of course, also been in America's
self-interest to defend Western Europe. Not surprisingly, in their
present mood Americans feel about Europeans: "if they won't
help themselves, let them stew".

There is, too, of course, the enormous cost to America of
maintaining a multiplicity of bases, guns, ships, nuclear weapons,
missiles, satellites and so on around the world. The 1968–70
mini-depression and the Wall Street mini-crash (which have
given many Americans for the first time an intimation of economic mortality, if not of a 1929–31 slump), the American Budget
and balance of payments deficits, the 1969 revaluation of the
German D-Mark, the devaluation of the French franc: all have
been timely reminders that the dollar is now among the first in
the firing-line come the next international monetary crisis.

All these factors encourage a continuing military withdrawal from Europe, as from Vietnam. The signs are there for

all to see, although America's NATO partners are apparently not anxious to see them. President Nixon has already hinted strongly that as far as the American commitment to Europe is concerned, nothing is sacrosanct after 1971. To the extent that the nations of Western Europe are not looking to their own defences, while there is still time, the 1970's could be a repetition of the 1930's. There are many who argue that Russia has fundamentally changed her spots; that, despite the rape of Czechoslovakia, she has achieved her last territorial ambition in Europe. That remains to be seen. Meanwhile, it will not have escaped an older generation that recalls the wasted years of appeasement of Nazi Germany that Russia has only climbed down when she has been met by firmness—as in Berlin or in Cuba. Russia *seems* to be more beneficent than she was in Stalin's day. But may that not be precisely because of the world-wide system of alliances America has so laboriously built, backed by her nuclear deterrent? It is true, of course, that the present regime in Russia is a good deal less "hard-line" than was Stalin's, and that it has relatively new preoccupations on its frontier with China.

Yet the price of Western Europe making a miscalculation about the intentions of Russia (and in the longer run of China) could be disastrous as America brings home her beleaguered legions from the Rhine. A new, deeply pacific mood in Russia can hardly be taken on trust along the borders of her East European empire. Moreover, it is not only the fact that America is tired of defending the ungrateful and complacent nations of Western Europe which argues that they should look to their defences. For the balance of power itself between Russia and America has changed, and is changing rapidly, to the latter's disadvantage.

The expansion of the Red Fleet in the Mediterranean is both obvious and ominous. At the same time Russia has achieved in the last decade a remarkable all-round expansion of military strength. Her land forces and those of her Warsaw Pact allies are far greater than those of NATO. Moreover, they are better trained, have more reserves, command the central positions in Europe, have shorter lines of communication, enjoy standard equipment, and have no problems about security, public opinion or moral scruples in their closed societies. Within a few days in a conventional war (that is, where nuclear weapons were not used) the Russian and Warsaw Pact armies could be on the Rhine. And, leaving aside the moral issue, how could the countries of Western Europe, in the aftermath of an American withdrawal, redress the balance with nuclear weapons even if they wanted to? They do not have the wherewithal in either conventional or nuclear weapons to take on the might of the Communist countries. They have nothing remotely to compare with the Russian and American deterrents. And in terms of national income they have cut their military budgets to about half that of America. As a result they now depend totally on American nuclear weapons for their strategic defence.

"Graduated deterrence", once the fashionable catch-phrase of NATO defence, is no longer credible. Owing to the gross inadequacy of NATO's conventional forces, America has neither the time nor depth in which to manoeuvre and so mount a gradually escalating defence effort. Thus if the Russians were to launch a major attack, America would be faced with the stark choice of either initiating a nuclear Armageddon or abandoning Europe. Not surprisingly, in this situation, America is anxious to reduce as much as possible the danger of a nuclear confrontation by an agreement with Russia. Hence the "SALT" (Strategic Arms Limitation Talks) on nuclear weapons in Helsinki which have pointedly excluded the mini-nuclear powers, France and Britain. Clearly Russia is seeking to sow disunity—greater than already exists—between the West European nations with her proposed "European Security Conference".

What then is to be done? The hour is late and the night far spent. It may be that Western Europe no longer wants seriously to defend itself, or believes that any need to do so passed long ago. But on the assumptions that the values of Western society are worth preserving, and that Russia's rapid expansion of her military might has some significance, certain things need to be done quickly.

For a start, the politicians of Western Europe will have to start admitting that there is a problem. Indeed they will have to point out for the first time what the problem is. Our own Denis Healey as Minister of Defence, having withdrawn at short notice, and in the face of specific pledges to the contrary, from so many of our overseas commitments, would have had to point out, had he stayed in office, that the buck stops at least in Europe. No doubt (see Chapter Two) much of Britain's withdrawal from her post-imperial commitments, if not the actual way it was done, was inevitable in the long run. But the case for maintaining her legions on the Rhine is quite a different matter and concerns her survival as a nation. It is inconceivable, in the strategy of modern nuclear, or even conventional, war that Britain could ever again hold out on her own, the beleaguered but unbowed island fortress, while Continental Europe was over-run. In any case her military effort was so run down by a Labour Government which actually boasted that it spent more on "welfare" than it did on defence, that she could be brought to her knees in a morning (as Holland was in 1940 by Germany) by a super-power intent on brandishing its nuclear armoury.

To the task, then, to the toil. As the American military withdrawal from Europe—long forecast and long encouraged by President de Gaulle: the ultimate in self-fulfilling prophecies—continues apace, Europe must look speedily to her own defences. There will need to be a rapid programme of military integration, a build up of conventional forces (it might even be necessary, despite its great wastefulness, to reconsider conscription in Britain), and the creation of a European nuclear deterrent. Its embryo already exists in the shape of the British and French mini-deterrents. On their own these will not retain what credibility they still have for much longer. The rate of their "built-in" obsolescence is too great for that, the financial and technical resources of Britain and France are separately, or even together, too limited for that.

France seems interested in a possible European defence deal. The prospect of what Britain and France, historic enemies until the Entente Cordiale of 1904, could do together in the world seems indeed to have been an important factor in the marked softening of the Pompidou Government's attitude to British entry to the Market. A European "technological community" could make a worthwhile start on the integration of France and Britain's military "hardware". And the precedent of Anglo-French co-operation on the Concorde airliner, expensive though it is, should be valuable if Britain and France decide to merge their technological destinies. Moreover, if only to lighten her own burden, America would amost certainly provide technical and military backing for her NATO allies' efforts to build a Western European Defence Community. American nuclear weapons are in any case already, under the "two-key system," dispersed around the Western European flank of NATO.

It would be essential for Britain and France to retain their vetoes while proper control arrangements for the new Community were worked out. They would no doubt insist on this in any case. And by so doing they would avoid infringement of the Non-Proliferation Treaty, which would in effect prohibit present non-nuclear NATO countries from individual control of the new combined deterrent. Then in time, and the sooner the better, common Community foreign and defence authorities could take over direction of this European deterrent from the founder nations.

There was a time, not long ago, when it was possible to argue credibly, if not wholly convincingly (for it mortgaged an uncertain future too much) that it was unnecessary for Western Europe to duplicate in any way America's vast defence effort. And it remains true that in an ideal world President Kennedy's vision of a "dumb-bell" Grand Alliance of America and Europe, co-equal and yet inter-dependent, would be the safest, the cheapest and the best. But in a dangerous and far-from-perfect world America's desire to withdraw much, if not most, of her conventional forces and nuclear umbrella from Western Europe must be taken as given. Those European countries—battle-scarred, historically divided, and complacent in peace time, but the common heirs of a common civilisation, of Marcus Aurelius, Charlemagne and Napoleon—must now make a great effort to defend themselves properly or risk fluctuating between the status of an insecure American satellite and Russian blackmail.

What sort of new authority would control a Western European deterrent? The Six are committed to common defence and foreign policies and, since the 1969 Hague Summit meeting, it seems only a matter of time before they achieve them, with or without Britain. The Common Market was after all from the beginning designed to prevent war between European countries, many of whom were traditional enemies; and to decrease the possibility of intimidation from the East by building up and uniting Western Europe's strength. It was hoped, too, that a successful Market might attract one day the beleaguered States of Eastern Europe. And there were those who, like General de Gaulle, dreamt of one Europe from Shannon to the Urals.

It is a truism that no great thing is achieved without effort and in this case the difficulties are undeniable. The "Community" method of uniting nations is after all new, and so far unique, in history. There have been plenty of federations before, many of them unsuccessful, as the British have demonstrated in the wake of their imperial withdrawal. But they have usually concerned, as at Annapolis where the American founding fathers gathered, relatively new political units or not long-established nation States. For this reason alone many have claimed, particularly in Britain (consistently wrongly so far concerning the limited amount of integration already achieved), that uniting Europe, with its different languages, cultures and traditions, in any degree was impossible. It had been done in Switzerland, it was true, but that was an inconvenient "exception" which, strangely enough, "proved the rule".

A new Political Community, which might be synonymous with the existing Economic Community, and a new Defence Community, would enable the countries of Western Europe to speak with one voice in world affairs. Successive crises of the 1960's such as Cuba, Berlin, Indo-China and the Middle East, have surely shown conclusively that the industrial States of Western Europe scarcely count for a fig in the counsels of the super-powers.

The British Foreign Office, it is true, has a "view" on almost every known world issue from Biafra to Tashkent, and successive British Prime Ministers have flaunted their alleged cosy "hot line" relationship with Washington. But such attitudes have told their allies and enemies more about the British in their present uncertain and confused state than about the great climacteric issues which they are supposed to be "influencing". At times, such as the 1965 Commonwealth Peace Mission to Hanoi such posturing on the world stage has bordered on the pathetic. "Upon what meat doth this our Caesar feed that he is grown so great?" Yet, to be fair, there has been a growing realisation that this is so in Britain, and the Foreign Office in particular has been steadfast over nearly a decade in seeking to find a new role against the wider European back-cloth. Its opportunity may soon come at last—but it will have to face formidable difficulties and problems of adjustment, as will we the British people.

Possibly the "hottest" political issues in Britain soon after Market membership would be: can a European central government authority be created (and if so how) so that if the combined Western European nuclear armoury has to be used, would there be one, or six, or ten, or even more fingers on the trigger? Just how big can a safety-catch be? Can such an authority be created without building in the process a fully-fledged super-state, a United States of Europe such as does not at the moment endear itself to the British?

A compromise is possible which, in the short-term at least and in the manner of the Market, might well be all things to all men—depending on how they thought it would eventually develop. It might be done by reviving parts of the old plan for a European Army in a European Defence Community. The French, with British assistance, killed it but the Pompidou Government is much better disposed towards the concept than was its predecessor. There would then be a new European Political Community, or union of States, with some kind of central Ministerial authority to merge finance, defence, technology and foreign policy. This would emerge over a period and there would be safeguards and balances to ensure that no State, and especially not a smaller one like Luxembourg, was submerged or over-ruled on matters which it regarded as of vital national importance.

"Community", an accurate description of the Common Market as it is now is thought to be a more acceptable and more intelligible term than the dread words federal or con-federal (whatever the latter means in practice). After the EDC idea was killed and the EEC rose phoenix-like from its ashes, the idealists who met at Messina to negotiate the founding Treaty of Rome argued that in order to persuade the member States of the proposed Common Market to get used to working together in such important fields as foreign policy, technology and defence they should start with trade and industry. Thus by a remorseless historical process, which would brook no reversal once under way, one thing would lead to another and a political community would be grafted on to the European Community's existing economic institutions.

With the departure of President de Gaulle and since the 1969 Hague meeting which, thanks largely to Chancellor Brandt of Germany, gave the whole European movement a big and overdue boost, the time has almost come to achieve that grafting. It will probably wait for the success or failure of the negotiations to enlarge the Community—but no longer.

There could be a new European Political Commission. Or, perhaps more likely, since the old Euratom and Iron Coal and Steel Communities have already been merged with the EEC, the existing European Economic Commission could expand into important new fields. It is certainly straining at the leash, like a greyhound in the slips, to do this. It now prepares and executes policy in the economic and industrial fields and cajoles, and if necessary forces, the Council of Ministers of the Six to make decisions. Both the Commission and the Council could be given similar powers to prepare and apply foreign and defence policies.

Such developments would need democratic safeguards, of course. And ironically in view of all their past hesitations about a "political" Europe, the British would probably be the first to insist on them. There is already a European Court of Justice in Luxembourg to see fair play and to ensure that the member States, the Market institutions themselves, and individual companies, all abide by the dictates of the Treaty of Rome. Its jurisdiction will almost certainly have to be extended as economic union develops in any case. So its further extension to politics and defence would be a matter of degree rather than of principle. Moreover, the Treaty decreed that there should also be eventually a directly-elected European Parliament to watch over the European institutions and ultimately to legislate for the whole of Europe if the other countries had by then joined the Community. President de Gaulle much disliked this concept and succeeded during his time in ensuring that the Brussels Eurocrats were no more than bureaucrats; and that the European Parliament continued to be nominated by member Governments (with Communists barred) and to have few effective powers except that of dismissing the whole Commission, and only then *in extremis*.

The British are being consulted during the negotiations for Market entry on further moves towards integration, if not as fully as they had hoped, on French insistence. If the negotiations seem to be heading for success, and certainly after their completion, the new Ten will have some difficult decisions to take. It could soon be agreed that the Council of Ministers will meet regularly as a supreme political council. This would take joint decisions on foreign affairs and on the building of a new political Community. In foreign economic affairs, in such matters as tariff reductions, and relations with America and much of Africa, the Six already speak to the world with one voice. And behind Herr Brandt's "Ostpolitik" initiative is the wish that the Market should eventually speak also with one voice in its relations with the Communist East.

None of this would be unacceptable to Britain. Indeed British Ministers have gone out of their way to emphasise that they want a political (if, by implication, non-federal) Europe. Britain has insisted, to the past annoyance of de Gaulle's France, on joint foreign policy discussions with the Six in the Western European Union which was her idea in the first place. The results may not so far be very tangible—but these are early days.

Certain it is that Britain is not achieving much on her own in the world. By joining the Market she would have specific and valuable things to do, quite apart from the general merits and attractions from her point of view of making and applying policies in such fields as East-West relations, the Middle East, disarmament and Africa, backed by the might and accumulated wisdom of the whole of Western Europe. She might make a good start by insisting that the countries of what are now regarded, in the anachronistic aftermath of imperialism, as Francophone and Anglophone (if not Anglo-phile) Africa should be treated in the same way, with equal access to the vast Western European market.

She might, too, succeed in diverting some of the funds of the European Investment Bank to her tiny dependencies ("these specks of dust" President de Gaulle called those of France) such as Gibraltar, Tonga, the Seychelles, St Helena, the Falkland Isles, Antigua and even independent Malta. Why not full union with the new Europe for those tiny countries which wanted it? The offer would rival in its generosity Churchill's 1940 (admittedly grandiose and vague) offer to the dying Reynaud Government at Bordeaux that France should merge her destiny for all time with that of Britain. Why not, as is suggested in Chapter Sixteen more there in sadness than in earnest, offer to share our institutions such as the monarchy, which are so widely admired abroad, with those who are interested? May not Westminster eventually be the model for the European Parliament, as it was supposed to be for the emerging Commonwealth (but in many cases has already been usurped by darker forces)?

Britain has much to do in Europe. If she joins the Market "the tide of destiny will flow down new valleys towards new seas". And who can seriously doubt that in the longer run they will be better seas than the troubled waters we have known in the first two-thirds of this century?

Members of the Market can take back sovereignty already pooled if national problems become sufficiently pressing. France, in particular, has already done this on occasion. No member has been forced to bow the knee to Brussels against what it considers to be its vital interests. Thus, by revaluing and devaluing their currencies respectively, Germany and France in effect temporarily contracted out of the Common Agricultural Policy, whose prices are—curiously—fixed in dollars. But they are enjoined to rejoin the party and accept again the full rigours and benefits of the CAP as soon as possible.

Over a period, and on the basis of each country making concessions for the good of the whole and not pushing its fellows too hard on their particular problems, the political community should emerge. The pace will no doubt be that of the slowest. But this is not likely to be Britain's fault. If she joins, she will almost certainly be anxious to make the new Europe as democratic as possible in the shortest practical time. France, with her less consistently democratic tradition and her recent phase of extreme Gaullist nationalism, may well be the sluggard.

No doubt in time European, rather than national, Ministers will be appointed in Brussels (although why crowded, unexciting Brussels? Why not historic, beautiful, symbolic Strasbourg? Or a new Celesteville, a new Brasilia, a new Washington to epitomise Europe's new beginning?). These Ministers would, of course, be answerable directly to the European Parliament, and they would be responsible for foreign and defence policies as well as for the whole range of policies already dealt with in Brussels. They would form, in effect, a European Cabinet. The Commission, invigorated by the arrival of perhaps Lord George Brown and Christopher Soames from Britain as her two Commissioners, would continue to service the Ministers, but on the basis of a wider brief.

The President of the European Cabinet, which position might rotate between the member States, would have his finger firmly on the trigger. The Germans, whose collective finger many would wish to keep firmly away from the trigger, might agree in the earlier stages of building "Europe" to allow Britain and France to control the weapons which they had contributed to the European "pool". And, however unpalatable the fact may be to many in Britain, the Germans are the key to Europe. There can be no permanent solution to the problem of that dynamic race of 80 million people, united, it is true, only briefly in history and then only under the iron will of Bismarck, the Kaiser and Hitler, except on the basis of uniting Europe. Her neighbours, and France in particular, thrice invaded in a century, would never allow the two parts of Germany to re-unite *in vacuo*. But within a Europe of 300 million or more people (that is including Eastern Europe) all things would be possible. No one could reasonably fear that the Germans could dominate—even if they wanted to, which is most unlikely—a unit of that size.

But, of course, domination is emphatically not the theme of the new Europe. Co-operation is the watchword of the Ministers and officials who meet so regularly in Brussels: often several times a week. In pursuit of the good of the Community, and increasingly so again since the shadow of "Samson" de Gaulle, who so nearly brought the whole temple down about his broad shoulders, has been lifted from Europe, differences and ancient hatreds are ameliorated. The Dutch, who, for instance, on the whole suffered as individuals in the last war much more than did the British from the Germans, have buried the hatchet more readily and realistically. The absurd question, a quarter of a century later, "who won the war?" is seldom on Dutch lips, because they know that they lost all the way until the Liberation—and they have drawn the appropriate conclusions, however painful they may have been.

As Churchill said at Zurich, in time friends become enemies and enemies friends. It is past time for the British to draw the same conclusions as the Dutch. Decisions are continuously being made in Brussels, by war-time friends and enemies, which deeply affect Britain's interests: she must be there to influence them.

There is a feeling among many in Britain that if she joined the Common Market people's everyday lives would be changed—for the worse—by a stream of dictates from Brussels, over which Westminster had no control. In other words for the centuries-old bogey of centralised, impersonal Government in London would be exchanged a new but similar bogey based on the European capital.

Yet few Common Market rules which affect people individually have yet been framed. And even if and when they are, the British Government and Parliament will stand as a bulwark, in the unlikely event of their being needed in this role, against encroachment of ancient British liberties, such as the Common Law and a free Parliament, from across the Channel. Although technically signature of the Treaty of Rome is "for all time", if most improbably the worst came to the worst and the British wanted to contract out of the Market, in practice there would be nothing to stop them doing so.

14—WES • •

If Britain joins the Market, people here will come to appreciate its benefits, as they have in the Six. The conversion of the French and Italian Communist parties from rabid opposition to the Market to at least acquiescence in its existence, and of most unions in the Six to enthusiastic support, is an interesting commentary on the beneficent effects of the Market on "ordinary people" who are supposed to be going to be worse off if Britain joins.

In time the effects on people's everyday lives of Britain joining the Market would be varied and beneficial. Thus British workers would be able—indeed would have the right—to move to any other country in the Market, and would enjoy there a similar job, pension, National Insurance and health benefits. This right might well be in practice but sparingly exercised. In the earlier years of the Market there was a large efflux of workers from the poorer parts of Southern Italy to, in particular, a Germany which was desperately short of labour after the building of the Berlin Wall sealed off East Germany. But since then Italy's growing prosperity within the Market has persuaded many of them to return home. Thus new growth industries in the Market can call on all available suitable labour within a population of 180 million.

In British folk-myth, held strongly in some trade union circles, workers from the poor countries of Continental Europe would come flooding into the prosperous off-shore island if it became part of the Market. In fact if there was much movement at all, which is doubtful (there are usually strong ties keeping people in the country where they were brought up or with which they are familiar), it would be largely in the opposite direction, owing to the generally higher living standards in the Market (see Chapter Sixteen). The Six might, however, have mixed feelings about Britain's relatively large Commonwealth immigrant population. The British, on the other hand, might very well welcome their dispersion, or at least dilution, around Europe.

The aim is that, similarly, all professional people should be able to work anywhere in the Market. The professional bodies concerned in the Market have made predictable objections to this, as no doubt their counterparts, recently under examination by the Monopolies Commission, would also do here if Britain joined the Market. But sooner or later there will clearly have to be mutual recognition of professional qualifications in the countries concerned. Doctors in the Six, for instance, are already planning common standards of hospital treatment and medicine. With Britain in the Market probably more scientists and technologists would go and work on the Continent, some of them people who might otherwise have gone to America. The extent to which such people leave will depend largely on how attractive Britain, notably by paying them more and reducing rates of direct taxation, makes it for them to stay here. There will in any case be, in part at least, an off-setting growth in the number of people with similar expertise coming to Britain from the Continent. The British who do go to the Continent will tend to work in large international companies, such as International Business Machines, or on joint research projects in European institutions for advanced technology, such as Euratom which was almost killed by France in her Gaullist hey-day. Inventors who stay in Britain will be able to protect their brain-children in a market of some 250 million people, rather than 55 million, by applying to one European Patent Office.

There is, too, the "right to establishment", which is basic to the Market idea. This means that in time industrialists, shop-keepers, publicans, hoteliers and so on will be able, as of right, to establish themselves anywhere in the Market. There is a strong urge in Brussels—rightly so—to create a European company law, which would make it much easier for industrialists to run their businesses in similar conditions throughout the Market. At the moment an international company might be discouraged from going to Germany, for instance, because of its relatively advanced views on "worker participation", including the obligation to have workers on the boards of companies. This is in a sense, whatever the merits or otherwise of "co-determination" itself, a distortion of the complete economic union which the Market has always sought to become. To avoid this there would need to be either less "participation" in Germany or, as will probably be the case, more elsewhere in the Market.

At the level of people's everyday lives, Continental holidays should become even more of a joy than they usually are now if and when Britain joins the Market. Gone eventually should be the embarrassing scenes at Orly (and Heathrow) where "foreigners" have to brandish passports and on occasion have their luggage searched. The complete abolition of cross-Channel tariffs, common currency allowances (if any), common immigration procedures and common approaches by airlines, should greatly speed up travel in the new and, it is to be hoped, enlarged

Europe. Frontier formalities should become a thing of the past, as they already are in much of the Market.

There will, moreover, be more to travel on—although much of this will happen, of course, in any case whatever happens to the Market itself. A Channel tunnel, and, it is to be hoped, one day a Channel bridge (primed by capital from a central Market fund?), will stimulate the building of European—"E"—roads from Land's End to Reggio. In that sense Europe will be one as it has not been since Rome's Antonine Emperors held most of the then known world in fee. There will probably also be jointly-run hovercraft and air-line companies. In time, and well within the life-time of most people now living, people should be able, if they so wish, to live in one country and work in another. A well-to-do Londoner should easily be able to have his country cottage in the Loire country or in Brittany, rather than in Rye or Little Gransden.

Consumer choice will be greatly expanded if Britain joins the Market. Food, it is true, will cost housewives more, as we are told *ad nauseam*. But their husbands' *real* wages should expand much more rapidly. And there should be a larger national income from which to more than compensate the poor, such as old age pensioners, for a somewhat higher cost of living. Consumer goods from the Continent, such as kitchen appliances, clothing and so-called luxury goods, will be cheaper (see Chapter Thirteen). Continental wines and liquor are likely to be substantially cheaper than their present prohibitive cost in Britain. France, Germany and Italy in particular will almost certainly insist on this; they will be right to do so in that the Rome Treaty provides for the free flow of goods of all kinds between its members. Britain's licensing laws might well have to be amended to suit Continental tastes—the number of tourists coming to Britain will no doubt increase even more rapidly than now—but that would not necessarily be a bad thing.

The poor areas of Britain, such as the Scottish Highlands, should benefit from Market membership, too, as has Sicily, for instance, from the funds of the European Investment Bank. There may even be one day an assembly, alongside the European Parliament, to cater for the regions needing special development help. Thus representatives of Sicily, Portugal and Greece (one day if and when they achieve full membership) and the so-called "Celtic fringe" of Britain, would discuss together ways and means of sharing the central Market funds available from, among other sources, the European Investment Bank for regional development.

There are yet other aspects of European integration at the level of the individual. In time people should have a greater choice of universities as educational and professional standards become more interchangeable between member countries. European students might even "rotate", from one term to another or from one year to another, between universities—as German students do now between, say, Saarbrücken and Heidelberg. Few developments would more surely and more effectively force the British to learn European languages as well as some of them once learnt the "imperial" languages like Swahili and Hindi.

Integration could even affect the arts and religion. Funds dispensed from Brussels might supplement national grants and loans for the restoration or preservation of European art and architecture. The great unique cities and towns of Europe, such as Florence, Bruges and Cambridge, might benefit from concerted, Europe-wide, efforts to preserve their heritage: that after all is in one important sense what "a certain idea of Europe" is about. And a united Europe could even help the ecumenical movement: the founders of the Market, such as Adenauer, de Gasperi, Schumann and Monnet, who happened to be devout Catholics, certainly hoped so.

Thus the ramifications of "Europe" are many and complex. That is what makes the venture so exciting for the young in spirit of all ages. For many of those who came to maturity in Britain before and during the 1939–45 war the dangers and risks of joining with former enemies to build something new in this part of the world seem more obvious than the excitement. Their reservations, doubts, and often downright opposition, are understandable. But even they may find well within their lifetime that if Britain joins the Market their worst fears were unjustified—as a nightmare of the small hours fades into perspective, or even oblivion, with the dawn chorus. Certainly they will come to see what it is about "Europe" which has so captivated so many for so long.

CHAPTER FIFTEEN

NAFTA and all that—Westward look the sea is wide

What then should Britain do if even now the European venture fails? For this country the alternative to not entering the Common Market is, quite simply, not entering. She would be on her own and would have to go it alone. Pipedreams of a meaningful resuscitated Commonwealth (all-white, or "bridge-building" multi-racial, you take your choice), or a so-called North Atlantic Free Trade Area (neither North nor Atlantic nor Free, but at least to do with Trade and indubitably an Area), or a revivified European Free Trade Area (which though hardly visibly Free in that it discriminates against third countries, scores rather better: three points out of four) are seductive but futile.

So are hopes that without Britain the Common Market would wither away of its own inanition. The Market has been sadly buffeted almost from its inception by French Gaullism. Its development has also been held back ironically, by the insistence of the Five that Britain should be allowed in on the great adventure. They will hold back no longer if it becomes apparent in 1971 that there is no hope of the candidate States being admitted within the foreseeable future. Even since the Hague meeting of Market Heads of State in December 1969—which agreed in principle on the completion of the Common Agricultural Policy and the means of financing it, and on other aspects of the Market's operations, as well as on enlargement of the Community—the Market has developed rapidly.

The Six would be disappointed if Britain did not join them in the Market. They would not, however, be stricken unto death. Without Britain it would be a different kind of Europe, a smaller Europe, a truncated Europe. But it would be Europe. It would be an economic Europe, a technological Europe, probably a defence Europe, increasingly a political Europe. It could even be a loosely federated Europe.

Meanwhile, back on their offshore island, the British would—perforce—be doing Trojan work to find a role in an unfriendly world. The super-powers, America, Europe, Russia, China and Japan, would inevitably ignore the smaller units around the globe. The present loose understanding between America and Russia that they will not get too much in each other's way, and certainly not go to the brink of nuclear war, would probably in time be broadened out to include as many of the super-powers as were prepared to take part in a civilised, pacific world order. There would eventually no doubt emerge a more complex version of the old balance of power.

The British might well in this situation, in the wake of their exclusion from Europe, dally with the North Atlantic Free Trade Area concept. They would be unlikely, however, ever to carry the argument of the NAFTA and anti-European stalwarts to its logical conclusion and apply to become the fifty-second American state. If only because the British dislike pushing arguments to their logical conclusion. And if only because there is no sign that the Americans would have any interest in undoing the work of George III and in being reunited with their separated brethren.

The Americans would have their good reasons, of course. The innate absurdity of union with a nation divided by 3,000 miles of water would probably be more obvious to them than to the Europe-less British. The latter would inevitably come cap-in-hand as suitors in such a situation. The Americans have their Puerto Ricas and Hawaiis, of course, but there seems to be no particular reason why they should welcome a nation of 55 million people (roughly a quarter of their own population) with a standard of living barely half theirs; unless it were as "quaint" poor relations. The Americans are, moreover, if possible more chauvinistic than the British. Statehood would mean for the British swallowing their understandable dislike of exchanging the certainties and strength of the Parliamentary tradition, with all its faults, for the unfamiliar, cumbersome maze which is American politics. But it would have the advantages of a common language, a common cultural heritage, a common law tradition, even in part a shared history ("westward look, the land is bright!" quoted Prime Minister Churchill to President Roosevelt, from Clough, in 1940). It would have the advantage, too, that some of the prosperity of what is still, despite all its contemporary troubles, by far the most successful economy the world has ever known, would inevitably rub off on a relatively undynamic economy far away across the Atlantic. American investment, in particular, might be expected to pour into Britain, if only to take advantage of the cheap labour there. Yet, although American statehood for Britain has a good deal more logic to it than the NAFTA, this beckoning concept of "the king over the water"— seductive, remote, romantic, redolent of happier times—is clearly not a serious possibility.

Nor, it might be thought, is the NAFTA, the poor country's answer to "Europe", really a starter. Until and unless Britain is excluded from the Common Market for the foreseeable future— and it could be for ever—canvassing of NAFTA is not helpful. It may even be that it is positively harmful. There are those who argue that the projection of NAFTA as an ostensible alternative to Europe actually strengthens the British negotiating position in Brussels. This is a time-hallowed British argument, which was even applied in its time to the establishment of the European Free Trade Area, the British-inspired scratch team of small countries on the periphery of Western Europe who happened to be excluded from the Common Market.

There is little evidence that such a gambit works. Most Continental Europeans can see as well as the British that the Emperor is naked and that there is no constructive alternative to Britain joining the Market. Moreover, the constant canvassing of so-called alternative options to "Europe" tends to strengthen the still widespread impression within the Six that Britain is not serious in its application to accede to the Treaty of Rome.

If it became clear in 1971, however, that Britain would not or could not join the Six in their European aspirations, then clearly the possible alternatives would need to be examined exhaustively. To go on waiting in the Brussels ante-room endlessly would only be to invite ridicule and humiliation. Even Heath that steadfast "European" and then leader of the Opposition, implied as much to his Paris audience on 5 May 1970.

Its enthusiasts are forced to admit that there is little interest in NAFTA at the moment in Washington, which is where it matters, but some are persuaded that this could change if it became apparent that British entry into the Market was a dead duck. The Americans have after all supported the idea of a united Europe, which included Britain, in good times and in bad—against their own short-term trading interests—ever since the launching of the imaginative Marshall Plan for the post-war economic reconstruction of Europe.

Most thinking Americans would still much prefer to see Britain take her rightful place in Europe to any other possible arrangement. Their idealism tends to equate, perhaps rather naively, the unification of Europe with the formation of their own federal union. And there has been the more practical, and more pressing, consideration that until the British balance of payments swung into surplus, this country was widely regarded as the sick man of Europe and a millstone round its creditors' (and particularly America's) collective necks. Radical solutions, such as British entry into the Market, have thus been thought of as the only possible way of forcing overdue changes for the better on the British.

Yet might Americans not feel differently in the wake of a possible failure of the negotiations in Brussels? Their change of heart would indeed have to be immense. The author checked out on the NAFTA concept in America in the autumn of 1969. Very few intelligent and otherwise well-informed Americans appeared to have heard of it at all. Although one Californian did comment under pressure that: "we get so many new types of gasoline I get confused".

Senator Javitts, former high-priest of NAFTA in British eyes, is said to be disillusioned and complaining of losing his friends since he espoused the Cause. And enquiries in Washington as to who in the Nixon Administration might be prepared to talk knowledgeably about NAFTA produce dusty replies. The idea of writing an article on American attitudes to NAFTA was thwarted by almost total American ignorance of what has been billed in some British circles as a great new imaginative démarche which would electrify the English-speaking world—possibly the greatest vision since Joseph Chamberlain's ideas for a united Empire seventy years ago.

Problems, even mutual problems, appear quite different when viewed from different ends of the trans-Atlantic telescope. America has a legion of allies of varying degrees of troublesomeness. Britain, *faute de mieux*, has become almost pathetically dependent on American goodwill and frequently on her money. Memories of the war-time grand alliance still linger, especially among older British people, much more in London than they do in Washington.

In contrast, the harassed world-weary Americans, bogged down in Indo-China, criticised on almost all sides, anxious to withdraw from their far-flung post-war commitments, beset by their own internal social problems, think little about Britain. Many have fond memories of the great war-time days; some such as Dean Rusk, have spent happy months or years here as Rhodes scholars and the like; some, too, regard Britain as America's most dependable ally.

Yet few Americans have either time or inclination to think much about Britain. And probably few regard Britain as important in the world as most British people do. Enquiries in London of the returning visitor from Washington as to how Americans regard Britain invite the reply "the Americans are not saying anything about Britain". It is important that this background of relative indifference to Britain's problems should be more widely realised in this country while the key Common Market negotiations hang in the balance. Nothing could be more unfortunate than a widespread impression that there is an easy, tailor-made alternative, such as the NAFTA or even American statehood, if Europe proves to be a chimera.

In such a situation there would certainly be no harm in exploring the NAFTA possibility, even though the chances of its coming to anything must be regarded as remote. The concept of a North Atlantic Free Trade Area, embracing America, Britain, the "old" Commonwealth of Canada, South Africa, New Zealand and Australia, with the Scandinavians granted economic citizenship as honorary Englishmen, and the Japanese perhaps offered country membership of the club (because, "lets face it, they are different") is beguiling.

In terms of total population and, even more, of total national incomes, such a trade grouping would be much more powerful in economic terms even than the Common Market of the Six. Like-minded nations, looking outwards traditionally to the world's sea routes for their trade, could do much together if the political will was there. And the economies of industrialised Britain and, for instance, agricultural New Zealand, still complement each other to a remarkable degree. Moreover, as Douglas Jay would argue, in theory there could be exciting longer term possibilities of linking together existing common markets and free trade areas into one vast free trade zone within which there were no tariff barriers: a sort of Kennedy Round of tariff reductions writ large.

Unfortunately, there appears to be even less interest, if possible, in NAFTA in the old Commonwealth, and certainly in Scandinavia and Japan, than in America. New Zealand would probably of necessity follow Britain in a NAFTA initiative. But Australia already trades more with Japan than she does with Britain. Canada's economy leans heavily on America's and in many ways is almost indistinguishable from it (some four-fifths of Canadian industry is owned by American capital). No doubt she would follow America into a NAFTA, but Britain is becoming progressively less important to her; and the Canadian mood, epitomised in the Trudeau Government, is to withdraw as much as possible from trans-Atlantic entanglements, such as NATO commitment. South Africa, thanks in part to past British actions, is increasingly estranged from Europe, and so thrown back on the old Boer concept of the laager—the covered wagons facing outwards towards a hostile world.

Denmark and Norway can hardly wait to join the Common Market and even Sweden might be prepared to swallow her traditional scruples about neutrality in order to come to terms with the Market. If Britain failed to join the Market, the Scandinavian countries, including Finland, would be unlikely to wait any longer. They would seek either to join, or come to a collective trading agreement with the Market as soon as possible. They could hardly afford to do otherwise: Germany, for instance, is Sweden's most important trading partner. Japan would probably see NAFTA as a restrictive, rather than a liberating, force in her trading arrangements in so far as it involved any discrimination between nations in tariffs or no-tariff barriers to trade.

Some of the same objections to NAFTA apply to boosting the European Free Trade Area as an alternative to British entry to the Common Market. EFTA has been as good as far (which is not far) as it goes, although it has hardly smoothed Britain's path into the Market, which was its chief original aim in 1959. On the contrary, in so far as it has created a new set of obligations for Britain, in addition to those to the Commonwealth (and in particular to New Zealand), it has complicated the task of negotiating British entry. This applied more in 1961–63 at the time of the first negotiations than now, however.

By the end of 1966 all tariffs on industrial goods between EFTA countries had been abolished, three years ahead of the target date of the founding Treaty of Stockholm. Since then EFTA has put more emphasis on the removal of non-tariff barriers to trade and the enforcement of fair rules of competition. Agriculture is excluded from EFTA co-operation.

But EFTA has from the start been bedevilled by unspoken suspicions that one or other member, and notably Britain, might "rat" on the others and do a unilateral deal with the Six. In the wake of the first French veto on British entry to the Market, President de Gaulle sought to woo the Danes, albeit without success. The Austrians are in almost continuous negotiation, if not communion, with Brussels in an attempt to get the full economic advantages of Market membership without jeopardising their neutrality—which would antagonise Russia. The Portugese are too far away and too poor to make much difference either way. The Irish seek largely to safeguard the British market for their agricultural produce. They will follow Britain whether or not she joins the Market, although they would much prefer that she should join, which could be the long-term answer to her border troubles with Ulster (that is, merging them in a wider union). In the same way as Belgium has for long sought to submerge her Walloon-Flemish difficulties in a wider European union.

There have been other running sores in EFTA. The long-standing dispute between Norway and Britain over the latter's proposed aluminium smelters is one example. Another is the protracted effects in terms of good will lost of Britain's unilateral action in 1964 in imposing without consultation an import surcharge of 15 per cent: memories of this still rankle among Britain's EFTA partners. And the Scandinavian countries have for some years been toying with the attractive concept of a do-it-yourself NORDIC customs union, which to some extent would cut across EFTA.

So EFTA will probably disintegrate in time whether or not Britain joins the Common Market. It certainly promises no "fall-back" position as an alternative to Market membership. Like trade between Common Market countries, that between EFTA countries has grown relatively rapidly: by nearly one-and-a-half times in the 1960's. There is no doubt that in some industries which need long production runs, such as the British car industry, the addition to the British home market which it has provided has been very useful.

Yet the fact remains that Britain accounts for about three-fifths of its total population and even more of its total income. And there is little more that EFTA can achieve except to integrate the agricultures of members, which no one wants except the Danes. And there is not, and can hardly be, any urge to political integration among nine disparate, and on the whole small, countries strung out on the periphery of Europe.

What then of the so-called Commonwealth alternative if Britain fails to join Europe? In those far away days before NAFTA was thought of, the anti-Europeans used to urge on a Macmillan Government belatedly applying to join the Common Market that the vast, rich, like-minded nations of the Commonwealth offered a much more attractive and larger market than the Europe of the Six. Less is heard of this theme than eight years ago. But still the Beaverbrook newspapers, for instance, urge their readers to lift their eyes to the beckoning prairies of Canada; to the measureless mineral wealth of Australia; to doughty, loyal, agriculturally-fertile New Zealand; to mistreated, gold-rich South Africa; to the beleaguered but trusty ex-Battle of Britain fighter pilots of Rhodesia.

These countries in themselves, it is true, whatever services they may have rendered the mother country in two world wars, do not amount to a great deal in population, nor even in terms of aggregate national incomes. But by sleight of hand the argument at this point is inverted, or at least distorted. For to these few relatively rich, and on the whole under-populated countries are added some of the poorest nations in the world. Most of the non-white Commonwealth is poor indeed, and India shockingly so. But these under-developed nations do have the merit of having, *in toto*, a vast population. India alone, with 550 million, is far larger than the Common Market of the Six (180 million).

Still letters are written to the newspapers showing what an enormous proportion of Britain's trade is done with the Commonwealth; and as often as not reminding readers of the ties of kith and kin; and of that brilliant summer of 1940, when the Commonwealth stood alone.

So the Commonwealth as a whole, with some 800 million people, can be presented as a mighty and exhilarating alternative to the puny countries of the Six, clustered on the tip of the

Eurasian land mass. The Commonwealth, moreover, is, by definition, multi-racial, a bridge-building exercise between rich and poor nations. The sun never sets on such a disparite, far-flung family of nations. They all owe, moreover, a good deal to Britain: a common legal tradition, many, though progressively fewer, Parliaments modelled on Westminster, a tradition of speaking English (at least in government), a network of personal and family connections, traditional trade links whereby manufactured goods from Britain are exchanged for food and raw materials and so on.

Why indeed should not the British people turn their backs on Europe—unfamiliar, speaking strange tongues, addicted to drinking the fruits of the grape, Catholic-orientated, romantically and unreliably Latin, home of wars and charnel houses, above all *different*—and lift their eyes to these delectable mountains? Surely Mr Pilgrim himself would turn aside at such a tempting vision?

In this case, alas, the grass is no greener the other side of the hill: on the contrary. The fallacy about the Commonwealth argument, as in part about the NAFTA argument, is that the countries concerned have little in common except tradition. Many of them, such as the new African nations, are intensely suspicious of the former colonial power. They remain members of the Commonwealth for what they can get out of it: not surprisingly, as Britain does (although in our case, and especially since the January 1971 Singapore conference, the advantage is less clear). They have no wish to prolong traditional trading patterns with Britain a moment longer than necessary. These are remorselessly weakening all the time.

India, for instance (by definition since its population is so large), is no doubt a vast potential market for British goods. But she is so poor that she has a voracious and growing need for aid and development capital. Already about half the aid she receives goes on servicing the interest charges on previous loans. With an income per head a tiny fraction of Britain's, there is no chance whatsoever of India within the foreseeable future buying with money she has earned from her own exports the relatively sophisticated manufactured products which are, or should be, Britain's staple exports.

The same is true in varying degrees of most of the rest of the non-white Commonwealth. In Africa, for instance, Kenya, Tanzania (one of the poorest countries in the world), Zambia

Ghana, Sierre Leone, and even Nigeria between them cannot begin to compete in buying power and prosperity with say Western Germany. It is an unpalatable but irrefutable fact for the exponents of the so-called Commonwealth alternative that trade between highly industrialised countries has expanded much more rapidly than that between the producers of manufactured and primary (such as food and raw materials) products. Moreover, there is no sign of this trend ceasing—much less of it being reversed.

This is the main reason why Commonwealth trade has accounted in recent years for a progressively smaller share of British trade. There is also the fact that the anachronistically-titled Imperial Preference, whereby Commonwealth countries ostensibly discriminate in tariffs in each other's favour against the outside world, has become one of the greatest one-way mirrors of all time. Britain still provides this preference for imports from all Commonwealth countries, plus Eire and South Africa. But the reciprocal privilege for British exports sold to those markets has been steadily whittled away as overseas Commonwealth nations have developed trade with their more immediate neighbours (for instance, Australia with Japan). In many cases, such as Ghana, the preference in favour of British goods is now non-existent.

Is there any chance of this trend being reversed? It would seem not: on the contrary. The fear must be that the world is increasingly dividing into the "haves" (largely the white nations) and the "have-nots" (largely the non-white countries); that the economic gulf between them will get wider, that the rich will get richer and the poor relatively poorer; that there could even be a *jéhad*, a holy war, between the races one day, born of ancient resentments and lack of mutual understanding In such a situation the tenuous bonds of the Commonwealth ("as light as gossamer but as strong as steel" in the rotund speeches of Commonwealth statesmen only a decade ago) are unlikely to noticeably deflect the course of history.

The "bridge-building" aspect of the Commonwealth should certainly not be decried. In so far as thirty or more statesmen of different racial backgrounds gathered round a table in Lancaster House or Singapore or Ottawa every year or two get to know each other better the Commonwealth is worth preserving. On the other hand, in so far as its existence delays the process of readjustment of British public opinion to Britain's changed and reduced circumstances in the world and in so far as it negatively limits Britain's "elbow-room" in world affairs it is actively harmful—not merely harmless, as many would maintain—in the domestic context. This process still has some way to go, especially among the older British generation which by and large still controls policy-making. Witness the British Foreign Office's apparently deep-seated urge to have a "view" on, and so be seen to be "influencing", almost every world problem.

The Commonwealth option then is a non-option if Britain does not enter the Common Market. The Commonwealth will probably go on existing, despite Prime Minister Health's anger over the treatment he received in Singapore on the South African arms issue, if only because London, where most Commonwealth conferences (by popular request) still take place, is such a pleasant place for overseas statesmen to visit. And because it gives many here such a cosy feeling: colonial anti-British prisoners into Commonwealth Prime Ministers and Presidents, foes into friends, Empire into Commonwealth, "the political genius of the island race" and so on.

In theory by a gigantic effort of will Britain could seek to reverse the tide of history and divert a higher proportion of her exports and overseas investment to the Commonwealth. There is no evidence that any Commonwealth countries, except perhaps Australia and New Zealand, wants this to happen, it is true. But no doubt, at the heavy cost of lost opportunities in trade and investment in the larger and more dynamic markets of North America and Western Europe it could be done.

This really is the so-called Commonwealth alternative. The poorer, and often anti-British, Commonwealth countries would on no account have any truck with an attempt to resuscitate the old trading links which they tend to regard as putting them in an inferior status *vis-à-vis* Britain as post-colonial helots. But Britain, with no certainty of reciprocity from the richer countries of the "old Commonwealth", might seek unilaterally to strengthen her trading links with countries which for years have been increasingly going their own way. Yet in terms of population and aggregate incomes they amount to little more than non-British EFTA. And even if by some miracle EFTA and the old Commonwealth could be kept together and fused into a new international trading group—a sort of NAFTA writ small—the result would be smaller than even the Common Market of the Six, let alone of the Ten.

So there are no meaningful *international* options for Britain outside Europe. She would be on her own in an uncomfortable world. She would be forced to make unpleasant adjustments, of the sort outlined in earlier chapters, which are long overdue in any case, in the most difficult way possible. But, of course, it could be done. A new Dark Age would not necessarily be upon us.

What chance was there of these things coming to pass?

The outlines of a deal between the Six and Britain, with the three other candidate states, was already visible by the end of 1970. It looked as though the net balance of payments cost of British entry might rise to some £300 million a year towards the end of the transitional period of adjustment to Market rules after membership, largely on account of a disproportionate contribution (more than a fifth of the total?) to the archaic Common Agricultural Policy. But that cost would then almost certainly tail away, and the industrial benefits accrue, as the enlarged Market reduced its "target" prices for food to more realistic levels. Meanwhile, British farmers—as opposed to some horticulturists—and especially large arable farmers stood to make a bonanza from those high prices which reflected the inefficiency of German, rather than of French, peasant farming and the tricky political operation of slowly transferring millions of farmers to industrial jobs in the towns of the Six.

Geoffrey Rippon, and his able and experienced deputy Sir Con O'Neill, were rightly holding out for a gradual adjustment to the full rigours of financing the CAP during the transitional period and for a further three years beyond that, and for a "trigger" clause in writing against the possibility that the balance of payments cost of Market membership might be temporarily too much for Britain at some stage. The special problem of New Zealand, so heavily dependent on the British market for her agricultural exports, had been conceded in principle, if not in practical detail, by the Six. Her dairy produce and Commonwealth sugar seemed to constitute, given good will in Brussels, no insuperable obstacle to the enlargement of the Market.

The French took the Chair of the Council of Ministers and thus spoke on behalf of the Six, for the vital first six months of 1971, which should settle for this generation, if not for ever, whether or not Britain would enter the Market on New Year's Day 1973, or soon thereafter. Maurice Schumann, France's Foreign Minister and for long a good friend of Britain, blew hot and cold almost daily about her prospects. President Pompidou, although also undoubtedly in favour of British entry in principle, as long as France gained her pound of flesh in the shape of new members fully subscribing to the CAP, which was so advantageous to France, spoke of the British sense of humour in asking for the terms she did in Brussels. He also agreed with Chancellor Brandt of Germany in January 1971 that the Werner Plan for monetary integration should go ahead.

The situation had the makings of a deadlock which might then be broken by a meeting of Heads of Government—notably between Pompidou and Heath. The latter had his problems if, as seemed on balance probable terms emerged in 1971 in Brussels which he felt he could recommend to the Commons. Ministers were anxious that the House (but certainly not the country via a much-canvassed and unprecedented referendum) should give its agreement in principle to at least the outline of an agreement with the Six before the House rose for the summer Recess and before the party conferences in the autumn, when much could go amiss.

Meanwhile, against a rising crescendo of shrill opposition from the curiously-named, all-party Common Market Safeguards Committee (whatever that was) the "Midlothian" campaign for British entry was launched by the European Movement and increasingly, but not before time, by Ministers. The anti-Europeans could boast such ex-Ministers as Douglas Jay and Derek Walker-Smith; the "Europeans" among others Lord Gladwyn, former Ambassador to Paris, and Lord Harlech, former Ambassador and "Camelot" courtier in Kennedy's Washington. The Europeans hoped with reason that public opinion, which only three short years earlier had been roughly two-to-one in favour of British entry, would swing again rapidly towards Market membership if and when the terms were known.

Yet in a sense the whole great enterprise could turn on the personal courage and integrity of one man. Nearly a decade ago Roy Jenkins, the future Chancellor, had resigned from the Labour Opposition front bench when Hugh Gaitskell, obscurely invoking "a thousand years of history", moved, to George Brown's manifest disgust, with many doubts against Market membership for Britain. Jenkins might soon face his own Gethsemane, which if the worst happened could even lead to his temporary withdrawal from public life, on the historic European issue.

In early 1971 the tide was running strongly against Market membership in the Labour constituency associations. And nearly half the Parliamentary Labour party had signed an anti-Market motion. To his great credit at the Blackpool party conference the previous September Harold Wilson had held the line on "Europe", and those closest to him said that he still believed in Market membership with all the enthusiasm of a convert. But could he fail to make party capital out of such an unpopular issue much longer? It seemed that he might eventually compromise (two-thirds of his Shadow Cabinet were "Europeans") and allow a free vote on the Labour side. In that case he and Jenkins, Michael Stewart, Geoffrey de Freitas, and between sixty and 100 other Labour MPs could go into the Government lobby in possibly the most exciting Commons debate since the fall of the Chamberlain Government in 1940.

There seemed little possibility of Heath not putting on in effect a five line Whip on the other side of the House. He had between thirty and sixty potential rebels, including Enoch Powell, that one time strong "European", but essentially an old-fashioned (not to say volatile) nationalist. But if Wilson put on the Whip against the Treaty of Rome, his deputy Jenkins and many other Labour Europeans would face an intensely difficult decision. Six months is a long time in politics but in early 1971 there was no sign of them not making the right decision if it came to the issue. Clearly, whatever Ministers might say, there were not enough Conservative votes without some help from the Liberal and Labour parties. It seemed that "Europe" might in the end be carried by a small majority as has many a great issue and as was the Treaty itself in certain Market countries. One is enough, as Churchill used to say. But such an outcome would be a sad denouement for an ideal which has haunted this generation.

CHAPTER SIXTEEN

The Sunshine Day

Britain would survive, and no doubt would get slowly richer, even if all the international options discussed in Chapters Thirteen, Fourteen and Fifteen—Common Market membership, NAFTA, EFTA, the Commonwealth—came to nothing. The outlook would be bleak in such a situation in that Britain would be the one advanced, industrialised country without a large home market for its manufactured products. The ill effects of this can be exaggerated in that tariffs, and even non-tariff, obstacles to trade (such as quotas) are on the whole coming down. The 1967 Kennedy Round tariff reductions, agreed through the General Agreement on Tariffs and Trade, alone reduced tariffs on a wide range of manufactured goods by a half over a period.

Even so, both experience and economic theory show that even relatively low tariffs can have a quite disproportionate effect on diverting trade. The Common External Tariff, for instance, was fixed in the earlier years of the Common Market's development at the reasonable average level of 11.7 per cent. Yet behind that modest barrier to the outside world, trade between the Six increased at a rate several times that of international trade as a whole. Clearly the danger for Britain would be that if her main competitors—America, the Six, Russia, Japan—had much larger home markets than she did, and if she resolutely refused to carry out the overdue reforms mentioned in earlier chapters, she might decline relatively into a backwater off the coast of Europe.

There are those who argue, of course, that such a fate would not matter; that Britain is in many ways one of the most civilised countries the world has ever known (which is undoubtedly true in some important respects), that in future she should lead the world in "living". Thus Harold Macmillan was fond of likening Britain

to ancient Greece and America to ancient Rome in their relation-
ships with each other.

This argument can be carried to a charmingly logical conclusion. Why have any growth if it is all rather a bore? Why do the
British not do what they are best at? Why do they not merely "do
their own thing"? Why do they not forget all about Concordes,
Channel tunnels, third London airports, high speed passenger
trains, nuclear reactors, and so on? Britain has after all the "social
overhead capital", as the economic text books say, to make a real
go of being Disneyland. It might, it is true, involve a few details
such as exporting 20 million people to the beckoning wide open
space of the Commonwealth. But, as every *Express* reader knows
they can hardly wait to have us anyway, and many Britishers are
straining to go.

For the rest, the 35 million-odd people who stayed, Britain
could become a demi-paradise, another Eden. Tourism would
boom as it had never done before. The "invisible" trade balance
would fructify as it has not done even recently. Ideally, indeed,
invisible earnings would overtake, and eventually almost wholly
replace, "visible" exports. The beauty of such a solution to
Britain's perennial economic problems is that it would involve
relatively little inconvenience, change, and difficult decisions of
the type that the British so much dislike.

The "social overhead capital" is there for all to see: Anne
Hathaway's cottage (or its successor), Hadrian's Wall, the castles
of the Welsh marches, the Cambridge Backs, the Ashmolean
Library, Stonehenge, swinging post-Christine Keeler London,
Carnaby Street and the Tower. Almost the only acts of modern-
isation required would be to put bathrooms in the many British
hotels where they do not now exist (memo to new English Tourist
Board), heat them and build more of them where necessary.

For the rest, dress everyone in beefeaters' uniforms, change
the guard at Buckingham Palace every ten minutes. Change it in
Sheffield, Manchester, Belper, Huyton, Hoylake, and Bexley, as
well as Westminster. Build, if necessary more castles like Edinburgh. Renovate Dingley Hall, where Dickens stayed and whose
name has been immortalised in his account of that most famous of
all English Christmases—the Pickwickians at Dingley Dell. Fly in
Germans from the Ruhr by the 'plane-load: "next Christmas you
too can dine at Dingley". Encourage the Duke of Bedford in his
plans to shoot deer and (at a price) to "do" the London season
round—Ascot, Wimbledon, Henley and so on—with wealthy

Americans. Think big. Drink mead. If necessary quadruple the size of Woburn. Row all tourists ashore in coracles through Spithead; paint them first in woad. Have thousands of Texans dining every night with Dukes, old and newly-created. Take a leaf out of Lloyd-George's book and multiply the peerage. Why should not indeed every free-born Britisher (happy the man that can boast 'civis Romanus sum') have a title of some sort?

Wider still and wider. Rent out the Queen. Why not, if she does not want to live abroad in the Commonwealth—and Balmoral, Windsor, Sandringham, and Buckingham Palace are perhaps enough homes for any normally-adjusted sovereign—and if those countries do not want her to do so, rotate her as Queen-President of Europe? Say once a week or once a month? Consider the Swiss Confederation, which rotates its head of State, and go and do likewise.

Those who argue (often well-to-do-middle class people with already many of the good things of life) that economic growth does not matter thus have much in their favour. A Shangri-La Britain would indeed be a restful Britain: no coronaries, no ulcers, no rush, no strain, no doubt the lowest crime rate the world has ever known, all tears wiped away from every eye: Ninevah.

The opposite case, that economic growth matters because it should, if properly managed, bring most people more of the good things of life, is often disputed—not least by economists. America today, with its riots, student unrest, racial strife and extraordinarily high crime rate, is widely regarded elsewhere, for instance, as an example of what happens when economic growth is carried to its logical conclusion (no doubt the wish is father to the thought). What price happiness in California, home of the Sharon Tate murders, dope-taking, divorce and alimony—yet the richest society the world has ever known?

However, those who point disapprovingly to the alleged fruits of such economic growth as even the British enjoy—traffic congestion, pollution, airport noise, erosion of the countryside, hydra-headed parking meters and so on—surely miss the point. For they throw out the baby with the bath water. Some of the fruits of economic growth must be used to mitigate its otherwise bad side-effects. Architectural planning, the best sort of planning, will have to be further tightened up. There will have to be stricter legislation on pollution, noise levels, car use (road pricing?) and parking. There will probably have to be more and bigger grants for those unlucky enough to be living near airports or motorways.

There must be no more Stansted fiascoes: surely the overwhelming case for Foulness as the third London airport is that it will cause a minimum of inconvenience to a minimum of people. It also happens, of course, that the project to combine the proposed airport with a new deep water ("Europort") sea-port is one of the most imaginative Britain has seen in a quarter of a century. But for those who are concerned about the "quality of life" in Britain in the late twentieth century, the main point is that the fruits of economic progress, such as much increased air travel, must not destroy the aspects of life which in times past were regarded as making it worth living—peace and quiet, privacy, the beauty of a June dusk in the country, space for children to play, good clean air, and so on. The best things in life may not necessarily be free, but it is as well that not too high a price should be put on their survival.

A reasonable economic growth rate, combined with a preservation of the traditional good things of life, should not be an impossible aim. But surely both are of great importance. If present trends continue Britain will decline *relatively* to become a sort of second Portugal within ten to fifteen years—a relatively poor island, a back-water, off the coast of a booming and integrating Europe, with extended communications from and to the Continent's geographical and economic centre of gravity.

After all Britain's economy has since 1964 expanded at an average rate of little more than two per cent a year and its chief international competitors in world markets, notably America, the Six and Japan, at least twice that rate. Japan is, of course, a law unto itself. Its growth rate of 10 per cent a year or more is as strange to post-Keynesian economics as is Britain's—in the opposite direction.

The argument is still sometimes heard in Britain (see Chapter Three) that much of this discrepancy in economic growth rates is inevitable; that, although most of them are already richer than Britain in income per head, her main competitors are merely "catching up" with Britain's nineteenth century, and even post-1945, start. There was indeed a head-start: in 1945 Britain had the fourth highest standard of living in the world, but it now ranks fourteenth!

The present signs are clear: within a generation (which is

usually taken to be twenty years) at the most Britain will be poorer in income per head than almost all of Western Europe. Quite possibly it could be poorer even than Eire or Southern Italy. By then, on present trends, Germany and Japan will be economic collossi, far more powerful and influential than Britain. A remarkable number of Americans fear that even they will eventually be dwarfed by Japan. This may be a special case, but the relative steady growth in the economic might, and therefore influence, of Britain's other main competitors (and even America, which is already far richer, expands more rapidly than Britain) is indeed worrying.

Whatever the views of certain British academic economists, it is difficult to see the British people as a whole ever regarding such a state of affairs as satisfactory. The British, like the French, are unusually preoccupied in the post-war Western world with power, "influence" (usually ill-defined) and at least until recently "moral leadership".

This will have to change and, of course, is changing. But it is difficult to see Britain ever voluntarily and willingly sinking into impotence, into such a situation that it could not, for instance, retain its links with India and the former British territories of Africa. For the foreseeable future the giving of aid and technical assistance to countries so infinitely poorer than any European nation must be important for Britain. In the short-term no doubt, despite a low growth rate, such worthy objectives can be accommodated out of a large, but it may well be transient, balance of payments surplus. In the longer run however, a relatively stagnant Britain must lose its capacity to do the things in the world which it considers most important.

There are those who argue, of course, that aid should not in any case rank among those top priorities. The case usually turns on the familiar complaint that much, if not most, aid is wasted. But again this is surely to throw out the baby with the bath water. If aid is wasted the solution is surely to tighten up the procedures for administering it—both among the donors and the receivers, and not to cut it off entirely.

In this context the growing relative importance of the international aid-giving and investment-providing institutions, such as the World Bank and its offshoots, is surely encouraging. Their procedures for assessing the most worthwhile projects to back are usually highly sophisticated and becoming more so. And they avoid the stigma which attaches in so many under-developed countries, which were until recently colonies, to receiving assistance of any sort from the former imperial power.

There is also the wider point: can the rich countries of the West afford *not* to do anything about the widening gulf between them and the poor and the heavy-laden of Latin America, Africa, and Asia? The so-called moral argument that such relatively rich countries as Britain *ought* to help the underdeveloped part of the world may be disputed. Yet it is difficult to see what the difference in principle and in logic is between the social and economic reforms—such as Factory Acts, old age pensions, children's allowances, decent housing—which gave the poor of this country at least a minimum standard of living, and which are now generally regarded as desirable, if not Christian, ways in which to treat one's fellow-citizens, and the present case for helping the poor nations.

Even on grounds of self-interest posterity will surely say that the £200 million a year (projected to rise to £300 million in 1975) which Britain now devotes to aid was well spent. Only about a half of it in any case is aid in the sense of a net immediate loss to Britain. The rest is largely accounted for by increased British exports. For a high proportion of British aid is "tied", that is conditional on recipient countries spending it on British exports.

Some British aid goes, moreover, to countries where Britain has substantial overseas investments, such as Kenya and India. To that extent by contributing to the economic and political stability of those countries, it is safeguarding an increasing return on valuable investments. In that context the argument for aid is similar to that for Britain maintaining a defence presence overseas—East of Suez and elsewhere—in order, *inter alia*, arguably to protect its investments. (It remains true, of course, that many poor countries, which desperately need foreign investment, are their own worst enemies in expropriating foreign companies.)

The fallacy in the argument that Britain should become a second Sweden, is, quite simply, that the British people do not want (and seem unlikely ever to want) any such solution. If by that Sweden in this context is meant a country with a neutralist foreign policy and a tradition of minimal involvement overseas (although this is rapidly changing in such countries as Tanzania where Scandinavian influence is expanding rapidly). Moreover, it is much more difficult for a country of 55 million people to contract out of the world scene than one of eight million.

For the British to exercise the "Swedish option" would be in a sense to turn their collective backs on their tradition of world-wide involvement. It may be doubted, too, whether such a solution is really any solution at all in that a quite exceptionally high proportion, roughly a third, of Britain's national product is accounted for by overseas trade. By that token she is unusually vulnerable to economic and political events all over the world. Examples are the Six Day War in 1967 which, with the seamen's strike, played havoc with her exports, and the worries in 1970 that the hard-earned improvement in the British balance of payments might have been (but was not) jeopardised by an American depression. Britain cannot contract out of the world even if she wanted to do so.

It is difficult, if not impossible, in any case to see the British *willingly* allowing their standard of living to fall far behind those of their immediate neighbours. The wage explosion of 1969–71, in the aftermath of years of "restraint" of wages, indicates just how powerful is the urge to better one's living standards. Aspirations for a better life seem to be if anything increasing more rapidly rather than the reverse. Governments willy-nilly therefore have to go for faster economic growth. And, although the electorate appears to have a short collective memory about quite recent deprivations, Ministers must be *seen* at election times to be improving living standards rapidly.

This Labour was demonstrably unable to do in 1970. But long before that it was apparent how much dissatisfaction there was. Thus a significant indication of how unsatisfactory many able people find Britain as a place to live and work in today— and, in many cases, how gloomy a view they take of her prospects if things do not change—is provided by the numbers of engineers, technologists and scientists "voting with their feet" by leaving this country, most of them never to return.

We hear much about the evils of immigration: including, curiously, that of the Asians from East Africa, who have much to contribute to the British economy, as had the Huguenots and Jews of the diaspora, whom Hitler drove out, before them. We hear much less about the blood-letting Britain is suffering from the steady loss of much of its best man-power. Most of this loss consists of men in their twenties and thirties, at the height of their physical and mental powers, and on the threshold of their most productive years. The calculation must inevitably be imprecise, but the loss to the British economy of an able young engineer who emigrates has been estimated at nearly £30,000.

Destinations of British and Commonweath Engineers,
Technologists and Scientists Emigrating (approximate figures)

	Engineers and technologists	Scientists
1961	1,900	1,300
1963	2,500	1,500
1965	3,300	1,800
1966	4,200	2,000
1969	4,685	4,830

Between 1961 and 1966 the flow of engineers and technologists to North America quadrupled, as the Table shows; and the American proportion of the total increased from just over a quarter to almost a half. There are similar figures for other professions, such as doctors and dentists. The plight of the National Health Service, whose Indian and Pakistani doctors are often, through no fault of their own, ill-trained compared with those who have left British medical schools for lusher pastures overseas, is well known.

Such professional people seek much higher real incomes, further enhanced relatively in almost every other advanced industrial country by substantially lower direct taxation than prevails in Britain. And they seek—at least as important—better opportunities in their jobs; to do well what they have been trained for. This, rather than the money alone, is probably why America takes so many British emigrants. In the last two decades or so she has made a massive investment in pure and applied science, such as the space programme, which has led to the establishment of well-endowed centres of learning and research in both industry and the universities. Thus a young graduate has many more choices open to him in America than here, despite recent cut-backs there in certain types of expenditure on technology.

It would not be possible, of course, for a country as small and relatively poor as Britain (compared with the Great Republic) to rectify this sad state of affairs overnight, and certain aspects of the problem, such as the sheer scale of modern technology, can only be dealt with on a continent-wide scale in the long run. Nor would it be desirable, in a free society, to make, for instance, a young doctor sign a pledge before he goes to his medical school that, in return for State aid during his apprenticeship, he would not emigrate for, say, three years on qualification.

The fact remains that a great deal could be done over a period—through wider salary differentials, lower direct taxation, a higher economic growth rate, more and better research facilities, and a much greater general and well-founded optimism about Britain's future as a place to work and in which to bring up one's children—to retain the services of our brilliant young men.

It is, after all, four years since an official working party urged that, *inter alia*: there was a serious brain drain of young engineers, technologists and scientists from Britain; the solution was to create more challenging opportunities, particularly in industry, for talented people; this would require a high and sustained level of industrial investment; there should be a greater recognition that the main source of wealth is industry; new ideas create wealth only if commercially exploited; there should be a more professional approach to management; more detailed statistics of migration of qualified manpower should be recorded; there should be greater mobility between jobs in Britain; pensions should be more readily transferable and other obstacles to mobility should be tackled; engineers, technologists and scientists should play a fuller part in the formulation of company policy; they should be appointed, where they deserve it, to the boards of companies; there should be closer ties between industry and the universities; and the latter should put less emphasis on training scientists towards academic achievement as an end in itself, and more towards the needs of manufacturing industry.

Most of these are unexceptionable—irrefutable—sentiments, and since 1967 something has been done in certain directions, such as management education, to improve the situation. But fundamentally the last state is worse than the first in so far as since then Britain had enjoyed a pathetic rate of economic growth, and hence of expansion of real living standards. To that extent the grass has become even greener the other side of the valley as other industrial countries forge ahead of Britain in almost everything which matters in economic terms.

Britain is not only suffering from the loss of so many expensively trained scientists and other professional people.

There has also been a large increase in total net emigration in recent years. And undoubtedly the average quality of the people who have left, and are leaving, this country is much higher (despite the influx of East African Asians) than those who have come here in recent years. British emigrants tend to be young, with their best years before them.

It is particularly hurtful to British pride that so many Britons have gone to work in prosperous Western Germany, already enjoying a standard of living (despite the higher prices of which so much is made in Britain) substantially higher than in this country. So much for the widely-held thesis that if Britain joined the Common Market hordes of impoverished Continentals would rush like lemmings across the Channel to enjoy the material blessings of the island Shangri-la.

German leaders predict a much bigger immigration of British labour in the future, and particularly so if Britain joined the Market. By 1971 over 15,000 Britons were working in Germany— not a large absolute figure, and small compared with the size of the other immigrant communities there. But in that it was nearly five times the figure of a decade earlier it was unmistakably symptomatic of a trend. British dockers who had moved to Hamburg, for instance, claimed that by working long hours they could earn up to £80 a week, or more than twice what they were getting at home. They tended to comment, however, that they really had to work for their money there with much more emphasis on punctuality, and much less on tea breaks and other such time-wasting nonsense.

Some interviews conducted at the Australian High Commission in August 1970 cast an interesting light on why people leave Britain. The sample was too small to be necessarily typical of the reasons for emigrating to Australia, let alone to the other countries where most British emigrants go (New Zealand, South Africa, America, and, increasingly, Germany). But it was certainly symptomatic of the dissatisfaction so many people feel about their life and prospects in Britain today.

The younger people interviewed made, among others, these points: the growth of their monetary wages in Britain was not sufficiently rapid to cover the increase in the cost of living: the country was "slowing down" and was not dynamic enough: they disliked the fact that there were so many Commonwealth immigrants around: and they objected to the dirty and crowded conditions in so many public places in Britain. The fewer older people, that is roughly those who lived as adults through the 1939–45 war, were on the whole content with conditions in Britain, but were usually emigrating to Australia to be close to relatives.

These were some typical comments. A flooring installer, Cardiff, married, aged forty: "We're fed up", climate bad for health, not enough money, might do more with what he earned in Australia. A driving instructor, Hertfordshire, married, three children, aged thirty-four: wanted a change and "more experience of life", felt to be in a rut here, would try Australia for two years. A self-employed bricklayer, London, married, two children, aged twenty-five: did not like British weather, nor Britain's immigration policies, against "letting in blacks", wages not "in comparison with" cost of living, wife said Australia would offer a better future for their children. A motor mechanic, married, no children, aged twenty-five; "I'm leaving because I feel London is running down", wanted something more challenging. An installer of heavy engineering machinery, Woking, aged about forty-eight: "if we work as hard there as we are doing here, we will do better there; working up to eighty hours a week in Britain, wanted to be near his daughter in Australia. A laboratory technician, Enfield, married with children, aged fifty-seven: wanted to be near daughter, who said Australia was wonderful, "so clean and so big"; he would work there. An engineering designer in London, married, two children, aged thirty: he had emigrated before to Canada but had returned to London, leaving mainly because his son was asthmatic, although life in Britain was good, "London, probably for the amount of work available to my particular trade is perhaps the best in the world".

As the world becomes more one, through more travel and improving communications, people will if anything become even more conscious of what goes on in other countries. An example is American influence, partly through American investment here, on British attitudes to, and enthusiasm for, such items as consumer durables, central heating, pre-packed food, self-service and so on.

Thus relatively high economic growth rates elsewhere must surely persuade the British to go and do likewise. But what should Britain do if she found herself excluded from the Common Market and the so-called alternatives to Market membership proved to be non-starters? The Swedish example has at least a certain relevance to Britain's predicament in such a situation. Sweden has dumbfounded the sceptics who said that such a small country could not thrive without a large home market and corresponding long production runs. Yet she has achieved the fourth highest standard of living in the world with a population of only 8 million!

The trick has been done by a single-minded concentration on certain industries where high wage costs and even higher productivity have gone hand in hand. The great modern pre-fabricated shipbuilding yards at Gothenburg, for instance, compete with the shipyards of other countries (not least the British) with much lower wage costs. And Volvo, which is renowned throughout the world for its reliability and competitiveness on the price of its cars, exports over two-thirds of its production.

Japan has if possible been even more successful in its single-mindedness. And an interesting aspect of this success has been the relative stability of its export prices. Exports of Japanese cars, for instance, have quadrupled in the last four years. They have penetrated the American market, to mention only one, in a way not seen since the original post-war success of the Volkswagen.

Japan's remarkable concentration on those things which it does best has paid impressive dividends. This despite, or perhaps because of, the fact that, like Britain, she has few raw materials (hence her voracious appetite for Western Australian iron ore). In her case necessity has concentrated the mind wonderfully.

The result has been a model for such countries as Britain, which have perennially low growth rates, usually weak balances of payments, rapidly rising unit costs, low levels of investment and relatively stagnant standards of living. Despite an at least average rate of overall inflation, Japan's export prices have on balance increased remarkably little for many years. This remarkable, almost unprecedented, stability, has given her a keener edge in the competitiveness of her exports in world markets.

Like Sweden, but even more so, she has achieved the economies of scale which modern large-scale industry requires by concentrating on certain products, such as cars and other smaller consumer durables, and exporting them in enormous and ever-increasing quantities. With an annual economic growth rate of 10 per cent a year or even more, this has enabled her to spread her rapidly increasing wage costs over this rapidly rising output. Hence her unit labour costs, the ratio between her wage costs and a given volume of output, have remained far more stable than those of other great exporting countries.

This extraordinary success story has important lessons for Britain. A faster economic growth rate here would avoid many of the harmful side effects of rapid wage inflation. A profitable concentration on the advanced industries—such as nuclear power, certain types of engineering, sophisticated motor components, even cars themselves—would surely pay great dividends in the longer run, rather than endless hand-outs to support industries which should be allowed to die if they cannot hold their own in world markets.

For the logic of the trend of recent years, at least until the advent of the Heath Government, is that the whole of Britain will become one vast development area. Regional employment premiums, investment grants or allowances, 'soft' loans from the Industrial Reorganisation Corporation, Development Certificates to stop businessmen investing where they most want to go, assistance to certain State industries and so on—all these can spread out in ever-widening circles, like ripples on a pond, to cover so-called "grey areas", and even eventually areas like the south-east which are now regarded as economically viable. Why should not every ailing industry have a subsidy? Why not the motor industry?

It is time, indeed, to be alarmed when pillars of the economy are making virtually no profits. The plight of the motor industry symbolises so much of what ails Britain. Thus mighty British Leyland's profits were exiguous in 1970. Loss of production from wild-cat unofficial strikes played a major part in such disastrous results, as Lord Stokes has rightly been quick to point out. But the progressive decline in the competitiveness of the British car manufacturers compared with their international rivals (as evidenced by the big increase in imports of foreign car to Britain, to around 15 per cent of the market, in the first half of 1970) also reflects the fact that there has been virtually no growth in the home market in the last decade. Meanwhile, the German car industry has doubled in size.

So bad is the plight of the car industry that it is now even being suggested that if Britain joins the Common Market, and even more so if she does not, there will be no major British mass-production car manufacturers by 1980. Giant international companies, such as Chrysler and Volkswagen, would dominate the European car market, Britain might be left to console herself with making sports cars, motor components, and commercial vehicles. The growth of sales of these products since the 1939–45 war has been one of Britain's most notable economic successes. The story of how, for instance, Guest, Keen and Nettlefolds expanded so rapidly in its production of motor components, persuading British car manufacturers to standardise their push-rod sizes and selling drop-forgings deep into Germany over the Market's common external tariff, is a remarkable tribute to British commercial enterprise at its best.

Yet no one can be happy at the prospect, at even only the possibility, that within years Britain will have lost one of the major industries on which modern industrial societies are built. From the car industry so much else stems. The jobs of millions of people directly or indirectly depend upon it, as does the prosperity of much of the engineering industry (including, of course, motor components). All this is now at stake. Britain could, of course, continue to make sports cars and motor components without a modern mass-production car industry. But there would inevitably be a serious danger that over a period the centre of gravity of even these activities would follow car production and shift to the great car-producing areas of Continental Europe: notably those around Wolfsburg in Germany and Milan in Northern Italy.

Great efforts would be made, of course, to avoid such a disaster for Britain ever happening—and more obviously so under a Labour Government. That is precisely the point. More long years of an abysmal economic growth rate for Britain and hence of a relatively stagnant home market (on which the profitability of exports depends) for British car manufacturers would put the industry into a tail-spin, a vicious circle of poor sales, low profitability, under-investment and declining competitiveness in world markets. As a palliative, as an inadequate attempt to reverse economic forces, Governments, certainly left-wing Governments, would no doubt shell-out an ever-increasing amount of taxpayers' money. The car manufacturers, most of which are already American-owned, would doubtless be duly grateful for such crumbs from the rich man's—alias taxpayer's—table. As British Leyland, the one indisputable major British car company, was when it received £25 million as a loan from the Industrial Reorganisation Corporation.

Yet grants, loans, hand-outs, investment allowances and other such artificial stimuli, will not in themselves reverse the march of history. The relatively poor performance of the British car industry since 1945 reflects in large measure its weak domestic base, which in turn has resulted from Government stop-go economic policies—but stands in stark and favourable contrast, nevertheless, with the tragic and avoidable decline of, for instance, the shipbuilding industry which has enjoyed a great deal of State aid. But it could come to resemble it if present trends go on long enough and especially if its relative decline accelerates. There could come a time, indeed, when most major industries became pensioners of the State (why not a hand-out too, for those Fleet Street newspapers which are losing so much money?). The only problem then would be for the State, with so few viable industries on which to levy taxes, to find the funds to support them.

The scale of Government's recent intervention in industry is not generally realised. In 1970 roughly £600 million was provided in investment grants, plus nearly £200 million to individual companies, and about £1,000 million of repayments of selective employment tax to manufacturing and certain other industries, such as those in the development areas. There have also been the IRC's "investments" (see Chapter Nine) and many nationalised industries have received help in roundabout ways, such as substantial write-offs of their capital (see Chapter Eleven). Yet, whatever the precise causes and effects, the last state is worse than the first, and Britain's non-growth remains a legend to the rest of the world. Much of the State aid to the development areas has been wasted in "assisting" capital-intensive companies which employ relatively few people anyway.

The conclusion is therefore clear. Britain will have to specialise in the future much more in the economic activities in which she has a "comparative advantage"—in other words, in those things at which she excels. She will have to refrain from retarding those historic and economic forces which decree that over the decades some industries rise and others fall.

She will have to do all this in any case, whether or not she succeeds in joining some larger economic unit. But if she fails to do this, the task, the need for rapid adjustment will be that much greater.

It is for this reason that the negotiations in Brussels for the enlargement of the Community should be brought to a swift and successful conclusion: Geoffrey Rippon is rightly pressing for speed and "action". It is desirable both for the Six themselves and for the candidate States who have waited for nearly a decade in the Gaullist ante-room to know at last where they stand. Britain in particular will have to make difficult changes whether or not she succeeds in Brussels. The sooner she can start the better. The difficulties for new members joining the Market have steadily increased as integration has continued apace. They will do so further as time goes by—so much so that if this latest attempt to unite virtually the whole of Western Europe in an exciting new economic and political structure failed, it would be only realistic to forget the whole concept in this generation, and possibly for ever.

The Six would not want to retard any longer their own integration in order to wait for the candidate States to catch up. And public opinion in those hitherto patient nations would almost certainly not suffer yet another approach to be made to the Six for membership. NAFTA and the Commonwealth may be pipe-dreams as "economic options", but so in those circumstances would "Europe" be for those left outside. Long years ago, in the aftermath of yet another terrible world war and in Strasbourg—the historic capital of Alsace-Lorraine, unhappy inheritance of King Lothar, Charlemagne's younger son—the ancient States of Western Europe made a tryst with destiny in forming the Council of Europe: an earnest of happier days for this Continent. The time has come to redeem that pledge of unity. As even Lord Attlee, never an ardent "European", said: "Europe cannot wait". For her, the best is yet to come.

It cannot possibly be predicted in advance with any certainty that the British people would respond to the challenge of "going into Europe". If they did not do so their country could conceivably become even more of a backwater than it will be if present trends continued and if Britain remained relatively isolated outside the Common Market on the periphery of the Eurasian land mass. And if Britain did go into Europe, even then she might decline into a depressed area of the Market, like Sicily far from the centres of economic might. Almost anything is possible in history.

By the same token, no one can be certain that the British would react favourably to any of the other radical changes suggested in this book—such as more competition, more flexible exchange rates, more incentives through lower taxation, much greater selectivity in the social services, a drastic reduction in the power and influence of the State, a streamlined machinery of government, and a legal framework for industrial relations.

If the British did not respond to a more bracing climate, that would indeed be their problem. To argue in advance that they would not do so (and all radical changes are acts of faith), despite their past as the world's industrial pace-setters, is surely to take too gloomy a view of their inherent energy and abilities given the right conditions; or to argue, against history, that national characteristics change drastically over a period. If, as seems probable, they did so respond, the late 1970's—and it will surely take some time for initially difficult, uncomfortable, unsettling changes to reap their reward—could herald a glorious period of British history, as good as any since the accession of Queen Anne. And, across the centuries, posterity has rightly called that the Sunshine Day. Why should not the year 1997 be as different for the better, from 1971 for Britain as 1971 is from 1945?

> When every morning brought a gentle chance
> And every chance brought forth a noble knight.

APPENDIX ONE

1967: Diary of a Crisis-laden Year

January		Unemployment exceeds 600,000. Wage freeze gives way to "severe restraint".
	20	Finance Ministers meet at Chequers.
	26	Bank Rate cut to 6½ per cent.
February	10	Prince Philip "sick and tired of making excuses for Britain".
	14	Record export figures for January.
March	13	Bank for International Settlements renews $1,000 million loan.
	16	Bank Rate cut to 6 per cent.
	21	"Voluntary restraint" White Paper on Prices and Incomes.
April	11	Virtual "no change" Budget; restraint on bank advances lifted. Quips Chancellor Callaghan: "No news is good news."
May	2	Prime Minister announces application to join Common Market.
	4	Bank Rate cut to 5½ per cent.
June	5	Six-Day War between Arab States and Israel begins; Suez Canal closed and Arab embargo on oil to Britain.
	7	Hire purchase restrictions on cars eased.
	13	White Paper on Productivity agreements and second National Productivity Conference.
	21	Increase in National Insurance Benefits by £230 million; but contributions also raised. End of period of would be "severe restraint" in incomes policy.
July	24	Chancellor says devaluation "a flight from

reality"; announces restraint of growth of public expenditure to annual rate of 3 per cent over three years.

August   Good trade figures for July; Treasury optimistic about balance of payments prospects. Pound firm.

20   Ray Gunter at Ministry of Labour tells trade unions to "stop equating profits with incest and lechery".

24   Group of Ten of rich nations agrees on Special Drawing Rights for International Monetary Fund.

28   Douglas Jay fired from Cabinet: Harold Wilson over-lord of Department of Economic Affairs, with Peter Shore to "mind the office".

29   Hire purchase restrictions on cars and domestic appliances eased.

September   Arabs lift oil embargo.

11   International Monetary Fund agrees on SDRs scheme. Dock Strike.

October 3   Common Market Commission ominously critical of British monetary system, and hints at "fundamental disequilibrium" in Britain's balance of payments in report on her application to join EEC. Gold reserves fall for fourth month running.

10   Swiss banks lend Britain £37.5 million.

30   Bank Rate raised to 6 per cent; pound remains under pressure. Liverpool dockers return to work, but some London dockers remain on strike.

November 2   White Paper on "Economic and Financial Objectives of Nationalised Industries".

5   Pound drops to lowest level for a decade.

9   Bank Rate raised to 6½ per cent.

12   Further credits arranged with Bank for International Settlements; France leaves gold pool.

14   £107 million trade deficit for October announced; pound has worst day ever.

16   Rumours of $1,000 million loan to support sterling; pound slumps further.

18   Pound devalued from 2.80 dollars to the pound

to 2.40 dollars; Bank Rate raised to 8 per cent; hire purchase terms tightened; £100 million defence cuts and £100 million reduction in Government expenditure; Selective Employment Tax premiums withdrawn; export rebates cut; $3,000 million stand-by credits arranged.

22 World-wide rush to buy gold starts.

27 President de Gaulle announces, in effect, second veto on British membership of Common Market.

29 James Callaghan resigns; Roy Jenkins Chancellor of the Exchequer. Publishes "letter of intent" (or good intentions) promising IMF more "hair shirt" policies.

December 21 Chancellor warns of forthcoming £600 million cuts in public expenditure. Followed by prolonged and well-published Cabinet discussions about which "sacred cows" should be first for the slaughter.

APPENDIX TWO

Labour and Conservative Versions of Industrial Relations Reform

The 1964–70 *Labour Government's* approach was evolved in four stages: White Paper, "In Place of Strife", published in January 1969 and hailed by Barbara Castle as the "most important charter of trade union advance for sixty years"; the short Industrial Relations Bill introduced after the 1969 Budget, when Roy Jenkins announced that the main provisions of "In Place of Strife" would become law; in the face of the opposition of the Parliamentary Labour Party, this was dropped in favour of the TUC's "Solemn and Binding Agreement", which promised, among other things, to modernise union structure, to intervene to help to settle strikes, and in part to "police" wage agreements; a new Industrial Relations Bill, introduced in April 1970 but overtaken by the election the following June, which omitted the proposals, such as cooling-off periods and strike ballots, to which the unions most objected.

The *Conservative Government's* ideas have emerged in stages from the Tories' policy-making reappraisal after they went into Opposition in 1964: "Fair Deal at Work", published in 1968, which introduced for the first time in Britain the concept of legally-binding contracts in industrial relations—the Industrial Relations Consultative Document, published in October 1970, which roughly followed that pamphlet's main proposals; and the Industrial Relations Bill presented to Parliament in December 1970.

Pre-Strike Ballot

Labour said in "In Place of Strife" that the Secretary of State would have "discretionary power to require the union or unions involved to hold a ballot on the question of strike action" in cases where he believed that the proposed strike "would involve a serious threat to the economy or public interest, and there is doubt whether it commands the support of those concerned".

Conservatives proposed in their Bill that the Secretary of State should be able to apply to the National Industrial Relations Court for an order requiring a ballot where he was satisfied that there were "emergency circumstances", or that the effects of the industrial action in question might be "seriously injurious to the livelihood of a substantial number of workers employed in that industry; or where there were reasons for doubting whether (*a*) the workers who might take part in a strike or other industrial act really wished to do so and (*b*) had had a chance of making known their wishes.

Differences: only one major one, that Labour would have had the Minister take the decisions, while the Conservatives would leave that to an independent Industrial Relations Court.

Conciliation Pause

Labour would have given the Secretary of State a discretionary reserve power to secure a conciliation pause in unconstitutional strikes and in strikes where, because there was no agreed procedure "or for other reasons, adequate joint discussions have not taken place". After warning both sides the Minister could issue an Order requiring those involved to return to work and to desist from industrial action for a period of 28 days. If either side failed to obey that order the Industrial Board "at its discretion could impose financial penalties".

Conservative proposals for a "cooling-off" period are restricted to circumstances in which an emergency has arisen. Thus the Industrial Relations Court would be able to make an order restraining the people and/or organisations which it named from being able to "call, organise, procure or finance a strike, or threaten so to do "in a specified area of employment from a specified date and for a specified period up to a maximum of sixty days".

Differences: the Labour proposals were wider in scope and the proposed length of pause shorter. The Conservatives' conciliation pause would be imposed not by a Minister but by an Industrial Court with a lawyer as Chairman. As with all the Conservatives' so-called penal clauses, penalties would not be imposed by the State on delinquent workers. Instead an injunction would be directed against the union rather than against individual workers.

Registration of Trade Unions

Labour proposed that trade unions should be registered with a new Registrar of Trade Unions and Employers' Associations (recommended by the Donovan Commission) within a prescribed period. Unions would be required to have "rules governing certain matters (e.g. admission, discipline, disputes between the union and its members, elections, strike ballots, and the appointment and functions of shop stewards) and to register with Registrar". Refusal would lay a union open to a financial penalty by the Industrial Board.

Conservatives would have the Queen appoint a "Chief Registrar of Trade Unions and Employers' Associations who shall hold office during Her Majesty's pleasure". There are guide-lines for the conduct of every workers' organisation, which cover applications for a termination of membership, the right to nominate for, seek and hold office, the vote without constraint, to take part in meetings, and so on.

Penalties

Labour by and large preferred the decision to act to rest with the Minister. He could sue both a union or individuals in quite a number of situations.

Conservatives propose that the decision whether or not to act should be left with the proposed Industrial Relations Court; and that action should be taken against the union, with penalties geared to the size of membership. Action would be taken against individuals only where they operated outside "the control and authority of the unions".

It is arguable whether the Labour or the Conservative approach is potentially the more severe.

Contracts of Employment

Labour would have reduced from twenty-six to thirteen weeks the period of employment after which both sides were required to give a week's notice of termination: and provided for six weeks' notice to be given to an employee after ten years' employment, and eight weeks' after fifteen years.

Conservatives would reduce from twenty-six to thirteen

weeks the period of employment after which both sides are required to give a week's notice; and they provide for six weeks' notice to be given to an employee after ten years' employment-and eight weeks' after fifteen years.

Unfair Dismissal

Labour and *Conservative* have broadly agreed, in their proposed legislation, on the details here. Both have laid down definitions of unfair dismissal, the role of the industrial tribunals has been made clear, and the remedies have been outlined. But the Labour proposals emphasised more reinstatement: and the Conservatives propose a greater maximum compensation for wrongful dismissal.

Disclosure of Information

Labour went beyond the recommendation of the Donovan Commission by proposing that trade unions should be able to obtain from employers "certain sorts of information that are needed for negotiations". The Secretary of State would be able to require employers to disclose particular kinds of information.

Conservatives: The employer has the duty to provide "information without which the trade union representatives would be to a material extent impeded in carrying on collective bargaining with him". There are proposed financial penalties for failure to comply with the regulations on disclosure or for providing false or misleading information.

Legality of Contracts

Labour was opposed to making *all* collective agreements legally-binding: "agreements could be made legally binding only by an express written provision in the agreement". In other words, agreements would not be legally enforceable contracts unless they contained an explicit written provision to that effect.

Conservatives provide that any written collective agreement "concluded *after* the commencement of the Act will be presumed to be intended to be a legally enforceable contract if it does not contain a provision to the contrary".

Differences are not as great as they seem as first sight, and certainly not as wide as Labour leaders tend to claim—although the problem is approached from opposite angles. In practice the results could be similar.

Summary

The major divergence between what was once the Labour approach to reforming Britain's industrial relations and the Conservatives' present approach are that: (*a*) Labour assumed that collective agreements were not legally enforceable unless specifically stated otherwise, while the Conservatives propose the opposite, and (*b*) Labour put the onus on the Minister to decide when the Executive should intervene to enforce "law and order" in industrial relations, whereas the Conservatives put the onus of decision on a judicial authority (which would in time no doubt build up a case law of precedents).

Other Points

Labour provided that grants or loans could be made to trade unions to make them more efficient or to encourage amalgamations. The *Conservatives* make no such provision. Unlike *Labour*, the *Conservatives* outline a new concept of unfair industrial practices, with compensation proposed for those injured by them. Among those practices are those discriminating against non-union members, and action to force anyone not connected with a dispute to break a contract with an employer who is in dispute (for instance, for the "blacking" of goods and sympathetic strikes).

External trade of the United Kingdom

	1958 £ million	1958 Per cent of total	1968 £ million	1968 Per cent of total	Percent- age in- crease 1958–68
IMPORTS[1] by geographical area					
Total	3,834	100	7,745	100	102
of which					
EEC	538	14	1,551	20	188
Continental EFTA[2]	436	11	1,161	15	166
Commonwealth	1,336	35	1,867	24	40
Rest of world	1,524	40	3,166	41	108
IMPORTS by categories					
Food, beverages and tobacco	1,490	39	1,900	25	28
Basic materials and fuels	1,345	35	2,109	27	57
Manufactured goods	977	26	3,627	47	371
EXPORTS by geographical area					
Total	3,250	100	6,183	100	90
of which					
EEC	448	14	1,196	19	167
Continental EFTA[2]	352	11	858	14	144
Commonwealth	1,239	38	1,408	23	14
Rest of world	1,211	37	2,721	44	125
EXPORTS by categories					
Food, beverages and tobacco	194	6	398	6	105
Basic materials and fuels	242	7	346	6	48
Manufactured goods	2,714	84	5,285	85	95

Source: Annual Statements of Trade of the United Kingdom
[1] Excludes United States military aircraft
[2] Including Finland
Note: Import values are c.i.f., export values f.o.b.
Source: Britain and the European Communities, An Economic ASSESSMENT, Command 4289

APPENDIX FOUR

Britain's Net Invisible Earnings and Payments

	£ million				
	1965	1966	1967	1968	1969
INVESTMENT INCOME	438	381	369	322	472
SERVICES					
Government	270	290	276	283	283
Transport	24	30	43	89	74
Travel and tourism	97	78	39	11	26
Financial and other services	270	299	383	452	496
TRANSFERS					
Government	177	180	188	179	174
Private	32	49	62	78	87
TOTAL CONTRIBUTION TO					
CURRENT ACCOUNT	156	113	230	334	524

Sources: U.K. Balance of Payments 1969
Economic Trends March 1970

APPENDIX FIVE

Administrative Class (at 1/1/67)

Year of Birth	Permanent Secretary	Deputy Secretary	Under Secretary	Assistant Secretary	Principal	Assistant Principal
1901 or earlier					7	
1902–06	2	8	19	28	36	
1907–11	12	26	71	109	65	1
1912–16	12	33	112	175	107	
1917–21	2	7	65	258	220	
1922–26		1	7	145	153	
1927–31				59	226	
1932–36				2	183	13
1937–41					64	127
1942–46					1	137
TOTAL	28	73	274	777	1,053	278

Of 2,483 total, 2,277 were men, and 206 women

Source: Fulton Report 1968

Index

Index

Acheson, Dean, 25
Added-value tax, 97–100
Aden, 28
Adenauer, Konrad, 144, 181, 185, 187, 213
Adjustment, British, to change in power-status, 23–5
Adjustment, British, genius for, 123
Africa, 14, 126, 206, 207, 233
  former British territories in, 232
  new nations of, 222
  see also East Africa; South Africa
Agriculture, Ministry of, 81
Agriculture, subsidies, 100, 191
  see also EEC, Common Agricultural Policy
Airlines, *see* BEA; BOAC; Sabena
Airmec, 114
Airports
  Heathrow, 20, 211
  third London, 139, 231
  Orly, 211
Aitken, Jonathan, 62
Allied Breweries, 121
Aluminium smelter schemes, 132–3
  dispute, 220
Amalgamated Engineering Union, 165
America, *see* United States
  Latin, *see* Latin America
  North, *see* North America
Amery, Julian, 106
Amory, Derick Heathcoat (Viscount), 41
Anglesey Aluminium Metal, 132–3
Anne, Queen, 244

Antigua, 207
Appeal, Court of, 84
Arabian sheikdoms, 28
Arkwright, Sir Richard, 22
Armstrong, Sir William, 59
Asia, 233
Asquith government, 124
Associated Electrical Industries, 116
Atomic energy, 15
Atomic Energy Authority, 132
Attlee, Lord, 243
  government, 36, 37, 38, 135, 145
Australia, 77, 221, 224
  British emigrants to, 237–8
  British entry to EEC and, 184
  NAFTA and, 218, 219
  taxation, 94
  trade with Japan, 223
Australian High Commission, 237
Austria, 220

Babcock and Wilcox, 116
Balance of payments
  (1956–9 and 1960–1), 42
  (1964), 34, 44
  (1965), 55
  (1966), 56
  (1967), 50
  (1968), 56
  (1969/70), 56, 71
  (1970), NIESR forecasts, 52–3
  External trade, UK, *table*, 253–4
Baldwin, Stanley, government of, 69, 163